TIE DOWN THE SUN

i

ii

WHAT REVIEWERS SAY:

The author displays a rare descriptive gift, blending ancient cultures with modern developments. Latin America comes alive!
—*J. Oswald Sanders, Overseas Missionary Fellowship.*
Author, former Bolivian Indian Mission council member

The penetrating eye of a journalist, the warm heart of a cross-cultural missionary, plus a remarkable gift of expression make Harold Fuller a uniquely qualified writer on missions today. His ability to link vignettes to the broad sweeping picture of Latin America makes this a fascinating and reliable book.As one who spent years in Latin America, I highly recommend it.
—*David M. Howard, International Director,*
World Evangelical Fellowship, Singapore

The style is lively and clear, summarizing a lot of information in a readable way. It is a book about very painful situations in one of the most difficult areas of the contemporary world.
—*Samuel Escobar, Eastern Baptist Theological Seminary,*
Philadelphia

Harold Fuller's previous travelogue, *Run While the Sun Is Hot,* is without doubt the most fascinating book I have read about Africa. Now he has turned his attention to South America--a continent of *coups d'etat,* cocaine lords, and charismatic churches. The reader will feel the pulse of a continent through a skilled reporter and sense the spiritual need through the heart of a veteran missionary. Must reading for all who are interested in how other parts of the world live.
—*Stuart Briscoe, Author, Conference Speaker, Senior*
Pastor Elmbrook Church, Milwaukee

The author has a way of putting things clearly and orderly, with very good illustrations. A useful book for people facing similar situations all over the world.
—*Arnoldo Canclini, General Secretary, Bible Society of*
Argentina

A tremendous job! Readers gain crucial insights as they travel with the author. I trust God blesses *Tie Down The Sun,* particularly in challenging people to pray and serve with sensitivity in the continent I love so much.

— William D. Taylor, Executive Secretary, World Evangelical Fellowship Missions Commission

The effective way in which the author writes and the extent to which he has been able to incorporate so much significant information is a tribute to his capacity as a reporter and journalist. I trust his treatment will have wide acceptance, especially since there is so much misunderstanding of the situation among evangelicals and others in Latin America.

—Eugene A. Nida, linguist, anthropologist, consultant American Bible Society

Most interesting! Fastpaced, insightful, and hard to put down, it brings together a wealth of information from an evangelical perspective. May it be used of God to generate increased prayer and missionary effort in our beloved Latin America.

—Allen R. Hatch, former Executive Secretary, Latin America Committee of EFMA and IFMA, Administrator COMIBAM Spanish Office, Ecuador

I highly recommend this work. The careful reflections come from someone intimately in touch with current realities in Latin America.

—Ruben Dario Ramirez, International Fellowship of Evangelical Students, Colombia

A sparkling and insightful book providing a picture in broad strokes of Latin America's secular and religious past and the status of evangelical churches.

— Wade T. Coggins, former Executive Director, Evangelical Foreign Mission Association

A graphic picture of South America. The book reveals diligent research, accurately giving details of great interest.
—*Joseph S. McCullough, General Director Emeritus, Andes Evangelical Mission*

A clearly-executed presentation. More than once I was moved to tears.
—*Lena Lau, former Assistant Professor of Linguistics, Hong Kong University; Manuscript critic*

A true insight of what is happening in South America. It was difficult to put aside. Thank you for taking time to put into print what a lot of us have only kept in our minds.
—*Hudson Shedd, General Director, Gospel Mission of South America*

This book will motivate people to pray more for the work in Latin America. It is a challenge for those who are serious about working there.
—*Tito Montero, Director, World Vision, Bolivia*

A timely overview of Latin America; a book of great value for new missionaries and missionary-minded Christians. Bible colleges, seminaries, and mission agency offices need this book.
—*Edwin L. (Jack) Frizen, Jr., Executive Director, Interdenominational Foreign Missions Association*

Very interesting! The travelogue format is ideal for putting together information and vignettes from the countries visited. Elements of zest, anticipation, surprise, and elation. I really didn't want to put it down.
—*Jack Phillips, Director, SIM Canada*

Striking contrasts: the deadly sense of oppression and fear; great wealth and extreme poverty; the amazing joy and vitality

exhibited by evangelicals. Harold Fuller's perceptive analysis provides revealing insights to this part of God's vineyard.
—*Betty Vetterlein, Missions Committee Park Street Church, Boston, MA, one-time resident of Argentina*

Immensely readable, with a ring of total authenticity to those who know well this exciting but increasingly sad continent.
—*Dennis Smith, General Secretary, Evangelical Union of South America, U.K.*

We need more people who are serious about reaching Latin America and who will pray for God's work there. Such people need to read this powerful and informative book.
—*George Verwer, Operation Mobilization*

TIE
DOWN
THE SUN

Adventure in Latin America
by W. Harold Fuller

*The ancients of South America
"tied down the sun" in solemn rituals,
seeking to control their world.
Today's citizens try other ways of coping
with their turbulent age.*

An SIM Publication

Tie Down The Sun

Printed in Canada

ISBN 0-919470-26-2
Library of Congress Catalog number 90-81670
All Scripture quotations in this publication are from the
Holy Bible, New International Version. Copyright © 1973,
1978, 1984, International Bible Society.

Cover art and book design by J. Douglas Thompson
Maps by Ronald W. Parlane
All photos by the author except where noted
Country Statistics (Appendix): International Research and
Education Department, SIM

SIM International Media
10 Huntingdale Blvd.
Scarborough, Ontario
Canada M1W 2S5
Phone: (416) 497-2424
FAX: (416) 497-2444

Dedication

To Lorna
whose mother prayed for
the pioneer missionaries
in Bolivia

CUBA

CARIBBEAN SEA

VENEZUELA

COLOMBIA

ECUADOR

PERU

BRAZIL

BOLIVIA

CHILE

PARAGUAY

ARGENTINA

URUGUAY

ATLANTIC OCEAN

PACIFIC OCEAN

General route of the travelogue
See chapter headings for detail

AUTHOR'S ROUTE

The High Andes:
Ecuador
Heart of Inca Empire
The High Plain
Lake Titicaca
The High Valleys:
Bolivia's Heartland
Cochabamba
The Chapare
Sucre
Oruro
The Central Lowlands:
The Beni
The Central Plains
Paraguay
The Southern Cone:
Uruguay
Argentina
Chile
The Pacific Coast:
Southern Peru
Coastal Peru: Lima
North-Central Peru
The Caribbean:
Cuba
Portuguese America:
Brazil

ACKNOWLEDGMENTS

The author gratefully acknowledges research assistance from the archives of SIM, AEM, McMaster University, and Southern Baptist Convention Research Department. The author has drawn from innumerable published and unpublished sources, including those listed in the bibliography. Missions and churches mentioned in the book have been most helpful in checking information and providing detail, as have the men and women I interviewed. To the Latin Americans and others who gave time to critique early drafts, I give special thanks. And to my own office staff, I express appreciation for painstaking checking and correcting.

CONTENTS

Your sun will never set again, . . . the Lord will be your ever-lasting light.

Isaiah 60:20

ABOUT THE BOOK

I sat on a rickety chair in the home of Isaias, a Peruvian church elder. The sun stabbed like a shaft of Inca gold through a hole in the roof of the shack. One of the elder's daughters kept watch at the front door as we talked about guerrilla bombings and secret informers.

But those weren't the things uppermost in my host's mind. He wanted to tell me how the gospel was making an impact-- about neighbors receiving Christ, about Christians growing spiritually amid trials.

"I've wanted to write believers in other countries to tell them what things are really like, so they can pray for us," Isaias said. "I've wanted to tell the missionaries who used to work here, to encourage them. But I don't know how to reach them. So I'm glad you're writing a book."

I asked Isaias to pray for me, because it would be no easy task to tell "what things are really like" in South America. As I traveled through the continent south of the equator, plus Cuba in the Caribbean, I came to realize there are different worlds within this Latin American universe of 27 countries.

My journeys covered some twenty thousand miles, from sandy shore through steamy jungle to snowy peak. I interviewed a cross section of Latin Americans: a distinguished senator and jungle Indians, businessmen and drug addicts, Christians and Communists, professors and peasants. I was awed by mysterious Inca ruins and fascinated by modern city towers--and thankful to escape a train bombing en route.

How to portray the gospel at work in all this? As I was reading the Bible one day, I realized that the Acts of the Apostles is really a travelogue. Luke wrote what he had "seen and heard." In other reading I discovered that an early missionary travelogue challenged the founder of the South American mission which had merged with my mission, SIM (an amalgamation of Andes Evangelical Mission, International

xv

Christian Fellowship, and Sudan Interior Mission). I decided I could do no better than take the reader along with me on my own journey, to see what I saw and to hear what I heard.

The travelogue is not short, because one doesn't traverse Latin America in a day! It's a living experience that I invite you to go through with me. I found the odyssey physically rigorous, mentally stimulating, spiritually challenging--but also thrilling. I hope the account will provide what each reader is looking for: exotic experiences for the travel enthusiast, hard facts for the academic reader, and fresh insight for the mission-minded. I also pray that the Holy Spirit will touch lives spiritually as He touched mine.

I've given bald facts and statements without editorializing, for the most part, knowing that you'll come to your own conclusions. However, if you want my evaluation, you'll find it in the Author's Evaluation at the end. If, before trekking through the entire continent, you want a quick look at a specific country, you'll find it in the list of contents under "Author's Route." If you wonder why I didn't put all the facts about a major topic (e.g., the Incas or liberation theology) in one handy section, remember that a traveler learns as he goes, gaining insight in different contexts. But readers who want topics cate - gorized will find them in the detailed index.

The book is essentially about the continent south of the equator. (Central America would need a separate book to do it justice.) Although some details will be different in the northern countries not covered, the major factors described in these chapters affect the entire Latin American context. Friends of SIM may wonder why I cover some countries in which SIM is not working. I feel it is important to give a wide overview, for each country contributes to the dynamics of contemporary Latin America. We're looking at a volatile continent. Some of the conditions I describe will change in the years to come, but the background will still be there.

In countries where SIM is ministering, I have sought to put its work in the context of other evangelical work. However, the list of missions and churches became so long that I reluctantly had to limit the names to a sampling. May the others forgive me! God is not unmindful of their work. I faced the same problem in telling the stories of people. Those who are mentioned would agree there are many others whose stories deserve to be told. With regret I had to leave out a number because of the limits of length. Again, God has them all recorded in His Book of Remembrance. (Incidentally, for security reasons, I've changed the identities of a few people.)

My research took several years and numerous trips, which I made while carrying out mission administrative responsibilities. When I finally came to write the narrative, tears came to my eyes at times as I relived some of the scenes. At other times I had to laugh aloud because of humorous incidents. But the end result of the odyssey is a personal burden for this remarkable part of the world.

Along the way, I fell in love with South America. Pinned on my office wall as I wrote, was a map of the continent that I'd bought on a Bolivian street. As I looked at it day after day, I imagined the continent was the shape of a bunch of grapes, or a throbbing heart, or an impish cartoon character--the northern nations forming his tassled cap, the Amazon a mischievous eye, and the Brazilian coast his bulbous nose and receding chin.

Whatever it reminded me of, the continent took on new shape and meaning as I wrote the story. It became the form of real people--very diverse people. People struggling to control their destiny, to "tie down the sun." That Quechua idiom described what the ancients tried to do through sacrifices, to keep the sun from forsaking them. Today's Latin Americans try to control their world in other ways, I discovered.

To tell you the truth, I found the kaleidoscope of South American life mind-boggling. I was groping for some way to sum it all up, when an Argentine artist explained her airport mural to me. "My people--they don't know who they are," she said. "They're fragmented!" (See chapter 14.)

That helped me understand the background to what I saw. In the mural was a sun. The Incas sought to placate the sun god to hold their world together. Modern Latin Americans are worshiping a materialistic sun, or following the deceptive light of ideologies and cults. But only the eternal Son of God can put real meaning into life.

To Isaias, the Peruvian elder, I say, "Thank you for praying for me. I'll try to tell it as I saw and heard it."

--W. Harold Fuller
Toronto, Canada
July 1, 1990

*In the heavens he has pitched a tent for the sun. . . . It rises
at one end of the heavens and makes its circuit to the other.*

PSALM 19:4,6

1

TYING

DOWN

THE SUN

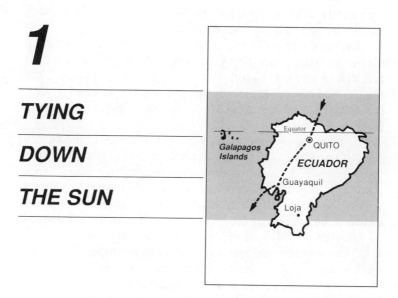

STRADDLING THE EQUATOR

I couldn't resist the impulse to straddle the equator. That's
where my odyssey started--on South America's northwest
coast, in Ecuador. The equator passes right through this
country. ("Ecuador" is Spanish for "equator.")

The government has thoughtfully built a 10-storey stone
observation tower capped with an enormous brass globe, right
on the equator. A line set in concrete marks zero latitude. I
straddled it, placing my left foot in the Northern Hemisphere
and my right foot in the Southern. Tourists were snapping

photos of one another standing on the line, and children tossed a ball from one hemisphere to the other. A honeymoon couple held hands across the equator. But this line, equidistant from both poles, is more than a tourist attraction, I noted. Several nations have built scientific research stations and museums in the vicinity to study equatorial phenomena. Those phenomena drastically affected the lives of the ancients.

Earlier, I had arrived in the nation's capital, Quito, high in the Andes Mountains. Ben Cummings of HCJB World Radio had driven me the 14 miles to the equator. Fortunately, the observation tower there had an elevator, for I found myself breathing heavily in the thin atmosphere at 9500 feet above sea level.

From the top of the tower we looked across to the snowy peak of one of Ecuador's 30 volcanoes. Several, like Cotopaxi, the world's highest active volcano, periodically shake with eruptions and earthquakes. Ben told me that shortly before I arrived, a thousand people died in three successive quakes, followed by a week of 40,000 tremors. The quakes destroyed sections of a 300-mile oil pipeline, causing the nation to suspend exports of oil and payments on its foreign debt. (Oil and bananas are Ecuador's chief source of foreign exchange.)

The volcanoes poke up from Ecuador's spine, the Andes. The longest mountain chain in the world, and boasting the highest peaks apart from Mount Everest in the Himalayas, the Andes start in the far north of the continent. They form its backbone, stretching 4500 miles along the western edge, from Venezuela and Colombia, through Ecuador, Peru, and Bolivia, and between Argentina and Chile.

We walked around the tower to the opposite side, facing west. I knew that 650 miles off the coast, right on the equator, were Ecuador's volcanic Galapagos Islands, made famous by the naturalist Charles Darwin. He identified species of plants and living creatures found nowhere else in the world, including giant turtles weighing up to 600 pounds.

The Galapagos Islands mark the juncture of two ocean currents that affect the rest of the world: the Humboldt and El Niño. Every few years, the warm El Niño ("The Child"--so-called because it usually starts flowing southward around Christmastime) pushes over the Humboldt and raises the surface temperature. Meteorologists link El Niño/South Oscillation (ENSO) and a colder system dubbed La Niña ("Female Child") with disastrous changes in weather patterns all around the world, from Australia to Africa to Asia. They leave a devastating trail of floods in some parts, drought in others.

My musings about El Niño were cut short by Ben's telling me that until the eighties the official line marking the equator was a few hundred feet away from where we stood.

"See that knoll a quarter of a mile away?" Ben pointed out. "That was the site of an Inca temple. When the equator was recently surveyed from space, calculations placed the equator on a line that runs right through the ruins. The ancient Indians were more accurate than our scientists! So the original monument was torn down and this new one was erected in line with the ruins."

SACRIFICE TO THE SUN

The Inca's priests tracked the sun as a matter of life and death. They believed that the sun god created the first Inca and then stalked off to the west across the sea. He did say he'd return each day to check that his instructions were being followed. That was why the people lived in constant fear. What if they offended him and he didn't return? They confessed their sins to shaman priests and made sacrifices of grain, woven ponchos, and llamas to make sure he'd come back. In some Indian cultures, captives were sacrificed daily for this purpose.

More frightening was the sun god's annual drift north. What if he kept going farther away, never to return with his life-giving warmth? As winter shadows lengthened on the frosty ranges, priests performed elaborate rituals. Finally, on the day the sun was farthest from the equator, priests sacrificed a black llama to "tie down the sun." The people were convinced that it worked every time, for on that day the sun stopped receding! (Our own English word for this day, "solstice," comes from a Latin verb, "to stand still.") Daily the sun god got closer, until he wandered off in the opposite direction, requiring more sacrifices.

Through such rituals ancient people tried to control the gods and spirits. The modern Latin Americans I was seeing on this trip faced contemporary gods--materialism, ideologies, cults, and more. These men and women had their own fears. How were they coping? How was the gospel faring among them? I was anxious to find out.

Ben brought me back to earth by pointing out the site of ancient fortifications once guarding this section of the Inca Trail--the "Roman Road" of the Inca Empire, traversing 3000 miles from the Venezuelan border in the north to the heart of Chile in the south. It was constructed in A.D. 1200-1500. In only eight days, relays of the sun god's messengers, bearing the sacred condor emblem, could run the thousand miles from Quito southward to the empire's capital of Cuzco, "The Navel of the Universe."

The tourist shop at the equator obviously felt *it* was at the center of things. I cast aside the wisdom of modern and ancient science and succumbed to tourism, buying a certificate that declared I had been at the Middle of the World. The officially stamped document stated poetically:

Welcome to the Middle of the World . . .
I embrace you with the igneous fire of the Andes,
With the clouds, the wind, and secret dust.
I toast you with the juice of the sun
In a clay vessel, spiritual ceremony of my ancestors.

Ben and I turned to go. A wet mist blew in our faces. The easterly wind, heavy with moisture from the steamy Amazon basin, rammed into the mountain walls, shooting upward a mile and a half to condense over the Andean snows. Was it defiantly showing the sun who was the master of the equator? Or was it angry at being obstructed in its westward race? In a black rage the wind hurled swirling clouds over the lofty ridge and rumbled off across the Pacific.

The ancient Indians would have said the god of weather was venting his wrath. Sun, wind, lightning, water, earth--to the Inca and his serfs, these were gods affecting daily life and eternal destiny. If they became angry, they could send El Niño to eat all the fish in the sea. (The El Niño current causes the anchovy-laden Humboldt to shift away from the coast, disastrously affecting the livelihood of fishermen in Ecuador, Peru, and Chile.) The gods could devour their farmland with torrential deluge and shake the mountains, causing Pachamama, the earth mother, to belch smoke, fire, and ash.

HARNESSING AN INVISIBLE FORCE

As Ben and I climbed into our van, I noticed a man listening to his transistor radio. "Talk about unseen power!" I said. "The Inca priests couldn't have imagined our use of radio today."

Back at HCJB's studios in Quito we heard the gospel being broadcast in the dominant language of the old Inca Empire, Quechua (spelled Quichua in Ecuador). I'd be hearing that language a lot in my travels, especially in Peru and Bolivia. Quechuas number around 12 million--over half the total of all American Indians. In the control room, an Ecuadorian technician slotted cassette tapes into a bank of machines, as though they were sandwiches stuffed into the mouths of hungry robots. A computer issued commands to start programs at the right time. Lights blinked, reels turned, and meter needles indicated sound levels.

As Ben pushed one button after another on a monitor panel, we heard the gospel in Spanish, German, and English. Chinese, Japanese, Russian and other languages would come on later. HCJB transmits 500 programs weekly in 12 languages, apart from local programs.

"In some Latin American countries a large radio station broadcasting all over the world would be under suspicion," I commented. "How does the government feel about HCJB?"

"I'll show you," Ben said. On an office wall was a beautifully illuminated citation presented to former HCJB President Abe Van Der Puy by the president of Ecuador in 1956, recognizing the evangelical community's contribution to the nation. On the wall beside the citation was Ecuador's highest civilian award, the Order of Merit, also granted to HCJB.

"In the late seventies, Ecuador passed a bill banning foreign ownership of radio stations," Ben explained. "But because of HCJB's long service to the nation, the government exempted it. In fact, in 1981, on our 50th anniversary, Congress unanimously passed a vote of appreciation to HCJB for its services, which included earthquake relief."

GLOBAL CHALLENGE

I was interested to see the radio station because my mission, SIM, along with HCJB and two other major radio missions, is involved in a challenging global commitment. In 1985 HCJB's Ron Cline, Trans World Radio's Paul Freed, and Far East Broadcasting Company's Robert Bowman made a covenant called World By 2000:

> We are committed to provide every man, woman and child on earth the opportunity to turn on their radio and hear the gospel of Jesus Christ in a language they can understand, so they can become followers of Christ and responsible members of His church. We plan to complete this task by the year 2000.

In 1986 the three initiators invited SIM to join in the project, because our Radio ELWA in Liberia, West Africa, completed the broadcast circle around the globe. Other broadcasters, like FEBC's associate, Far East Broadcasting Association, worked with our four organizations. We in turn sought to provide tools for missions and churches already ministering in many of the languages.

I could almost hear the Psalmist burst into singing Psalm 19:1-4 upon hearing about this radio fulfillment of creation's witness:

> *The heavens declare the glory of God;*
> *the skies proclaim the work of his hands.*
> *Day after day they pour forth speech;*

night after night they display knowledge.
There is no speech or language
where their voice is not heard.
Their voice goes out into all the earth,
their words to the ends of the world.

From personally working with the other three executives, I knew that the World By 2000 commitment was one of the biggest challenges we have faced. First, we had to find out who can't yet hear the gospel by radio. Even if there isn't a gospel broadcast in their own tongue, can they understand a trade language? We recognized that many small groups are better reached by agencies such as Language Recordings Incorporated (formerly Gospel Recordings).

Which of the unreached groups are within the scope of our transmitters? Will we need new equipment or additional power to reach the others? Will our constituencies catch the vision and provide the major resources needed? Where will we find writers and narrators in some of the new languages? How can we challenge Christians to pray in faith?

"If the Lord wants us to fulfill this commitment, He'll have to help us find the answers," said HCJB World Radio President Ron Cline. "I'm sure God is pleased with our worldwide cooperation. It helps avoid duplication and enables us to plan jointly."

COLONIAL HERITAGE

My time in Quito was too brief to do justice to this beautiful city, a reminder of Latin America's colonial past. Some have called it "The Florence of the Americas" because of its art treasures. Quito's Cathedral of San Francisco has altars and ceilings that shine with Inca gold. UNESCO has declared the ancient churches and other buildings in the city's old quarter a World Heritage site.

These reminders of the Spanish past are upstaged in the archaeological museum by a collection of Indian ceramics dating back to 3100 B.C. Jugs shaped like birds and frogs make the sound of the respective creature when liquid is poured out of them.

Quito became the northern capital of the Inca Empire. Now it is a city of one million people, one-tenth of Ecuador's population. The nation was once officially dedicated to the Sacred Heart of Jesus and was solidly Catholic.

Now I saw something of the recent growth of evangelicals in the nation. Rachel Saint was in town, reminding me of the response among the Auca Indians, jungle dwellers who, in 1956, murdered her brother and his four missionary companions. Evangelicals represent only 3.2 percent of the 10 million population of this nation, which is the size of Nevada or New Zealand. But there were no evangelical churches when the first interdenominational evangelical mission, Gospel Missionary Union, arrived in Ecuador in 1896. Now GMU churches number 500.

SIM conferred with GMU and other mission and church leaders after HCJB urged SIM to send teams into unevangelized areas to follow up gospel broadcasts.

"There's a lot to be done in gospel outreach," said GMU President Dick Darr. "For a long time Ecuador had the lowest percentage of evangelicals in Latin America, but praise the Lord, that's changing."

The southern province of Loja (population 260,000), near the Peruvian border, was the most unreached, according to research by the Latin American evangelical research office, Puente. Although evangelistic teams were finding response in other parts of the nation, in the south entire communities were isolated by the terrain and by deep-seated opposition. SIM was working in close cooperation with Ecuador's Evangelical Missionary Association, Mission to the World, and others.

LATIN AMERICA: SIMILAR AND DIFFERENT

Robert Allen Hatch, who lived in Quito at the time, gave me a helpful overview of Latin America. Al had his hands full as executive secretary of the Latin America Committee of EFMA and IFMA (Evangelical Foreign Missions Association and Interdenominational Foreign Mission Association), coordinator of Puente (Spanish for "Bridge"), and administrator of the Spanish office of the Iberoamerican Missions Committee (COMIBAM).

"Puente's first activity was in 1976--a consultation on church-mission relations and theological issues. Those were delicate and explosive topics, and a lot of emotion was involved on both sides," Al told me.

Al's work as Puente coordinator took him all over Latin America, making him keenly aware of current issues. He developed many close friendships and could easily have been taken for a South American, with his dark eyes, heavy eyebrows, and fluent Spanish.

"People in the Northern Hemisphere tend to think of Latin America as one huge entity. How accurate is that?" I asked.

"Not at all!" Al answered. "Any Latin American will tell you that although there are certain broad cultural elements that link them, there are also major distinctions--and the countries are proud of them."

Al listed the common factors: language and culture, widespread problems of underdevelopment, the struggle for self-reliance and identity, and the Catholic religion.

As to distinctions, Al pointed out that the Andean countries of Ecuador, Peru, and Bolivia have strong aboriginal elements, whereas Chile, Uruguay, and Argentina are more influenced by the culture of Europe. The tropical countries on the northern coast of South America, along with Central America, have a vivacious character.

"I'm trying to understand the major issues affecting Latin America--the context which the gospel has to work in," I said. "I've talked with Latin American leaders, and they list poverty, the drug trade, guerrilla activity, and a Catholic veneer over animistic beliefs. Would you add anything to that list?"

"All of those are major issues," Al agreed. "And so often it's the church and the local believers who suffer. As they suffer, God ministers to others through them. I wouldn't wish suffering on any country. There has been an incredible loss of life--excruciating persecution that has left wounds in society. And yet this tribulation is purifying the church and shaking the very foundations of society, resulting in a new openness to the gospel. I think Christians in the rest of the world can learn a lot from the evangelical churches in Latin America." How were those churches faring in face-to-face struggle with the major forces currently shaping the continent? I looked forward to finding out during my travels.

(Since this book was written, Al died from a heart attack while ministering in Mexico. He was a young-looking 47. He will be greatly missed.)

A SOUTHERN CROSS

Leaving Al, I walked out into the night. It was only 7 p.m., but at the equator there is no twilight--darkness descends like a drawn blind. The soft lights of the city glowed on the hillsides, as though the stars had fallen out of the sky. Otherwise everything was dark--except for three red lights on an HCJB antenna planted high on Mount Pichincha, a volcano that had recently been rumbling. To me, those lights looked like a Southern Cross of hope, shining in the darkness of a turbulent continent.

Before I left Ecuador the next day, Ron and Barbara Cline of HCJB took me out to a buffet luncheon served with Latin flair: a long line of tables laden with platters of hors d'oeuvre, soup, salads, vegetables, fish, fowl, and other meats. Another row of tables displayed tempting desserts. Ecuador does not know famine. All was produced within the country, and many of the vegetables, such as corn, tomatoes, potatoes, were indigenous to the area.

"Tell me what I'm eating!" I said to Ron and Barbara when we found a table on the crowded floor. Quechua musicians played while we ate.

"That's *ceviche* you're starting with," they explained. "It's made with marinated seafood. Here, put these kernels of toasted corn on top. That white pasty thing is hominy, also made from corn. You can eat it with your roast guinea pig."

We finished the meal with demitasses of strong black coffee and exotic fruit: tart prickly pear and mild granadilla-- black seeds in milky pulp.

As I was leaving for Simon Bolivar airport, an equatorial deluge burst on the city--hail mixed with driving rain.

The airlines have a unique way of coping with the rain in Ecuador. There wasn't a covered departure ramp or a bus to take me to the plane. Instead, an airline attendant handed me an umbrella at the departure gate. When I boarded the aircraft, I handed it back to an attendant, who had his arms full of wet umbrellas. Our Air Ecuadoriana flight taxied toward the runway, passing planes of other airlines I'd never heard of: SAETA, TAME, and AVIANCA.

Up we soared until we broke through the ragged clouds into a clear sky. The blazing sun was *north* of us across the equator. So, too, were the five nations that form the northern cap of the continent: Colombia, Venezuela, Guyana, Suriname, and French Guiana. They look toward Central America and the circle of the Caribbean. I'd be in the middle of that political cauldron near the end of my safari when visiting Cuba.

But for the present, I headed south toward Cuzco, the Navel of the Universe, high in the Peruvian Andes. From my airplane seat I wondered how often the Inca's wizards had wished they could fly into the sky and tie down the sun!

As for me, I was looking forward to being reunited with my wife, Lorna, who would meet me in Cuzco. Our guides there would be veteran SIMers Bill and Gloria Kornfield.

When you look up to the sky and see the sun, the moon, and
the stars . . . do not be enticed into bowing down to them.
DEUTERONOMY 4:19

2

NAVEL

OF THE

UNIVERSE

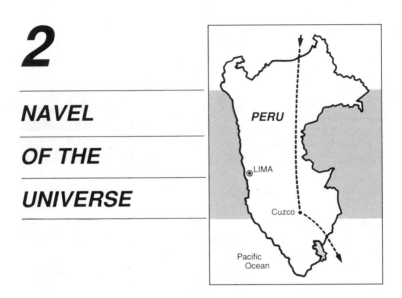

Traditional flags in rainbow colors fluttered over the streets of Cuzco, the Inca "holy city"--in earlier days as sacred as Jerusalem to Jews, or Mecca to Muslims. Lorna and I followed Bill and Gloria Kornfield onto a bus headed for the site of the Inti Raymi festival. One of the most important Inca festivals, it takes place on the day of the southern winter solstice--when the sun reaches its furthest distance north of the equator.

"We want to know something about the background of the people," we told Bill and Gloria. "Then maybe we'll under-

stand the significance of what's happening today, especially the impact of the gospel."

We couldn't have had better guides into the heart of the Inca Empire. Bill has a doctorate in cultural anthropology, specializing in Andean cultures. Both he and Gloria speak Spanish fluently and relate easily to every stratum of society.

On the bus were people from all over the world. The festival site is in the fortress ruins of Sacsayhuaman (Quechua for "satisfied eagle"). There we were swallowed by a vast crowd of Peruvians. The rocks of the fortress, looking out over Cuzco ("the navel"), were covered with colorfully attired men, women, and children who had come to witness the important event.

The size of the fortress boulders boggled my mind. Some of them were taller than I, and weighed up to 300 tons each. How did the Quechua artisans move these boulders, let alone shape and fit them so perfectly? One rock is carved into the shape of a throne overlooking a flat parade ground, where the Inca used to sit and review his warriors and receive the homage of the people.

FESTIVAL OF THE SUN

For today's ceremony, a huge dais had been built in the middle of the ancient parade ground. The roll of drums and the mysterious sound of large conch shells, blown like French horns, announced the arrival of the Inca's queen, enacted by a university student. Men swept her pathway as barechested braves carried her throne, surrounded by beautiful maidens.

They were followed by more maidens throwing flower petals on the path in preparation for the Inca's arrival. At last he came, carried on his throne by young warriors. As the royal procession moved around the arena, the young men and women stretched out their arms and bowed to the ground. The cheering of the vast crowd echoed from the fortress ramparts.

When the Inca (whose part was enacted by a dignified university professor) was seated on the dais, a torchbearer ran around the quadrangle setting fire to a haystack in each corner, representing the four corners of the empire. Governors came forward to present their gifts and recount their exploits.

At last the moment arrived to divine the coming year. Priests placed a black llama, its legs tied, on the altar before the Inca. As the governors solemnly watched, the high priest raised his golden sacrificial knife. With swift strokes he stabbed into the animal's chest, cut out its heart, and lifted the heart high toward the sun.

The priest announced that the llama's heart was still beating as he removed it. A murmur of approval went around the vast crowd. It was a good omen. Then there was prolonged silence as the high priest brooded over the entrails, divining what they foretold. He finally announced that the year ahead would be one of prosperity. A cheer went up from the crowd.

The high priest lifted a golden dish toward the sun, with a libation of the llama's blood. He walked over to the Inca, who dipped his fingers into the blood and drank a few drops from the cup. The governors did likewise, and then, along with the Inca, raised their hands to the sun, chanting a Quechua hymn to the sun god. The maidens encircling the dais raised their arms to the sun and swung them back toward the Inca, to indicate his inherited deity. In a rhythm accompanied by reed flutes and drums, they chanted: "O great and very powerful lord, son of the sun, only ruler, may all the earth obey you!"

Now the chief priest's voice boomed out over the loudspeaker, assuring people they would get all their desires and the maximum harvest from their crops. In an ancient benediction, he invoked the strength of the puma, wisdom of the snake, and fertility of the falcon--the powerful trio of Inca tradition.

Silence fell over the people as the Inca stood to exhort them. "The eternal sun commands good for our great empire, based on your zeal and your work!" he intoned. "We should be useful people, so that all will work out well for us."

To us and the other tourists, it was only a dramatization of an ancient ritual, but it was obvious that it had deeper meaning for the thousands of Quechuas around us. It was a somewhat eerie scene: the backdrop of boulders covered with humanity, looking like colorful rock gardens shrouded by the gray smoke of the quadrangle bonfires. Maidens held up their votive offerings toward the sun, and braves raised their spears in salute to the Inca. The haunting strains of Quechua flutes added to the illusion that we had been whisked back in time a thousand years.

RISE AND FALL OF AN EMPIRE

"The Inca and his officials had a genius for organization," explained Bill as we rode back to the city. They used that genius for nearly three centuries, although as an empire, the Inca civilization lasted only from 1476 to 1532--about half a century. It absorbed the textile, ceramics, metalworking, and stonebuilding skills which earlier Andean civilizations had developed. Writing, however, was unknown, perhaps because of superstition that "letters" would bring evil from the gods. A system of knotted strings recorded special events. The wheel was not used by the Incas or other American Indians, although there is evidence that the concept was known by some. Was it also banned because of superstition?

At its height, the Inca empire covered 1.2 million square miles (half the size of contiguous U.S.A.), rivaling the Roman Empire in size. A 10,000-mile road network aided travel throughout the domain. The Inca ruled over perhaps six million people representing 100 Indian tribes. Inca means "king" in the language of the largest ethnic group, the Quechuas. There was only one Inca at a time, but the term "the Incas" has been loosely extended to the people of the empire.

"It's amazing to think that this tremendous empire was conquered by an uneducated Spanish soldier!" Bill exclaimed.

That soldier was Francisco Pizarro, who arrived in 1532 in search of gold. He and his men had heard reports of an Indian ruler who dusted himself with gold before ceremonial bathing. The Spaniards dubbed him, El Dorado, "The Gilded One." (There actually was a ruler further north, in what is now Colombia, who practiced such a ritual.)

Pizarro had only 37 horses and 183 armed men. The Quechua warriors had never seen horses or firearms, but fought bravely. Probably the biggest factor in their defeat was the weakening effect of a civil war between the Inca Huascar, ruling from Cuzco, and his half brother Atahualpa, ruling from Quito. Atahualpa had killed Huascar and was sole ruler when Pizarro ambushed him. The Spanish promised to free the Inca if his men filled one room with gold and another with silver. Pizarro then treacherously assassinated Atahualpa before pushing on to Cuzco, center of the empire. With its "divine" emperor dead, the theocracy quickly collapsed.

Because Atahualpa had killed Huascar, the people of Cuzco at first welcomed Pizarro as their avenger. Soon, however, their own blood was flowing on the streets as the conquistadors took the city. While driven by lust for gold and silver, the Spaniards also believed they were divinely commissioned to destroy every vestige of paganism in the Inca Empire, in the name of Christianity.

POWER CLASH

Now we were here, in the Navel of the Universe, where the fanatical religious zeal of the Spanish conquistadors met head-on with the entrenched religious fervor of the Inca Empire. To Catholic Spaniards, Inca worship of the sun was an abomination that had to be destroyed. To animistic Indians, Catholic destruction of the Inca and places of worship threatened not only the existence of the empire, but also their very lives.

The Incas considered mankind and earth to be inseparable. Man was created from the earth, and every rock held a spirit. Priests and artisans had to carefully calculate how to cut each stone so the spirit inside would not be offended. It was not just craftsmanship or artistry that made them fit the stones so perfectly--it was a matter of ensuring the spiritual unity of a building.

In one wall we noticed a large rock with 12 different angles, or planes. Surrounding rocks were made to fit perfectly against these facets. In some cases a small protrusion from a rock had to be fitted into the next rock, although it would have been so much easier to knock it off and make two flat surfaces. I couldn't understand why some projections were cut off and others not. But Inca priests divined which ones were spirit manifestations. The result was a wall face intricately fitted like some vast neolithic jigsaw puzzle. Ancient Inca structures have withstood earthquakes, while Spanish-era buildings have fractured.

To demonstrate that Christianity had replaced paganism, the Spaniards forced the Quechuas to pull down the Inca temples, square off the stones, and build churches with them. They erected the imposing Cuzco cathedral on the site of the Inca palace, dominating the city's main square. The conquistadors buried alive one of the Inca's successors in the wall of the cathedral. Each time there is an earthquake, many Quechuas expect him to break out of the wall and return to life.

While outwardly conforming to their master's new religion, the Quechuas had their way of retaliation. They hid an idol under the altar of the cathedral as they were building it. Later, when they came to worship, they were in fact bowing down before their idol.

"There's a difference between Quechua Catholic religion and the Spanish Catholic religion," explained an elderly guide who showed us around the cathedral. "To the Quechuas, the Virgin Mary is Pachamama, the earth mother goddess. The Spaniards didn't believe that."

However, Catholic elevation of Mary lends itself to the Quechua belief. The archway of a Jesuit church across the square carries the inscription, "Come unto Mary all you that are burdened and weary with your sins, and she will give you rest."

Our guide showed us the religious paintings and figures that fill the cathedral. Jesus was inevitably shown as a pathetic figure in anguish. One of the saints held his own decapitated head on a Bible. Most of the paintings were depressing, mournful, bloodstained figures. There was no joy in this religion. Mary was the only healthy looking figure, striking a queenly pose.

The Quechua artists were good at contextualizing. Some figures were obviously their beloved Pachamama. In some frescoes an Inca sun shone over a patron saint, and a sacred condor, not a dove, represented the Holy Spirit. The artists often used as models their own faces or those of the sponsors who commissioned the paintings as acts of penance to gain merit after death.

"Mary Magdalene has a rather masculine face!" I commented in front of a huge portrait. The guide explained that her face was that of the man who paid the artist. Another large painting showed the Last Supper à la Quechua, complete with baskets of tropical fruit, hot peppers, potatoes, and a roasted guinea pig--its four legs sticking straight up. Judas is holding his bag of money as he peers furtively around.

"Judas' face is the sponsor's face," explained our guide. "He asked the artist to paint his face on Judas' body, as an act of penance."

About fifty people were attending a special Mass in a side chapel, in honor of St. John the Baptist Day, the Catholic alternative to Inti Raymi. Worshipers went forward to kneel at the altar rail to receive the wafer they believed was the actual body of Christ. Some had lit candles to burn before the figures of saints.

The peaceful silence of the cathedral was suddenly shattered by a succession of explosions. We rushed to the side door and were met by a fanfare of brass instruments and drums played by a group of Indians standing in the main entrance. I thought some pagans had come to disturb the solemn Catholic Mass, but our guide explained that this was all local custom connected with the special Mass.

Outside, the blasts had set off a verbal row. Policemen accused the celebrators of not having a permit for explosives. While the men shouted and gesticulated in the best Latin tradition, their womenfolk merrily passed champagne around to celebrate the success of the operation.

As we paid our guide, Bill asked him when he had become a Christian.

"When the Spaniards came, they did away with the old idol worship, and everybody became a Christian," he replied.

"But there's a big difference between Christianity as a religion and personal faith in Christ as your Saviour," Bill explained. "Here are several Bible verses I've written out for you. They'll tell you how to receive Jesus. Will you read them and ask the Lord Jesus Christ to be your personal Saviour?"

"I will," promised the guide.

SYNCRETISM AND TRUTH

"We were planning to take you tomorrow to the ruins of the ancient city, Machu Picchu," said Bill, back at the hotel. "But I've the feeling we should change our train reservations to the following day. Lorna and Gloria are tired from traveling, and we can use the day to get some insights from friends in Cuzco."

We readily agreed, for the effects of the city's 11,000-foot altitude were getting to us. In the morning, Bill tracked down a French priest he had known years before. Fray Miguel coordinated the rural development work of the Catholic church throughout the Cuzco valley. I was interested to ask a Catholic priest what he thought about the syncretism we had witnessed.

We'd noted that the Inti Raymi parade started from Santo Domingo church with two blessings: one from the Catholic priest, and one from the Inca's high priest, who poured out a libation to the sun on the ancient foundations. (The church was built on the foundations of the Inca Temple of the Sun.)

"Catholicism here is very far removed from the original meaning of the gospel," Miguel agreed. "We want to integrate evangelical values into the total life of the people."

The "evangelical values" turned out to be "the solidarity of mankind, sympathy, and affection." Commendable values, we agreed, but lacking the essential of spiritual rebirth by faith in Christ.

"I don't think the Indian concept of the Virgin Mary is an idolatrous one," Miguel told us. "Rather, they have a spiritual concept of her as the spiritual power of the earth mother. They think of the Virgin and Pachamama as being the same. We work with and through their customs, instead of trying to change them."

I next asked the priest what he thought of liberation theology--the concept that sin is institutional and must be overthrown, by violence if necessary, before the people can find salvation, namely, liberation from exploitation.

Miguel said his diocese doesn't espouse liberation theology and violence. In fact, he's received threats from the Peruvian Communist guerrilla movement, called *Sendero Luminoso* (Shining Path).

"Three times my team members have received messages threatening them with annihilation if they don't stop their village development work," Miguel said. "University students have accused me of helping the government and not being revolutionary enough to bring about real change. But the archbishop of Cuzco has accused me of being subversive and a Marxist because I'm working among the peasants!"

I looked at this dedicated man, ready to face danger in order to help people. I longed that he might personally have eternal life and be able to lead others to the knowledge of Christ as Saviour.

As we were leaving Miguel, we noticed two clean-cut American young men in business suits striding past, each with a black briefcase.

"They look like Mormons," I observed.

"Yes," Miguel said. "There are many of them! They don't have any program to help the people--they just go around witnessing." I learned that the Mormons operate a copper mine in southern Peru to finance hundreds of their missionaries.

After the discussion with the priest, it was refreshing to meet Pastor Luis Guisada, local superintendent of the Peruvian Evangelical Church *(Iglesia Evangelica Peruaña--IEP)*.

Besides pastoring the main IEP church in Cuzco, Luis is responsible for coordinating the work of 200 churches. He also supervises theological education for 500 churches, a ministry SIM assists him in. The young pastor had clear-cut ideas on the people's needs and how to meet those needs.

"Cuzco is surrounded by 350 pagan altars," Pastor Luis told us. "There are dozens of Catholic churches; many of them are trying to help the poor. But they aren't able to provide the most important thing--the life-changing power of the gospel!"

Luis was encouraged by changes he saw in men and women

who received Christ as personal Saviour. At the same time, he and the churches weren't neglecting the physical needs of the poor. They've helped with disaster relief and with rehabilitating needy families. They too had received threats from guerrillas.

There was an air of unrest around Cuzco. With people there from all over Peru, plus many foreign tourists, it was an ideal time for political groups to get attention. Police were on the watch not only for agitators but also for pickpockets, because Cuzco is called The Pickpocket Capital of the World.

As we walked back to our hotel (the name, Royal Inca, was regal, but the price was right, at $15 per person per day), a group of 30 young men marched down the cobbled street toward us. They waved clenched fists and shouted political slogans. I took photographs of them as they shouted angrily. As soon as I put my camera down, they grinned at each other, probably thinking their photos would appear in some overseas newspaper.

THE TRAIN BOMB

"Bomba!" That's the word we heard as we entered the hotel. The manager and his staff were huddled together. The antique clock on the wall pointed to 1 p.m.

"Any problem?" we asked.

The manager turned and looked at us.

"The tourist train to Machu Picchu was blown up this morning!" he said grimly. "Three of our guests were killed."

The train had been crowded because tourists who come to Cuzco for the Festival of the Sun usually go to Machu Picchu the next day, before continuing their journey. That had been our original plan, too. Seven people died and 40 others were injured when explosives ripped through the two-car train.

We hurried to our rooms and prayed for those who were injured and for the relatives of the dead. Three of the dead tourists had been with us in that very hotel the night before.

We also thanked the Lord that He had protected us from injury or death. We marveled at His guidance, for we could have been on that train. I looked at the Scripture verse my sisters had given us before we left Canada: The angel of the Lord encamps around those who fear him, and he delivers them (Psalm 34:7)--"from guerrillas or *whatever!*"they added.

Who blew up the train? Why did they do it? All kinds of speculations were going around the hotel. One was that it was a reprisal for the deaths of several hundred Shining Path guerrillas who were killed the week before, when police bombed their cells in Lima to end a prison rebellion. Perhaps the Shining Path guerrillas were using the presence of the crowds in Cuzco to make a public statement--or to further upset the economy by discouraging tourism. Although an estimated nine thousand Peruvians had been killed over the past eight years by the guerrillas, this was the first time they had attacked tourists.

Bill and I headed for the station, but armed soldiers wouldn't let anyone in.

"Bill, look to your left," I whispered. "There's a TV crew trying to get in that small side entrance. Let's go!"

It was a government television crew, and we followed hard on their heels. The guard took a look at my telephoto camera and my Canadian passport, and let us inside.

The damaged passenger cars were on a siding. While the TV crew photographed the exterior, Bill and I climbed inside and were shocked with the scene of carnage. A vast hole was blown through the roof of one car, and seats were torn from the floor. Both cars were splattered with blood from injuries caused by flying glass. The TV crew told us that shortly before the train was due to leave, a young man, perhaps a university student, had placed a covered basket on the overhead luggage rack in one of the cars and then left. As the train started moving, a bomb in the basket blew up.

Outside, while the TV camera rolled, the newscaster asked us what we thought of the tragedy. We expressed our condolences and shock. Bill added that such an act of terrorism was far removed from anything to do with the gospel of Jesus Christ.

"Are you still planning to go to Machu Picchu?" the interviewer asked us.

"Yes, indeed!" we replied. "We're planning to go tomorrow."

Clips of the TV interview were shown in Lima and

overseas, we later learned. But SIM missionaries in Bolivia heard only a radio report of the bombing. They were very worried, because they knew our original plan was to travel to Machu Picchu that day. When we eventually got through by telephone, they were greatly relieved.

OPERATION PICKPOCKET

Bill and I walked back towards the hotel with heavy feet. We had caught a glimpse of the violence which some Latin Americans face daily. It was hard to imagine. Life on the busy streets around us looked so normal. These were lovable, industrious people. Everyone seemed to be selling something. A round-faced woman, wearing a straw hat and multicolored shawl, wound wool on a bobbin. Another woman squatted on the curb of the cobbled street and wove cloth on a traditional handloom, stretching the threads with her toes. A little man sold a woolen blanket, making the sign of the cross with the money before pocketing it. A farmer, his woolen cap flapping with each step, peddled potatoes from an enormous sackful on his back. Another farmer had a slaughtered pig tied on his back with a shawl. A woman, cheeks red from living at a high altitude, led her family's llama past parked cars.

Bill and I stopped to take photographs of a picturesque archway. A peasant woman, baby tied to her back with a colorful shawl, suddenly stumbled and fell at my feet. She grabbed my left leg as if to protect herself as she fell.

Mindful of the warnings about pickpockets, I instinctively placed my hands over my safari jacket pockets. I could feel the wad of folded paper *intis* which I kept handy to give people whose photos I took. My camera bag was safely slung over my right shoulder, protected by my arm.

Bill saw the woman sprawling on the ground and courteously stooped to help her get up. As she did so, she grabbed a cloth that a woman behind me had dropped, and the two disappeared in the crowd.

"That was strange!" I said. "But if they were pickpockets, they didn't get anything!"

Later that evening Lorna and I went for a walk to enjoy

seeing the floodlit colonial churches. Their bells, cast in Spain 300 years ago, tolled softly. As a security measure I left my camera bag, in which I usually kept my wallet, back in the hotel room. The night air was chill, so I thrust my hands into my jacket pockets. To my surprise my left hand went right through. Thinking the pocket seam had fallen apart, I examined it and was amazed to find a long slash right across the face of the pocket--in fact, through three layers of fabric. The roll of paper money was still lodged in a corner.

"My pocket . . . it's slit!" I exclaimed. We rushed back to the room to see if my wallet was in the camera bag. It wasn't there! I must have put it in my pocket by mistake after getting change from it at the station.

Suddenly I remembered the woman who had fallen at my feet. Lorna and I put together the scenario. By the time my hand reached my pocket to protect it, the woman behind had already slit it, whipped out my wallet onto the ground, and dropped a cloth over it. I felt nothing except the woman in front grabbing my leg to distract me. She picked up the cloth with my wallet under it and made off.

"Just to think you were overcome by two market women!" Lorna chuckled after we regained our composure. I had to admit they were very clever!

Our *South American Handbook* stated: "If you are robbed, the police will not normally investigate your complaint; getting things back is largely up to you and fate. Stolen items often turn up in the local market and can be bought back cheaply."

But we met friendly tourism police and headed for their office. There we found half a dozen forlorn-looking foreigners, each with a story of ingenious pickpockets.

A dejected European couple told us they had just lost everything on a train. At a station, some men on the platform were putting on an act, and all the passengers peered out the windows to watch. That's when thieves got the bags which the couple had safely stowed under their seat! Two other tourists lost their expensive mountain-climbing gear. It had been in a bag over one man's left shoulder. When a stranger asked him the time, he raised his left arm to look at his watch. An accomplice slashed the strap from behind and made off with the bag.

A policewoman took down details and had me sign a statement with my fingerprint on it. She told us we must go and purchase two sheets of foolscap white paper from a local shop and bring these back for an official report to be typed. We also must go to the bank to purchase an official form as proof of our declaration. But by then all offices were closed. After a number of visits to the police and the market, we decided there was no point in pursuing the matter. We just thanked the Lord that our loss was so small in comparison to the tragic loss of life on the bombed train.

Cuzco really had turned out to be not only the Navel of the Universe, but also the Pickpocket Capital of the World!

LOST INCA CITY

The Cuzco flag was at half-mast over the railroad station when we arrived early the next morning to take the train to Machu Picchu. *DINAMITAN TREN A MACHU PICCHU* (Machu Picchu Train Dynamited), screamed the headline of a newspaper flown in from Lima. Inside was a series of drawings showing tourists boarding the train, a young man placing the bomb-laden basket in the baggage rack, and passengers being blown to bits. As our train proceeded to Machu Picchu, soldiers with submachine guns at the ready stood in each railroad car. There were plenty of seats available, because a number of tourists had canceled the trip. They feared the guerrillas might follow up their attack on the train by blowing up bridges or tunnels.

"This probably will be the safest journey this train has made in a long time!" remarked Bill. "The security is tight. The government doesn't want to lose the tourist traffic."

We knew our lives were really in God's hands, and so we bowed in prayer, thanking the Lord for His continued protection, and committing the trip to Him.

Our train, with only three cars, zigzagged out of Cuzco's "navel." The grade is steep, with no room for hairpin turns; instead the train reverses back and forth up to the rim of the valley. Once over the top, we descended to the Urubamba River and followed its serpentine course, soldiers standing alert at the carriage doorways. The train suddenly stopped at a bridge. Two crew members jumped out and clipped telephone wires to a box at the base of a telegraph pole.

"They're reporting back to Cuzco that the bridge is O.K.," Bill explained.

Farther along the track everything suddenly went black-- we were in a tunnel. After the mountain disgorged our train at the other end without incident, the train stopped again and the crew jumped out to telephone another report.

It was interesting to see quaint mountain villages from the train. Some of the stone huts had crosses on their roofs, with a miniature bull on either side. The villagers were obviously taking no chances, and were using symbols of both Christianity and pagan religion to ward off evil spirits. The surrounding hillsides were terraced all the way up, for farming.

By the time we reached the station at the foot of Machu Picchu Mountain, the previously placid Urubamba had turned into a frothing serpent writhing through the jungle-covered gorge. It had taken us only three hours to travel the 70 miles from Cuzco, but in 1911 it took a young archaeologist from Yale, Hiram Bingham, a week on muleback and on foot before he discovered the lost city of the Incas. He paid a Quechua the equivalent of 50 cents (two or three times the daily wage) to show him what the Spanish conquistadors had never found.

"The sight held me spellbound," wrote Bingham, whose father and grandfather were missionaries. "Would anyone believe what I had found? It is the work of a master artist."

Although Bingham became famous as the discoverer, the first foreigner to find the ruins may have been a British missionary, Thomas Payne. Some people believe that Quechua friends led Payne to the site before Bingham heard of it. Payne wrote to the Royal Archaeological Society to recommend exploration of the ruins.

The only way in at that time was over the Inca Trail, but now we took the easy way in a minivan that crawled along the edges of 14 hairpin curves from the train tracks up to the top.

In spite of the descriptions we had read and photographs we had seen, we were hardly prepared for the mysterious scene that lay before us.

Since the Incas had no written language, to this day no one knows the actual name of this fortress city, 7000 feet above sea level. Simply known as Machu Picchu, or Old Mountain, it is carved from the pinnacle of a granite "hound's tooth" that rises 2000 feet above the river.

We entered the city through a trapezoidal stone arch--the only access in Inca days. This self-contained fortified village was able to feed several thousand inhabitants from terraced gardens. Water flowed along an aqueduct from a mountain spring a mile away. We could see how the city was divided into sections for agriculture, military barracks, clan residences, and a temple. A cemetery had been excavated, unearthing a royal mausoleum containing gold-encased mummies. Most of the skeletons turned out to be those of women, leading to speculation that Machu Picchu may have been a refuge for the fabled Women of the Sun, who performed temple rituals.

"The Incas knew there was life after death, because there was a word for it," our Peruvian guide explained. "In fact, the use of 'three' in the temples may have referred to a trilogy rather than a trinity: life, death, and life after death."

The Inca Pachacutec, who may have built Machu Picchu, apparently looked beyond the sun god, Inti, to the sun's creator, known as Viracocha. Inca hymns passed down from the 15th century indicate that Pachacutec questioned worship of the sun and ordered his household to worship their creator god.

"Notice how perfectly these steps are made," Bill pointed out as we climbed to the temple of the sun. Back in Cuzco we had nearly stumbled headlong down flights of steps, because more recent carpenters and masons did not make them uniform. That was not the case during the Inca regime. The same care for detail and craftsmanship was shown in the temple. An eight-foot-high vertical slab was perfectly shaped, with the surrounding stones fitting precisely against it.

NO EXTRATERRESTRIALS!

How was the city built? Who built it? Who lived there? Tour guides come up with all kinds of stories to satisfy visitors, but the truth is that archaeologists are still searching for some of the answers. Meanwhile, strange theories are put forth, such as the one about the Incas having discovered the secret of melting stone and casting it in any shape they wanted!

Those who believe in visitors from space are convinced that Machu Picchu is the workmanship of extraterrestrial visitors. That upsets the Peruvian government. They were particulary unhappy with the American mystic, Shirley Mac-Laine. She claimed that her spirit floated out of her body when she was soaking in an Andean mineral bath, inspiring her to return to Machu Picchu to make a film about unidentified flying objects and extraterrestrials.

"How did the Inca workmen get such enormous flats of stone up to that height without iron tools and without the wheel?" the film's producer asked. "It isn't known for sure how they did it, and that leaves room for speculation."

The National Institute of Culture took exception: "It doesn't matter to us if people have contact with extraterrestrials. What does matter is whether someone tries to profane our historical monuments with the idea they were made by extraterrestrials."

A Peruvian physician employed to treat the filming crew for altitude sickness had another thought: "All this filming apparatus is very impressive. For people here, it's something coming from outer space!"

Archaeologists have demonstrated how the Indians could move mammoth blocks from quarries and split them with bronze crowbars and stone tools. Another method was to drive wooden wedges into cracks, pour in water during the winter, and let the expanding ice finish the job. The stippled surface of many rocks shows how they were carefully shaped through patient pounding. Temple stones were polished with sand.

Under the organizational genius of the Incas, the Quechua people worked tirelessly, considering it a privilege to build temples for the worship of the son of the sun. Didn't the earth goddess Pachamama give birth to each boulder? And didn't each stone contain a spirit? Their religious beliefs motivated them, and their craftsmanship and patient toil produced results which seem incredible today. For instance, archaeologists think that 20,000 Indians worked for 30 years to build the fortress of Sacsayhuaman outside Cuzco.

On Machu Picchu's highest point we found a sacred sundial carved from a huge block of stone. This was where Inca priests "tied down the sun," to keep it from wandering farther away. From this vantage point we looked around on the lost city. The stone buildings blended into the mountain top, as if it had given birth to them. Many would have been indistinguishable from the natural outcroppings had not the sun cast shadows, embossing them in the clear mountain air.

MOUNTAIN CONQUERORS

The Inca people truly conquered the mountains. They made them their servants, using their pinnacles as lookouts and their ramparts as fortifications. From mountain springs they irrigated their farmland, terraced down the steep slopes. With mountain granite they built temples and houses, and with mountain grasses they thatched their roofs. Their women decorated themselves with gold and semiprecious stones found in the riverbeds.

From the shrubs and trees which blanketed the mountain's flanks, they picked fruit and seeds that provided color to dye llama wool. The leaf of one tree was a treatment for rheumatism, and a certain herb was a thousand times sweeter than sugar. Another shrub with pink berries provided a sticky substance like eucalyptus, used for embalming their dead. From sisal they wove baskets, and from bamboo made flutes to provide entertainment. They planted crops at different levels, and if one failed, they could survive on another grown at a different altitude.

A small straggly tree, the *quebracho,* provided them with very hard wood that could be shaped while it was green, but dried almost as hard as steel. From this they made clubs and spears, hoes and plows.

The Inca people crisscrossed the ranges on the Inca Trail and domesticated the sure-footed llama for transport. From llama fleece they wove garments to ward off the chill winds, used llama dung for fuel, and with llama meat and potatoes they satisfied their hunger. They developed 600 species of potatoes suitable for growing in different altitudes and soils, mixing the strains so that plague would not wipe out an entire crop.

Although we found the mountain altitude exhausting, the Quechuas apparently thrive on it. In one village, census takers found nine people over a hundred years of age, out of a population of 819. The average in U.S.A. is only three centenarians per hundred thousand!

While catching my breath, I stepped out on a natural promontory and looked straight down 2000 feet to the Urubamba River below. It glistened in the sun like the jade and silver necklaces Lorna had looked at in the Cuzco market. Flowing like a moat around the giant fortress of Machu Picchu, it then was swallowed in the dark folds of the gorge on its way to the Amazon.

That was probably why the Incas built this fortress city in the first place. The ferocious Anti Indians (speculation is that the word Andes was derived from their name) of the river jungles raided high Inca villages and even penetrated Cuzco with their poison-tipped arrows. Long before the Spaniards arrived on the west coast, Antis knew of Inca gold and silver, which could be traded from tribe to tribe along the Amazon until it reached the ports of the east coast.

The Incas established a series of forts along the valley routes used by these jungle marauders. Lowland Indians probably never knew about Machu Picchu, for it could not be seen from the river. As I stood on the mountain peak, the sun's shadows deepened between the gorge walls as if seeking to preserve the mystery of this lost city. A condor floated silently by and disappeared into the clouds that swathed the rugged granite spurs and forested ridges.

The explorer Bingham thought Machu Picchu was the last holdout of the defeated Inca warriors fleeing from the Spaniards. However, other fortified cities since discovered could have been the last refuge. In 1986 Kuelap, twice the size of Machu Picchu, was discovered from the air. Other jungle sites are being uncovered. Fortunately, they have been inaccessible until now, so have not been looted.

It was time to catch a minivan back down to the rail line. While we were waiting for one to arrive, we refreshed ourselves with bottles of Inca Kola, a Peruvian soft drink.

"Do you know who was the last Inca?" Bill asked a young Quechua he'd been talking with.

"Of course--Atahualpa," replied the student.

"No," Bill grinned. "Inca Kola!"

The Indian roared with laughter. Bill explained to us that *cola* is Spanish for "the tail" or "the last."

Also waiting in line for the van was a well-educated Hindu couple from India. They had once lived in South Africa and were interested to know that the four of us had visited there as missionaries.

"May we ask you a blunt question?" they asked. "These ruins around here show what a great civilization the Incas developed. They had their own way of worshiping God before the Spaniards came. Is it right for anyone to force his religion on someone else?"

"Of course not," I replied. "Unfortunately, it's been done throughout history. That's what the Spaniards did in the name of Christianity, and before that the North African Moors did it in the name of Islam when they invaded Spain. It's also what the Roman army did when it invaded Britain."

"We didn't know that!" they replied.

I told the couple that invaders who carried out atrocities in the name of Christianity were not acting according to the Scriptures. We missionaries came not to impose a foreign religion, but rather to tell people about the living God, the Creator himself, who so loved them that He sent His own Son to redeem them.

I went on to tell the couple about communities we had seen freed from the fear of evil spirits and transformed into emancipated, healthy men, women, and children. It all started with an inner spiritual change, not an imposed foreign culture, I explained.

"I wish we could talk more," the couple said as the minivan arrived.

Back in Cuzco the next morning, we took a taxi to the airport to leave for Bolivia . I purchased a copy of *Newsweek,* which carried the cover headline, BLOOD BATH IN PERU. That referred to the bombing of the Shining Path prisoners in Lima. It took another week for us to get the issues of *Newsweek and TIME* which reported the dynamiting of the tourist train in Cuzco. Lorna and I also received a clipping from our hometown paper in Canada, with a front page report: SEVEN KILLED IN BOMB BLAST ABOARD PERUVIAN TRAIN.

Our plane lifted toward the sun as we settled back in our economy class seats. I asked myself the real reason I was thankful we weren't killed in the train blast. Naturally, I was thankful I wasn't among the injured, although I was concerned for those who were.

As a human being, I was glad to be alive. As a Christian, I was glad to have more time to help the people around us who have such great needs. Thousands live on the high plains of the Andes, which stretched out beneath our aircraft. Many of them were driven either by fear of evil spirits or fear of purgatory. They needed to know the Giver of eternal life. Maybe that was one of the reasons God had spared all four of us.

From our aircraft we could see azure Titicaca, the fabled lake the Quechuas believe gave birth to the first Inca. Snowy peaks lined the horizon.

"We are about to land at La Paz airport," a cabin attendant announced. "Make sure your seatbelt is fastened, and when leaving the plane, do not hurry. Please walk slowly! Do not lift heavy luggage!"

He causes his sun to rise on the evil and the good, and sends rain on the righteous and the unrighteous.

MATTHEW 5:45

3

LIFE

TWO

MILES UP

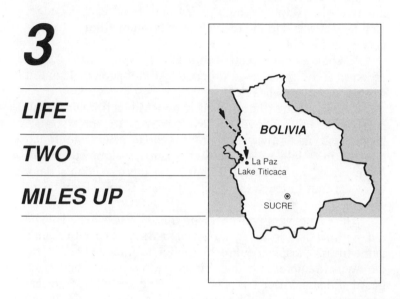

"**L**a Paz has the highest commercial airport in the world!" Bill said as our plane hit the tarmac. I noticed it took longer than usual for the aircraft to come to a stop in the thin atmosphere. In fact, La Paz runways are twice the length of sea level runways for comparable aircraft.

"It's over 13,000 feet here--2000 feet higher than we were in Cuzco," Bill added. "That's about two and a half miles above sea level."

I learned that early U.S. astronauts wore parachutes

programed to open at 10,000 feet--until the space agency realized that astronauts often orbited over Bolivia and would be buried before their chutes opened! Ironically, after taking off from La Paz, light aircraft don't *ascend* to their regulated cruising altitude--they're already above it! Instead, they keep low over the Altiplano (high plain) until they reach its edge; then they *descend* to the regulation maximum altitude for un-pressurized cabins.

As soon as our aircraft cabin doors swung open, the air pressure and oxygen level dropped. All at once our legs felt weak and our arms heavy.

As we walked to the terminal, snowy Mount Illimani, rising nearly four miles above sea level, provided a travel poster backdrop 25 miles away. Earlier that year an airline pilot found that the mountain was no poster when he slammed into it. Members of an SIM-related church on the mountain's flank were the first to reach the crash site--and found all on board dead.

"Illimani never gives up its victims, because it needs to be fed with souls," local Aymara Indians say. The mountain's name means "resplendent royal condor," for legend has it that the Aymara supreme being, Viracocha, assigned condors to guard Illimani. After the plane crash, Indians whispered that the royal condor had been victorious over man's flying machine.

SOROCHE STRIKES

"I'm sick!" Lorna gasped when I awoke in the morning and asked how she'd slept. Lorna is not one to admit she's feeling ill, let alone announce it. So I knew she really was sick. *Soroche* (altitude sickness) had struck! Difficulty in breathing, diz-ziness, headache, nausea, diarrhea, insomnia, and a general willingness to die: she had all the symptoms.

Many visitors travel across the Andes without being af-fected, especially if they arrive at lower altitudes and become acclimatized before traveling higher. It also has a lot to do with one's rate of metabolism, and hemoglobin count. Infection, tiredness, or overexertion can bring it on.

We were staying with the Kornfields, at that time based in La Paz. Bill telephoned a Bolivian doctor, who prescribed *soroche* pills with herbal tea, and 10 minutes of oxygen every hour. Where to find oxygen? The Kornfields asked a Brethren mission couple in the apartment building. They were out of oxygen because several of their missionaries from lower altitudes had recently visited them, but they scoured the city and brought over an oxygen kit. Within a few hours Lorna recovered enough to be able to read in a Bolivian tourism book that there was no such thing as altitude sickness!

"We didn't want to say anything to worry you," the Brethren couple said when I later returned the oxygen kit; "but just two months ago a 55-year-old visitor came down with *soroche,* developed heart congestion, and died right here in the city. We're thankful Lorna has recovered!"

A Bolivian church elder told us how his wife collapsed and died at the airport as she was returning from visiting her parents at sea level in the Caribbean. Bill and Gloria said it usually takes them about three weeks to adjust to the altitude when they return from furlough. The body has to produce more red blood corpuscles to carry enough oxygen to the brain. Andinos have developed larger lungs, more efficient hearts, and more red blood than their lowland cousins.

CITY OF PEACE

From the Kornfields' apartment we looked up at the edge of the Altiplano around us. We were 1000 feet lower than the airport. This city of 1.3 million lies in a basin in the Altiplano, looking as if a meteor had crashed into the high plains, leaving a vast crater strewn with rubble--the adobe, brick and stone huts of the squatter population.

Squatters account for nearly half of the city's residents. The Aymaras (400,000) predominate, for this is their heartland; in the rest of Bolivia the Quechuas are more numerous. The other half of the city's population is of Spanish or mixed European-Amerindian descent. They tend to live as low in the basin as they can, where there is more oxygen and warmth. The year-round mean temperature is 10 C (50 F), but there is wide variation between the heat of the day and the cold of the night. La Paz reverses the norm of many North American cities, where the poor crowd the inner city and the affluent flee to the suburbs.

The Spaniards were attracted to this hole in the high plains because there was gold in the river running through the canyon, and it was sheltered from the Andean winds. The city's full name is *Nuestra Senora de La Paz* (Our Lady of Peace). This was all part of what was called High Peru before Bolivia declared independence in the 1820s. There had been a power struggle between Lima, capital of Lower Peru on the coast, and Sucre, capital of High Peru on the eastern edge of the Andes. La Paz, situated between the two capitals, became a symbol of peace. Sucre is still the constitutional capital of Bolivia, but La Paz is the seat of government and the major center of commerce.

At the time of our visit, the Kornfields lived in one of the high-rise apartments crowding the canyon floor. At night I could imagine I was in a vast amphitheater. The lights of houses lining the sides of the canyon looked like spectators in the grandstand.

ASSIGNMENT: REACHING PEOPLE

"This apartment is a lot different from our first home in a Bolivian village," Gloria said, dusting an intricately painted *kero* --a wooden cup predating the Incas.

"But living among the Andean villagers when we first arrived was probably the most important postgraduate study in anthropology I ever did," Bill added. "It taught us to look at things through the eyes of the people. It also motivated us to learn more about them and the culture, while we told them about the living God."

Bill and Gloria moved from the village to the city of Cochabamba to teach at the Spanish Bible Institute, which later became a seminary. Several of their students are in ministry leadership, including the current seminary principal.

"As the churches grew, the sons and daughters of believers wanted to go on for further education," Bill said. "In the sixties, the Mission became concerned about the increasing number of these young men and women who were losing their faith because of Marxist influences at the university. The Mission had done a good job among the uneducated villagers, but not among the educated people. The gospel and its values were not making an impact on the more influential levels of Bolivian society."

Concerned Christian students suggested Bill approach the university in La Paz about teaching a course in anthropology. To everyone's surprise, the university gladly accepted. Bill's course on "The Origin of Man and Anthropology" was well attended, not only by students but also by several professors. One of them was a card-carrying Communist, head of the Sociology Department. His students demanded that Bill give him time to state the Marxist view of man. As the Communist professor lectured for 45 minutes to a packed session, missionaries and Bolivian believers prayed much.

Then one of the other lecturers, although not a Christian, told the Marxist that he had not answered the points Bill had earlier presented. As a result, that session was the turning point in Bill's gaining acceptance of his creationist view of origins.

"Tell me about the philosophy of limited good I've heard about," I asked Bill.

"It's common in Latin America, but is also found elsewhere," Bill explained. "It arose from the view that there is only so much good in the world, and that if one person receives more than his share, others are limited in what they can receive. Therefore, anyone who rises above the rest is attacked for being successful.

"This has developed into a culture of distrust, on the supposition that everyone is out to hurt the other person. It's become a deadly drag on society, even affecting the development of leadership in some churches. I saw a lot of it in the university. Professors would cut each other down and not associate with the students. I rarely heard a Bolivian compliment anyone."

"So you can imagine how surprised the students were when Bill encouraged them to excel!" Gloria chimed in. "They also were amazed when we invited them to our home for refreshments. We got to know a lot of them that way. One Sunday the students wanted Bill to go with them on an archaeological dig, but when he said he couldn't because he was preaching, several of the students went to the service instead."

COMMITTED COMMUNISTS

"How'd you like to meet some of our student friends?" Bill and Gloria asked. "We're having the Gonzaleses over for lunch. Pepe is leader of the major Communist society at the university. He won last year's student election by a landslide. Pepe was one of my best students when I taught anthropology at the university."

Pepe, wearing horn-rimmed glasses above a boyish smile, didn't look like an agitator. But embroidered on his shirt was "ST" for *Sociedad Trostkiska*, a party which advocates revolution by violence. He'd turned against his affluent parents' Catholic social circle because of the hypocrisy he'd seen. Pepe and his wife Juanita lived very simply while studying political science and economics.

Bill told the Gonzaleses about our visit to Cuzco, mentioning the train bombing. Pepe asked what I thought of that incident. I simply replied I was sorry others had been killed, but thankful we were not on the train. Pepe's eyes narrowed. There was an awkward silence, and I changed the subject. While Gloria served chicken casserole, I asked about hyperinflation in Latin America.

"It's a mess!" Pepe replied. "In some countries 50 percent of the government expenditure is paid as interest on the national debt, 30 percent on the civil service, and 20 percent on the police, army, and security--the mechanisms of maintaining a repressive regime.

"The main economic problem in Latin America is lack of productivity. Production has decreased, but the government has kept on printing money, increasing inflation. The inflationary problems began when countries received massive foreign loans. Now they can't afford to pay these back. We don't think they should repay the loans, but should use that money to encourage the use of foreign capital to increase productivity."

Pepe also blamed problems on bribery and corruption. I asked what the solution was.

The young couple hesitated before replying, "It's very complicated." After all, they were guests and, with Latin courtesy, did not want to offend their hosts. They did say that the necessary changes could never be brought about by the present government system. It was obvious they believed that only a Communist revolutionary government would be able to bring about the needed changes.

The two ardent Communists hadn't heard of liberation theology and its main exponent, Gustavo Gutierrez. That was interesting to me, because some liberation theologians flatter themselves that Communists respect their work. It seems that Communist ideologues tend to dismiss liberation theologians as ineffective experimenters. Religion is still religion and has no place in dialectic socialism, they say.

I asked Pepe and Juanita what they thought about evangelical Christians.

"We don't know much about them," they replied. "It seems they aren't working among the people who really need help. They should be doing more practical things."

Bill explained to the couple that evangelical missionaries have traditionally concentrated among the poor rural peoples, and that SIM missionaries are involved in agricultural and health projects. Of course the Gonzaleses had known only local missionaries who were involved in evangelism among educated urbanites. I added that SIM had extensive relief and development work in Ethiopia, where the Marxist government asked us to help people affected by famine.

At one stage, as I gently pressed my questions, Pepe looked uncomfortable. He began tapping his glass with his fingers while Juanita answered a question hesitantly. Suddenly he stood up, looked around the room as if wanting to leave, and then sat down.

"What's your profession?" he demanded. I told him I was a missionary gathering material for a book on South America, and that I wanted to meet Bolivians like them, even as they would want to meet my people if they came to Canada. Pepe relaxed and we continued. Finally he looked at his watch and said they had to go.

The young couple across the table from me were obviously sincere and committed--in part the product of Communist ideology. I thanked them for sharing their concerns with me and asked if I could share my faith with them since I didn't know if I would ever see them again. They nodded their agreement.

"I agree with the statement of Karl Marx, that religion is the opiate of the people," I started. They looked surprised.

"To me, religion by itself is only a system which man creates in order to try to cope with life and the unknown. The Incas tried to do that with their religious rituals of tying down the sun. Religion without Christ can dull the senses of the people, acting as an opiate--like cocaine."

I went on to explain that Christianity did not start out that way, but that it began as a personal relationship with Jesus Christ. It was only in later centuries that it became corrupted with manmade systems of religion. "Evangelicals," I pointed out, "are trying to bring people back to the original personal relationship with Jesus as their Saviour. When people have that personal relationship with God, they also care more for their fellow human beings, we find."

Pepe and Juanita thanked me, and we parted with a traditional embrace. As they were leaving, I wished Juanita success in her economics course.

"Thank you," she replied, her dark eyes flashing; "--so I can save my nation!"

Obviously the Gonzaleses valued their friendship with the Kornfields. Apart from that friendship, they might never have heard the gospel. Bill and Gloria were praying for a spiritual revolution in their lives--the new birth.

THE REAL AUTHOR: SATAN

"I'm going for the mail," Bill stated. "Want to see the university the Gonzaleses attend?"

As we passed a plaza, a crowd of demonstrators held up placards: "Down with taxes! Down with Yankees! Down with Imperialism!" A platoon of riot police, armed with tear gas and billy clubs, marched toward us. Bill swung down a side street. Later we learned that 90,000 people, mostly rural peasants, had joined the demonstration against tax reforms.

The university was in the heart of town, a cluster of rectangular cement boxes with peeling whitewash. In the lobby of the main building, students in jeans and shirts sorted through tables of used books on sale. Most of the books were Marxist. A poster on the wall stated that voting for student elections was obligatory. Another gave the political platform of one of the students running for leadership: "Open university. A tradition of struggle. Budget, autonomy, science, and revolution!" Another poster declared: "We salute the triumph of power and sociology through unity and change. We shall overcome!"

Some posters advertised courses in Marxism and used slogans from historic Indian uprisings. The Trotsky party had their posters: "Don't pay taxes. Put down the miserable salary increases. Every sector has repudiated the criminal decree of the government!" The Trotskyites had won 49 percent voting rights on the university governing council and had closed down the university on occasion. There seemed to be no voice other than the political left. Bill said the student body is filled with hatred for U.S.A.; no American ambassador would dream of visiting the campus. Yet Bill, an American, had developed personal friendships there.

On the eighth floor we found the classroom where Bill had lectured. Scrawled across the blackboard was the slogan of the Bolivian Communist Party. On each side were posters of candidates declaring, "Vote for the Left. The Right Will Never Change!" "Death to Imperial Fascism!" was chalked across the back wall.

I noticed bare wires sticking out of the wall where electrical sockets used to be. Bill explained that the army had shown their disdain for the university by ripping out switches and wall sockets. When he lectured, he had to twist the electric wires together and insert a light bulb in a socket dangling from the ceiling. He also brought his own chalk and eraser. Classroom chairs were broken.

"In spite of these conditions, the students do reasonably well academically," Bill told me. "There are 25,000 students on five campuses."

Obviously, I decided, one cannot judge academic standards by the appearance of classrooms! Floors, walls, and windows were coated with grime.

Lecturing at the university was a challenging assignment, causing Bill to think through a scriptural view of politics. He wrote a book on Communism, describing its appeal, methods, and weaknesses, as well as the Christian's attitude toward it.

"It's easy to be upset with Communism," Bill said, "but we need to approach the whole matter in humility. Perhaps God may divinely permit it as a scourge of Christless religions and a chastening and purifying of His own people. We need to exercise faith. Instead of being pessimistic and defensive, can we count on the Lord's victory? Have we ever prayed for the conversion of a Communist? Christ died for them as well as for everyone else!"

"We also need to recognize the spiritual conflict," Bill added as we left the university. "The real author is not Marx or Lenin, but Satan. Scripture shows we're engaged in a tremendous spiritual conflict."

PLAZA AND PEOPLE

As we drove through La Paz, I noticed it is a town of plazas--one of the pleasant features of South American cities. In fact, it is an essential part of society to have a plaza for citizens to meet and chat in. Shrubs are watered even in the driest season. Most plazas have a monument, which might be of a local hero or heroine, an unknown soldier, a saint, Christopher Columbus--or best of all, Simon Bolivar himself, after whom Bolivia is named.

Monuments were usually cast in Spain. We saw one which was supposed to be of a Bolivian national hero, but during the Atlantic crossing it had become switched with a monument of a Colombian hero. So the two ended up in the wrong countries. Never mind, a monument is a monument!

We saw some ancient stone monuments dating back to the pre-Inca Tiahuanaco era. Very typical of Tiahuanaco figures, the right arm of one was folded across the figure's chest, with the palm facing outward, an awkward position, but probably of religious significance. One Tiahuanaco statue has a moustache, an impossible facial growth for a true Indian. One theory is that this culture may have borrowed from Melanesia in the Pacific, where some men do have facial hair. The figure was probably carved a thousand years before the first moustached Spaniards stepped ashore.

"Notice the Asiatic features some people have," Bill pointed out. Their ancestors came across the Bering Strait in the Arctic and made their way southwards. It was certainly true that I had seen very similar facial features in Korea and China. Some South American Indians could have come right out of Mongolia! Anthropologists believe there were also early immigrants from the South Pacific, and possibly from North Africa.

La Paz is a microcosm of Bolivia: the poor washing cars to make enough to buy food, the rich shopping in fashionable boutiques, professional men and women striding to their offices, Marxist students, drug dealers, and Indian market women resplendent in black bowler hats and wide, colored skirts. In the fetish section of the market, bronzed men and women carefully selected herbs, powders, liquid concoctions, snake skins, stone figurines, and the dried fetuses of llamas. They needed one or another of these to help them secure a job, overcome illness or a curse, ensure pregnancy or a safe birth, or pass an examination.

"Some people use fetuses when they build houses," a Bolivian guide explained. "When a man and woman marry, their families help them build a house. The young couple will bury a llama fetus in the foundation as a sacrifice to the earth mother so they will have children. They also sometimes burn a fetus along with special powders and herbs as an incense, to prepare their new house for occupancy.

"If the couple do not have children for some time, or if someone dies in the house, they may leave the house and move elsewhere. That is why you sometimes find houses abandoned."

"Houses not only have witchcraft items in the foundation, but also a cross or Catholic shrine in a room," Bill added. "You'll notice this mixing of old and new all around you."

Not far from the fetish market was a good example. The facade of the San Francisco Cathedral, built in 1547, is baroque, a style introduced by the Spanish, who learned it from North African Moors. I was fascinated to note that the decorative friezes on the church walls include the figure of the earth mother goddess at regular intervals, the handiwork of Quechua artists.

"I'm going to take you to Lake Titicaca and Copacabana tomorrow," Bill announced. "There you'll see how ancient Inca and more recent Catholic cultures have met. Gloria will stay with Lorna while she recuperates."

From the rising of the sun to the place where it sets, the
name of the Lord is to be praised.

PSALM 113:3

4

"THE

WOMB OF

MANKIND"

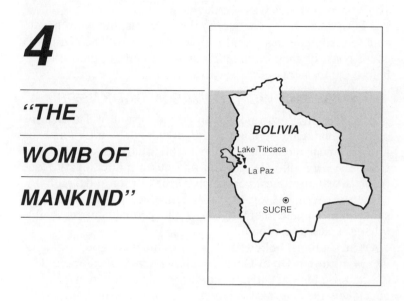

There before us spread "The Womb of Mankind"--Lake
Titicaca, shrouded in morning mist.

Bill and I had driven across the bald high plain of the
Andes, pockmarked with the adobe huts of Aymara farmers.
Unlike some other Indian groups, they do not traditionally live
in villages but in compounds separated from one another by
farmland. There are about a million Aymaras on the fertile land
surrounding the lake.

Piles of rocks attest to their burial customs. They believe

they would offend the earth mother by putting a dead body in the ground, so instead they place the corpse on the surface and pile stones on top. Passersby add a rock now and then, in memory of the departed. When the Spaniards came, they forced the people to bury the dead in graves, as a hygienic measure. To the Aymaras, this was sacrilege.

Earlier, the Incas conquered the Aymaras, but were never able to assimilate this proud people completely. The Aymaras could boast of their ancient Tiahuanaco culture, dating long before the Inca era--perhaps earlier than the first century.

WHEN THE WORLD WAS IN DARKNESS

"Maybe the Inca ruler invented the legend of Titicaca in order to subdue the Aymaras," a Bolivian guide in La Paz had told us. "When the whole world was still in darkness and people lived like wild animals, the sun and moon miraculously rose from the waters of the lake and gave birth to a son and daughter, Manco Capac and Mama Ocllo--the first Inca and his wife. The sun commissioned them to show the people how to build villages and harvest food."

The Indians believed that Inti, the sun god, trekked westward to the Great Ocean, walking across its surface. He did promise his son and daughter he would return every day to check how they were carrying out his commission. Each night he swam beneath the water and land to get back to the eastern side, to reappear the next day.

Meanwhile, the god-man Inca and his wife went off to Cuzco some 250 miles northwest of the lake, and established it as the center of their empire.

Bill and I stood in awe on The Shore of the Eternal People. We could understand how the Indians believed this was The Womb of Mankind. As the blue-green water stretched out before us, currents etched dark swirls stretching to the distant pastel blue shore. Tall reeds formed a green border. White sails of fishing boats caught the early sun. Rising higher, it gilded a backdrop of snowcapped peaks, as if Inti were restoring the gold stolen by the conquistadors. Off on the horizon were the Islands of the Sun and the Moon, with their temples to the sun god. There's also a temple to the puma, a deity prominent in Inca folklore. In fact, the name of Lake Titicaca may mean "gray puma."

The Aymaras still practice Inca ritual for their annual planting celebration. On that occasion, an Indian from the Island of the Sun paddles to the shore in a reed boat to fetch a white llama which is decorated with charms prepared by sorcerers. At dusk, a priest cuts the llama's jugular vein for islanders to drink the blood or to sprinkle it as an offering to the earth mother goddess. Coca leaves are used to divine the best sacrifice sites, and priests burn incense to placate evil spirits so they will not harm the crops with frost, hail, or lightning. Throughout the day, men and women drink homebrew and dance to the music of bamboo flutes.

THE REED CANOE BUILDER

Bill and I had started out early. Now as we stood looking out over the lake, frost was still on the tufts of grass at our feet. Overhead, a falcon poised motionless on an updraft, searching for breakfast.

"Since we're this early, we might have time to get out to Suriqui Island where reed canoes are made," Bill said as we walked over to a small inn. "Maybe the innkeeper will rent us a boat."

The innkeeper, Samuel Choque, owned the Festival of the Sun Hotel, a little adobe bungalow on the shore. It turned out that Samuel's father was the first evangelical in the area, brought to the Lord through the work of the Canadian Baptists. He told us how the mestizos (mixed race) had stirred up the Indians against the two remaining women missionaries, even throwing stones at them. (One of those missionaries had been Lorna's Sunday school teacher back in Canada.)

After the missionaries withdrew, the Indians realized they had been manipulated by the mestizos, who took over a farm commune the mission had parceled out to the Aymaras. The Indians appealed to the government to restore the land to them. The government did so, because it looked upon the Baptist project as a worthy model. It was a prototype of the 1952 Land

Reform Act that enabled Indians to farm their own plots of land. Since 1952 there has been remarkable church growth among the Aymaras.

Samuel asked an Aymara youth to take us out to Suriqui Island (The Place of Birds) in a motorboat. In crossing the water, did we skip back a millennium? There on the island before our eyes was a weathered Indian shaping the upturned prow of a reed canoe exactly as his ancestors had done.

"I am Paulino Esteban," the diminutive Aymara announced, the flaps of his colorful woolen cap dancing in the breeze. "I helped build the *Ra II.*"

We had found the master builder himself! I recollected reading about him in Thor Heyerdahl's story of the *Ra II* project. The Scandinavian explorer wanted to prove that North Africans could have made the voyage to the Americas on rafts centuries before the Spaniards and Portuguese sailed in their sturdier craft. Heyerdahl noted that reed canoes were constructed on Lake Titicaca in identical fashion to reed canoes in parts of Africa.

In 1970 Heyerdahl took Esteban and three other men from Suriqui to Morocco to build a reed raft 18 meters long, five meters wide, and three meters high. The voyage across the Atlantic was risky but successful. In 1973 Esteban and his team went to Oslo to reconstruct the raft for the Kon-Tiki Museum.

Now we watched while Esteban thumped on the bundles of reeds to compact them as he pulled a vine tight, lacing the bundles together. He showed us a replica of the *Ra II.* Before we left the island, Esteban autographed one of his miniature reed canoes for me.

Although the air was cool, my hands and face burned from the sun's ultraviolet rays in the thin atmosphere. We were on the highest navigable lake in the world--12,631 feet, according to Bill's altimeter. That is more than two miles above sea level. The lake stretches 135 miles from north to south, is 41 miles wide at its broadest point, and is more than 1400 feet deep. The Incas supposedly threw a lot of their gold and silver into the lake to keep it from the Spaniards.

The British provided the first steamer to make the nine-hour crossing of Titicaca. Bolivia has a navy based on the lake. The vessels are mostly small patrol launches, plus two hospital boats that serve the Indian villages around the shore.

"You've just been to the traditional birthplace of the Incas, Lake Titicaca!" Bill said as we returned to shore. "Now I want you to see what happened when Catholic and Inca religions clashed. Let's head for Copacabana. We'll have to cross the strait on a car ferry."

ROCKS AND CROSSES

Copacabana means "blue vista," and it lives up to its name, jutting into the blue lake. The town was a major government seat for the Incas, and therefore had a sacred temple to the sun god. To combat pagan idolatry, the Catholics built a massive shrine to Bolivia's foremost saint, the Virgin of Copacabana-- also known as the miracle-working Dark Virgin of the Lake.

"Vehicles will be blessed at 2:30 this afternoon," Bill read from a notice on the church door. On the way to Copacabana we had passed taxis, buses, and trucks decorated with paper flowers, showing they had been blessed on previous occasions. Now the church square was filled with vehicles, their drivers washing them and buying garlands to prepare for the ceremony.

"You must see the Stations of the Cross," Bill said. "They are on that hill, and we'll have to hurry to get there and back before the vehicle ceremony is over, or there'll be so many cars and buses on the road that we'll never make it back to the ferry in time to cross over this evening."

We hurried toward the dome-shaped hill overlooking the water. The Holy Sepulcher shrine at its summit is Bolivia's main pilgrimage attraction. By climbing the hill to the shrine, the faithful can do penance for revelry they indulge in during Bolivia's frequent fiestas.

Alongside the steep, cobbled pathway leading up the hill are 14 Stations of the Cross--large concrete crosses with descriptions of Jesus' sufferings on His way to Calvary.

Pilgrims carry small rocks up the hill, to place one at each station as a form of penance. They place the remaining rocks on an altar at the top, in a shrine that looks out over the town.

For most of the pilgrims, the stones carry more significance than the inscriptions on the crosses, for the stones identify them with the earth mother who, in their opinion, is the Virgin of Copacabana.

Our feet were heavy after the half-hour climb, but our hearts were even heavier as we realized that those who made it to the top past all those crosses still had no knowledge of how to accept the Saviour's redemption. There was enough gospel in the inscriptions to cause a sinner to trust in Christ's sacrifice, but the message was distorted. The pilgrims did not accept by faith Christ's sacrifice for their sins. Rather, they believed they could pay for their sins--gain merit for salvation--by suffering through the pilgrimage. Jesus' journey to Golgotha was reduced to an example of suffering.

Halfway up the hill was a flat area where pilgrims paid pagan shamans to burn incense in front of crosses. At the top the Quechua priests made pagan incantations beside the Madonna's shrine.

Even though the climb was tiring for us, we had actually made it the easy way. Some pilgrims do it on their knees, after walking the one hundred miles from La Paz as penance, to ensure their prayers will be answered. In a couple of weeks, 50,000 Indians would make the climb to celebrate the anniversary of a miracle accredited to the Virgin.

We could hear the distant crackle of firecrackers down in the village square, fired during the church ceremony to scare evil spirits away from the vehicles.

"We'd better get down in a hurry!" Bill exclaimed. As we bounded down the trail, our tired muscles protested.

The smell of beer was strong in town, making us thankful that we got ahead of the long procession of jubilant, drunken drivers returning from the ceremony along the tortuous switchback curves. As it was, there were sufficient buses ahead of us to raise a continuous dust screen, making the drive extremely dangerous. At the ferry ramp, Bill's car slid off the slippery planks, and the ferrymen had to lift the car out of the water back onto the ramp. Back on the other side we looked for fuel, and found a man selling it out of metal barrels in a shack.

He carried an open bucketful to the car and poured it into the tank through a funnel. I looked around nervously to make sure no one was smoking.

As we drove back to La Paz, darkness descended and the air became freezing cold. We nearly ran into a truck stalled in the middle of the highway. It had run out of gas half an hour before, and the driver turned off the lights because his battery was low! Two children and four adults were huddled inside trying to keep warm. They were grateful when we let them siphon some of our fuel. They turned out to be members of a Nazarene church. We reminded ourselves that the spiritual darkness we'd seen that day wasn't impenetrable. Evangelical believers were shining through the darkness like the stars in the black sky now above us. As we went on our way toward La Paz, we turned on Bill's car radio and heard a gospel broadcast from The Southern Cross, the radio station of the Bolivian Baptist Union.

I felt I had traveled through a time-warp machine that day, condensing centuries into 16 hours: medieval European superstition imposed on ancient Andean beliefs, resulting in a melding of East and West, of Christianity and paganism. Bolivia presented us with a missionary task as challenging as any the pioneers had faced. Different, but still challenging, as we'd soon see in La Paz.

THE UNREACHED PEOPLE

The last time Lorna and I had been together with Eldon Porter was in Nigeria where he was the MK (missionary kid) living next door. Now we met him and his wife Becky in La Paz, where they were SIM missionaries.

"I didn't resent mission life in Africa, but I just wasn't positive about spiritual things then," Eldon told us as we talked about the years since we had last met. "Later, when I was studying in U.S.A., another MK I had gone to school with in Nigeria was killed by lightning while playing soccer. That really made me get serious about setting some goals in life."

Eldon and Becky live among the people they are trying to reach--the educated class of La Paz. The Porters lived 1000 feet lower than the Kornfields' apartment building. La Paz is probably the only city in the world where there's a difference of 3000 feet altitude between its suburbs.

"It would be difficult to feel superior to our neighbors," Eldon and Becky told us. "They have many cultural similarities with us, and have a wide worldview. A number have studied in U.S.A."

"And if we run into problems or make a mistake, we get good advice from our neighbors on the ground floor," Becky added. "The Monteros are a big help to us, and our kids enjoy playing with their kids."

Tito Montero, director of World Vision for Bolivia, was well able to advise the Porters about church planting--he had been president of the churches with which SIM works: *Union Cristiana Evangelica*, or UCE--pronounced "oosay."

Eldon and Becky were seeking to share the gospel with other educated Bolivians, most of whom would not enter an evangelical church. They were really the unreached people of the city. All had a strong Catholic background, making them suspicious of evangelicals. At the same time, many had turned from the Catholic church in disillusionment and had become totally wrapped up in materialism. A few had espoused Marxism intellectually, if not in practice.

Establishing bridges of friendship among the city dwellers is not easy, and sometimes comes in unusual ways. The Porters were praying especially about reaching older people, who were not as open as younger ones to attending Bible study. One woman over 65 stopped coming to a Bible study group because she said she couldn't relate to the problems the others were expressing.

One afternoon Eldon found himself climbing several flights of stairs in an office building because the elevator was broken down. He was on his way to visit a Bible study member, Ruffo. The director of a large import trading company, Ruffo had often asked Eldon to pray for his father-in-law, who adamantly refused to have anything to do with evangelicals.

On his way up to Ruffo's office, Eldon heard someone frantically pounding on the inside of the old-fashioned elevator, which had stuck at that level. He was able to pry open the outside door, slip his hand past the inside door, and blindly push buttons until the door opened. The trapped passenger turned out to be Ruffo's father-in-law, whose eyes opened wide when he saw who was at the other end of the greasy arm that had opened his prison. They have since become good friends.

NEW TESTAMENT HOUSE CHURCH

We dropped in on a Bible study held in Ruffo's house. The group had been started by Wycliffe Bible Translators missionaries, and now the Porters were helping to develop it.

"We're glad to see you!" Ruffo's wife Maria said as we entered the door of their small bungalow. "Our group prayed for your safety when we heard of the train bombing in Cuzco."

There were 16 adults and 13 children crowded into the small parlor. After we sang choruses, the children left for their own time of worship in a bedroom. A businessman named Marcelo, won to the Lord by Eldon, led the Bible study.

"Our Bible study is going to be very simple today, because this is my first time to lead one," Marcelo started, timidly. "But I have found how powerful the Word of God is by itself. Fifteen minutes of reading the Bible showed me the uselessness of the previous 15 years I had spent in Marxism and materialism. That was just two months ago, and already I've seen great changes in my life."

After reading verses from Romans 6 about being dead to sin and living in newness of life, Marcelo turned to Hebrews 11:1 to show that salvation is based on faith and not on works or material things. He pointed out that it is possible for us to be self-satisfied with our salvation and not live any differently.

Marcelo made his brief comments very quietly, but it was powerful theology for people with a background of Catholic salvation by works, or of Marxist materialism. The illustration sat in front of us--the once aggressive businessman quietly opening God's Word and his heart to us. He asked if anyone else had comments on the passage.

"I've seen a real change in Marcelo's life," said a woman who was a niece of the president of Bolivia.

"So have I!" Marcelo's wife added. "That really shows the power of the gospel."

"This morning I woke up early feeling very lonely," testified an attractive divorcee. "Then I prayed, and I almost felt as if God reached out to touch me and assure me of His presence and protection."

A chunky, black-haired man said that before he found Christ as Saviour, he attended Catholic Mass regularly, but his life remained unchanged. "I felt very pious during the Mass, but a few minutes later I was committing the same sins."

A smartly dressed woman asked for advice about helping a friend who had become a Christian but who still dressed provocatively. The other Bible study members gave counsel on how to "put off the old" and to "put on the new" way of life. Then a thin man with sad, brown eyes told us he had a problem with drugs and with sex, which had caused his wife to leave him. He wept as he asked us to pray for him.

"Let's pray for our brother right now!" Ruffo said. Several prayed with love and sincerity.

I sat there realizing I was in a New Testament church--"the church that is in Ruffo's house." After the Bible study we all stood outside to enjoy fellowship in the warm sunshine.

While we were in La Paz, we met a number of other professional men and women whose lives God had touched. There was Dr. Carlos Vargas, whom we bumped into on a city street. Dr. Vargas was one of the most prominent surgeons in the country. He and his wife helped the Kornfields conduct Bible studies and Christian marriage seminars.

The Bible study groups have had some far-reaching results. For instance, Bill and Gloria met Dr. Edgar Ladesma and his wife, Terry, in a group of professionals who invited Bill to speak on Bolivian archaeology. Gloria struck up a friendship with Terry and discovered that at one time, after attending an evangelical meeting, she had made a personal decision to follow Christ. But she had not grown spiritually.

The Kornfields invited Terry and her husband to a Bible study in their home, but Terry would come only if Edgar accompanied her. An eminent surgeon and strong Catholic, he grudgingly attended on and off for several years, usually glowering over folded arms. Then one day Edgar dropped his arms and sat up in amazement. Bill had just read the text for the Bible study from John 1: *In the beginning was the Word, and the Word was with God, and the Word was God.*

"You mean God was actually in Christ Jesus?" Edgar asked. He became interested in reading the Bible for himself and took a more active part in the group. Then he went to Japan to study under a specialist surgeon. In the evenings he had nowhere to go, but sat in his cramped hotel room with not even a Bible to read. When his wife heard this, she and the other Bible study members sent him a card with Psalm 23 written on the back. Edgar read that psalm night after night, until God convicted him of his personal need of the Good Shepherd as Saviour. Now back in Bolivia, he is an active witness for the Lord and pauses for prayer before every operation.

Of course the SIM church planting teams have disappointments, such as when a businessman who had trusted in Christ decided to return to Catholic ritual with his wife, who had not yet made a profession. However, the woman later testified at a women's luncheon how she had found Christ through the Bible studies.

"HOW CAN I CHANGE?"

Eldon met a young couple while he was climbing Chacaltaya, a snow-capped mountain overlooking La Paz. The man was just finishing engineering studies and the woman worked for an airline. Eldon and Becky showed them how to make ice cream, went to soccer games together, and built a friendship.

"How'd you like to go up Chacaltaya yourself?" Eldon asked me. "It has the highest ski lift in the world, and we can get up to the snowline in just about an hour from here."

"Fine," I said. "You can tell me more about your urban church planting while we enjoy the scenery."

Frost was on the windshields of cars as we drove through the satellite town of El Alto (literally, "the High") on the edge of the high plain at 13,000 feet. The UCE pastor there is a lawyer, I learned, and his church is filled with university students. Although he doesn't have a car, he has started six churches within a radius of 60 miles.

"Tell me more about the group we met in Ruffo's house," I asked Eldon as we drove. "What's *your* role?"

Eldon explained that the group's concept of a church was greatly affected by their strong Catholic background. They had broken with that through accepting Christ alone, and not the church, as their salvation.

"They reacted against their former concept of the church, but they didn't understand what the church really is," Eldon continued. "So we had to study the New Testament church. They saw that it's not an authoritarian hierarchy ruling the lives of its members, but rather the local body of Christ, made up of believers, fulfilling its responsibilities to the Lord and each other through worship, teaching, and witness."

After that study, the group decided they'd like to fulfill those responsibilities themselves, and they committed themselves to being a local church body. One volunteered to be responsible for teaching the children, another for looking after the music, and another for keeping the finances. No one volunteered to preach. They assigned that to Eldon.

"While I was out of town a few weeks later, I got to thinking I shouldn't keep that responsibility--it should be taken by members in the group. How was I going to tell them? When I returned to the city, I telephoned Ruffo and asked how their Bible study had gone."

"We had a good Bible study," Ruffo replied. "By the way, we also had a business meeting. We decided we aren't growing fast enough in Scripture knowledge; so we'll lead the Bible studies ourselves--then we'll *have* to study."

"I thanked the Lord that He answered my prayer before I had to confront the group," Eldon said. "They're going to be stronger for that."

As our car climbed the dusty switchbacks up the mountainside, we met a truck coming down with a load of crusty snow for making ice cream and refrigerating meat. The road ended at 16,896 feet altitude, at a ski chalet perched dizzily on a rocky point. A glacier covered the peak ahead of us, reaching up to the world's highest ski lift at 17,129 feet. Within the past year a Japanese world champion skier had gone over the top of the glacier and disappeared without a trace. Below us was the high plain, stretching as flat as the ocean to the snow-covered peaks on the horizon, with La Paz in its haze-filled canyon. We entered the empty chalet to find refuge from the bitterly cold wind sweeping across the glacier.

"What problems do you find in developing the Bible study groups?" I asked as we sipped the hot coffee we'd brought.

Eldon said one major problem is how to broaden the groups. Bolivians tend to move only within their extended family circles, and even Christians tend to meet only at their own social level and not mix with others. The Porters also found resistance to the idea of discipling in depth. "Having a discipling relationship with someone else is a foreign idea to them. We'll have to study that in Scripture before they'll accept it."

Reaching the educated people of a Bolivian city is not an exciting time of vast city rallies, the missionaries found. Rather, it takes a lot of patience, wisdom, and prayer, working one on one.

"Yesterday the vice president of a leading bank gave me a fairly typical response after I explained the way of salvation over lunch," Eldon said. "He told me that he knew he should trust in Christ, but then he added, 'My father, my grandfather, and my great-grandfather have all taken the other way. How can *I* change?'"

Change--that's what the gospel does within lives. That's what the pioneer missionaries came to see happen. George Allan, founder of the mission that merged with SIM, had seen revolutionary changes take place not only in Bolivians, but also in the nation itself. As Lorna and I left La Paz for Bolivia's interior, we were curious to know how that came about.

Joshua said to the Lord . . . : "O sun, stand still". . . . The sun stopped in the middle of the sky. . . . Surely the Lord was fighting for Israel!

Joshua 10:12-14

5

MESSENGERS

OF THE

SON

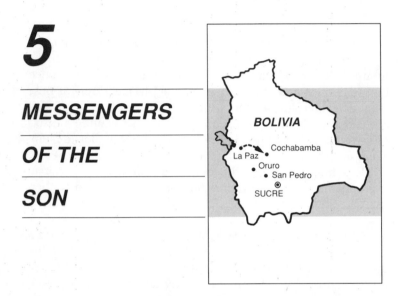

TARGET: THE QUECHUAS

How did George and Mary Allan get down in there!" Lorna exclaimed, looking out our aircraft window at the rugged scenery below. We had left La Paz on the high plains of Bolivia, and were flying eastward over the high valleys in the middle of this country of 424,164 square miles, more than twice the size of Spain.

The term "valleys" is deceptive because they may be anywhere up to 9000 feet above sea level, set between fractured ridges. In any other country they would be called the "mountainous area." But the term "high valleys" distinguishes the area (20 percent of the land surface) from the much higher plateau (10 percent) in the west, and the tropical lowlands (70 percent) in the east. The word *Quechua* may mean "warm-valley people"--another contrast to the windswept high plain, or Altiplano. Over a quarter of the country's 6.5 million population is Quechua.

Lorna's question about how the Allans got into this heartland was a good one. The answer was, "Not easily!" But George and Mary Allan got there as a result of vision, commitment, and courage. The story started a quarter of the way around the globe, in New Zealand, a century before. Lorna and I could well visualize George's upbringing, because we once stayed on a farm in the area where he was raised, on the southern tip of New Zealand. Seventh in a family of 10 children of pioneer British stock, George fell in love with a farmer's daughter, Mary Stirling. George and Mary both became interested in missionary service and went off to Australia to prepare at the Angas Missionary Training College near Adelaide, where they were later married.

Many missionaries had gone to Asia and Africa, but South America was looked upon as "the neglected continent." That was the title of a book by E.C. Millard and Lucy Guinness, reporting on a missionary expedition made in 1893 by Lucy's brother Harry and two other evangelists, under the leadership of G.C. Grubb. George and Mary avidly read *South America: The Neglected Continent.* They learned about American Indians living not only in abject conditions but also spiritual darkness. They spent time praying for the largest linguistic group, the Quechuas, and on one occasion Mary and a friend received assurance that great numbers would be saved. In faith, they thanked the Lord.

DEATH PENALTY

Bolivia formed a major part of the Quechua heartland. At that time its rugged ridges and valleys were considered inhospitable to foreigners. How to get there? Who would send missionaries? The Allans heard of a new mission in Canada, the South American Evangelical Mission, working in Argentina. George and Mary joined SAEM, hoping they could eventually enter Bolivia from Argentina. They knew it would not be easy, because not only were Protestant missionaries unwelcome, but also the nation's constitution actually imposed the death penalty for evangelical preaching!

There were two main routes to the heart of the continent, both extremely arduous. The shorter route from New Zealand was via a port in northern Chile on the west coast, and over the Andes by train to the mining town of Oruro. The other route took three weeks by sea, around tempestuous Cape Horn on the southern tip of South America, up the east coast to Montevideo in Uruguay, and across to Buenos Aires, Argentina. A train ran northward to La Quiaca on the Bolivian border. Either way, to get to the most populous high valleys of the Quechuas meant further weeks of muleback trekking.

George and Mary took the longer but cheaper route through Buenos Aires, arriving there in May, 1899. It was a flourishing European-style city, and the Allans and two other missionary colleagues set up base there. It was a time of learning the culture and valuable lessons of faith.

TESTED FAITH

Mail from home took four months to reach them, and on one occasion when finances did not arrive, they ran out of food. For three weeks George and Mary were reduced to the smallest rations, and then had nothing for three days. Tensions between the missionaries at the time may have kept them from knowing one another's needs. Anyway, it was the Allans' personal conviction that they should not inform anyone but God.

One morning Mary, weakened by hunger, found she was unable to nurse their new baby, Margarita. Once again George and Mary prayed for God's supply. Then they heard someone at their gate. It was a neighbor carrying a tray of bread and tea. She came to ask Mary to sew clothes for her boys. The food was a courtesy gift.

That evening an out-of-town miner asked if he could rent one of their rooms to stay in when visiting Buenos Aires--and he insisted on paying in advance. Their larder was already restocked by the time money arrived from New Zealand.

"They learned that no matter how hard the trial might be, our needs would be met," their daughter Margarita later wrote.

Meanwhile, they kept asking about the Quechuas of Bolivia. Their vision was strengthened by Andrew Murray Milne, who had arrived in Argentina in 1864 as the representative of the American Bible Society. He endured the most rugged traveling conditions to distribute Scriptures from Cape Horn all the way north to Quito, Ecuador. Between 1883 and 1902, he made more than 20 journeys into Bolivia, carrying boxes of Bibles and books on muleback. In 1901 he issued a special call to prayer for the descendants of the Inca Empire, especially the Quechua-speaking Indians. His great burden was for a complete Scripture translation in the Quechua vernacular.

On one occasion, Milne had to make a special trip to Peru to free a shipment of Bibles held by customs for 18 months. When the shipment had arrived in town, the local priest led a mob armed with axes to the customs house, to demand that the heretical volumes be handed over for destruction. That had been done in the past, but this time the customs authorities simply impounded the shipment until Milne was able to intervene.

Later, when a Catholic educator translated the Gospel of Luke into the Cuzco dialect of Quechua in Peru, it was hailed by the local newspaper and the public as a great achievement, because very little had ever been printed in Quechua. This caused the government of Peru to consider teaching Quechua children how to read in their language.

"Nothing can raise the Quechuas but the gospel!" Milne often repeated. He saw the arrival of the Allans and their colleagues as one answer to his prayers, and he encouraged them to make Bolivia their objective.

The Allans knew of other attempts to establish a gospel base in Bolivia. Anglican pioneer Allen Gardiner, founder of the South American Missionary Society, reached Potosi in 1846. The government closed his mission project shortly after. Another Englishman, Robert Lodge of Regions Beyond

Missionary Union, reached La Paz in 1896, but within weeks he died of typhoid.

PIONEERS MEET

Three years after the Allans arrived in Argentina under SAEM, the Canadian mission disbanded and the British branch merged with the Evangelical Union of South America. However, other missionaries from New Zealand and Australia arrived to work with the Allans; so they formed their own mission society--the Australasian South American Mission.

In August 1902, George Allan and a fellow New Zealander, Charles Wilson, guided by the Bible Society colporteur, Pedro Guerrero, headed off to the Bolivian border to survey a possible base. They knew that another Argentine colporteur had received death threats for selling Bibles in Bolivia and had been killed on his way back to Argentina. But they pressed on.

It was a grueling trip, climbing and descending ridge after ridge into the heart of the high valleys. Their boxes of Bibles were doused in water when the mules slipped while crossing rivers. At times they slept under the stars, and their main food was dried llama meat (called *charqui* in Quechua, from which we get the word "jerky" for dried meat).

Allan and his party trekked on to Oruro, a mining town on the high plain at the end of the rail line from the west coast. There George met the Canadian Baptist pioneers Archibald and Jean Reekie. Halfway around the world, the Reekies had responded to the same book *(South America: The Neglected Continent)* that challenged the Allans, and initially applied to the same mission (SAEM). However, they went to Bolivia under the Canadian Baptist Foreign Mission Board in 1898, the first Protestant missionaries to establish a base in Bolivia. The Reekies and Allans developed a deep friendship and helped each other in numerous ways in the years to follow.

During his 1902 visit, George Allan became more burdened by the desperate state of the Quechuas, neglected by the government and oppressed by landowners. Spiritually, they were held in the grip of a superstitious form of Catholicism, which in Bolivia's isolation remained unchanged from its medieval origins. It thinly veiled the Quechuas' spirit worship.

By the time George returned to Argentina, he was convinced he should move into Bolivia as soon as possible. A businessman in Buenos Aires provided the money for George, Mary, and their two children to travel the less risky route by sea to Chile. Near the end of 1903 they arrived in Antofagasta on the west coast. George dropped in on a "very much alive" Methodist church service while waiting for a train into Bolivia.

"Our pastor is up in Bolivia seeing what can be done to give the gospel to the Indians," an elder announced. "We've been praying to the Lord for some months to send missionaries to them; here is one who is on his way to them. His wife and children are in the hotel. Our prayers are being answered!"

The church gave the Allans sufficient money to pay both their hotel bill and their train fare to Oruro, where they stayed with the Reekies at the Baptist Mission. It was an era of missionary vision and cooperation among the major denominations: The Bible Society, Methodists, and Baptists were quite ready to help this missionary couple of Presbyterian background start an interdenominational gospel outreach in order to evangelize Quechuas.

The Allans went on to Cochabamba, 4000 feet lower, to establish a base. George Allan began the translation work which would eventually fulfill the vision of the Bible Society's Andrew Murray Milne--the completion of the entire Bible in the Bolivian Quechua vernacular.

"Mr. Allan's greatest service has probably been his translation of the New Testament into Quechua, thus preparing the way for Baptist work as well as for that of his own mission," wrote the General Secretary of the Canadian Baptist Foreign Mission Board, H.E. Stillwell, years later. He called its publication "one of the greatest events in missions in Bolivia in many years."

For a while, when the Baptists did not have missionaries available for Cochabamba, the Allans ministered to Baptist converts. Once when the Reekies were visiting, they and

George were stoned by an angry mob seeking to chase the evangelicals out of town.

Faced with the tremendous needs around them, the Reekies felt they should concentrate work among the people of mixed race in the cities, while the Allans would concentrate on rural Indians. This was confirmed by the Allans' New Zealand Council as well as supporters in London, England. The Allans' ministry should "be directed mainly toward the evangelization of the Indians," they wrote. In 1907 George and Mary took their first furlough, sailing via London to establish a council there under the name, Bolivian Indian Mission. Going on to New Zealand, they recruited three new missionaries and returned to South America as the BIM in 1909.

This time they followed the route which George had taken on his very first survey trek: Buenos Aires to the Bolivian border by train, and thence a three-week mule trek into San Pedro de Buena Vista (Saint Peter of the Good View). Its population was small, but from it radiated trails to hundreds of Quechua villages nestled between the Andean ridges.

"So that's how the Allans got down in there!" I said to Lorna as we took less than an hour to fly across an area the pioneers took weeks to traverse. I searched for words to describe the buckled terrain. The nearest illustration I could think of was a crumpled ball of paper, but that didn't fully describe the zigzagging corrugations across the rugged landscape.

The first evangelical church was built by BIM in San Pedro. From that small beginning, hidden away from the attention of the outside world, the gospel had spread from village to village and valley to valley, eventually reaching back into the cities. In 1950 the scattered congregations came together as the *Union Cristiana Evangelica* (UCE). In 1965 BIM expanded its horizon, changing its name to the more encompassing Andes Evangelical Mission, and in 1969 it entered Peru. Facing the need for wider representation to keep up with the growing call for missionaries, AEM "married" into the SIM family January 1, 1982. (AEM's British branch previously had merged with

Britain's Evangelical Union of South America. EUSA entered Bolivia in 1937, and its churches became part of UCE in 1959.)

INTERMARRIAGES

Lorna and I chuckled to think that before the AEM-SIM marriage, there had been intermarriage between personnel of the two missions. In fact, one was the granddaughter of George and Mary Allan, Muriel Hudspith, who married Richard (Dick) Fuller; the two served with SIM in Nigeria.

Muriel was born in Capinota, a Bolivian village where her parents, Tom and Margarita Hudspith, worked among the Quechuas. Muriel, with her husband, recently went back to Cochabamba, where, as a child, she had often visited her grandfather and grandmother Allan. She can visualize Granddad Allan listening intently as Quechuas and fellow missionaries came to him for advice. Her grandmother, a tiny woman, was busy working beside him, answering letters or bringing account books up to date. She was a midwife and nurse, and often traveled by mule to remote villages to provide medical help in an emergency.

"Granddad Allan really loved the people," Muriel told us. "When most educated Bolivians and foreigners thought Indians were mere animals, good only for the meanest labor, my grandparents were teaching them to read and write and helping them improve farming and living conditions."

The missionaries also taught the Indians carpentry, bricklaying, printing, and other skills that had been denied them.

"And our generation talks as if it discovered social action and community development!" I thought to myself. Missiological research isn't new either: Allan was constantly researching new opportunities for the gospel.

George Allan once found himself in a jail cell along with Quechua men imprisoned for various offences. The local priest had got his drinking buddy, the mayor, to imprison George for preaching the gospel in the open air. Mary supplied her husband with food and bedding in the rat-infested cell. When the British ambassador, visiting nearby mines, heard of the imprisonment, he addressed a telegram to the Mission saying he would arrive on Saturday, knowing that the telegraph operator would quickly spread the word. George was suddenly released from prison, charges dismissed.

The ban on non-Catholic religious teaching was lifted in 1905, but priests continued to intimidate evangelicals or have them arrested on trumped-up charges. One illiterate farmer who turned to Christ lost his crops, his water rights to an irrigation stream, and his land. He finally had to leave his home to look for work as a laborer.

"They have taken my land and my home," he told the missionaries, "but I am still richer than they are!"

Lola Turnbull was the other BIM MK who married an SIM missionary. Her parents, Johnson and Mabel Turnbull, were in the pioneer party that set up base in San Pedro in 1909. Young Lola spent several years in Oruro because the Canadian Baptists asked if they could borrow her parents to superintend the Baptist work during the furlough of the director. Things went so well, the Turnbulls continued with the Bolivian Baptist Mission.

I remembered Lola showing us a photo of her family, clipped from a New York newspaper dated May 27, 1926. The Turnbull family passed through New York on their way to Canada for furlough, and the photo showed the Turnbull parents plus their 11 children lined up according to age. ELEVEN--COUNT 'EM--ELEVEN! the headline announced.

"That's nothing!" Lola laughed. "My mother came from a family of 13 children."

In Toronto, Canada, Johnson Turnbull met SIM's founder Rowland Bingham, who for several years had been secretary-treasurer of another small Bolivian mission, which had grown out of the defunct, Toronto-based SAEM. By coincidence, it was named The San Pedro Mission, but was located in a different town than the San Pedro in which the Bolivian Indian Mission was initially based, San Pedro being a common name for a town. Turnbull asked Bingham if four of his children could stay at SIM's home for missionary children in Collingwood, Ontario, when the family returned to Bolivia in 1928. Lola was one of the four.

When Lola later became office secretary for Canada's Inter-Varsity Christian Fellowship, she married Melvin Donald, who had been appointed director. Melvin helped organize Inter-Varsity's first missionary conference, held in Toronto in 1946. Subsequent conferences met at the Urbana campus of the University of Illinois--becoming famous as IVCF's "Urbana." Mel and Lola moved on to serve with SIM in Ethiopia.

I met Mel and Lola in Cochabamba, where Lola was visiting after 60 years' absence.

"It's exciting to see the growth of the churches!" Lola told us. "And there's such freedom. Visitors nowadays just can't imagine the problems my parents and the Allans faced."

PRAYER ENCOUNTER

Lola's father told about those early days in his book, *From Mule to Jet in Bolivia.* The year the pioneers arrived in San Pedro, the rains were late starting. The rural Indian people became very worried. They paraded through town with statues of the Virgin Mary and St. Peter, chanting prayers for rain.

The local priest spread word that the new evangelical missionaries in town were the culprits. "What did you expect?" he demanded in his sermon on Sunday. "God is very angry with you! You've allowed the heretics to live among you; so He withholds the rain. Get rid of the heretics, then God will bless you and give you rain!"

The townspeople knew what a drunken mob could do, and they warned the missionaries of the impending Indian attack. The villagers armed themselves with guns to protect their own properties, but the Allans, the Turnbulls, and their single companion, Annie Cresswell, had no firearms. Instead, they appealed to the God who sent fire and rain when Elijah challenged the priests of Baal. The God who caused the sun to stand still in Joshua's day could also stop a frenzied mob's advance.

Tension mounted as the hubbub of the gathering Indians grew. All at once it began to rain. Big drops splattered on the cobblestones at first, and then came a torrential downpour. The mob scattered for shelter, their angry shouts changing to cries of amazement. Their earlier sacrifices to the spirits and prayers to the saints had not brought rain. Had the priest misled them by blaming the missionaries? Perhaps the evangelicals were right! To the Quechuas, the sudden rainfall was a convincing demonstration of God's power over the spirits who controlled the elements.

From that day on, the missionaries won the confidence of the Indians. They helped them with health and farming needs and told them the good news of salvation by faith. The Quechuas responded in such numbers that when the resident priest moved out of town, he advised the bishop not to send a replacement. "The town isn't worthy of it!" he wrote.

"It's difficult for people at home to understand the hatred and violence most Catholics showed evangelicals in those days," Lola continued. "Catholics today are so different--many are open to Bible reading and are tolerant of Protestants."

AN UNHOLY WAR

It really was a different day when George Allan first explored the highlands of Bolivia. The Republic's death penalty for evangelical witness had a historical background, with roots across the Atlantic in southern Europe.

Spain and Portugal had barely survived 700 years of battle with the invading Muslim Moors, who were finally expelled in 1492. In 1493, the year after Christopher Columbus discovered the West Indies and 40 years before the fall of the Inca to the Spaniards, Pope Alexander the Sixth divided the New World. Portugal got most of the east, now called Brazil. Spain got all the rest.

At the time, Spain was reacting to Muslim proselytization and to the Protestant Reformation in northern Europe. This was the era of the Spanish Inquisition (1480-1834), when anyone suspected of disloyalty to the total authority of the Catholic Church could be tortured into recanting. In the Saint Bartholomew's Day Massacre of 1572, over 3000 Protestant Huguenots were slaughtered in Europe.

Discovery of the Americas seemed almost like a reward from God for resisting both Muslim blasphemy and Protestant "heresy." As the New World opened, the Roman Catholic church became obsessed with exporting a purer form of Catholicism than that which Martin Luther had encountered in Germany. Protestant "heresy" and evangelical teaching must not be allowed to gain a foothold. Both church and government became fired with a sense of holy war similar to the Holy Land Crusades and to Islam's sweep across North Africa.

Although the Spaniards came professing to be on a divine mission, the atrocities some of them committed rivaled the most barbaric orgies of Indian rulers. Death by sword or firearm was merciful in comparison to some horrendous tortures. Captives were forced to watch relatives being burned alive, wives and children had their tongues torn out, and prisoners had their eyes gouged out. Soldiers shipped baskets of chopped-off ears back to the army base to convince their general that they were subjugating the people. One descendant of an Inca was torn apart by having his limbs tied to four horses which were spurred to bolt in opposite directions.

Spanish voices were raised against these atrocities. In 1511 a Dominican priest, Antonio de Montesinos, preached a sermon decrying "sins against the Indians." He indicted his countrymen "for the tyranny you use in dealing with these innocent people. . . . For with the excessive work you demand of them, they fall ill and die, or rather you kill them with your desire to extract and acquire gold every day." Several leading priests and soldiers sent reports back to their homeland, arousing a public outcry. In 1550 King Charles I of Spain ordered an end to military conquest, and new laws were published to protect the Indians. However, New World Spaniards revolted against these edicts and carried on with the devastation of the land and people.

The Catholic Church took the place of the Inca priests' authority, and so the Indian peoples transferred their fierce loyalty to the church. As they had obeyed their pagan shamans out of fear, they now feared and obeyed the Catholic priests. Quechua taboos and superstitions, on which they depended for life itself, became sublimated in the rites of the church. Government and church were one in maintaining control of the country, and their paranoia was increased by border wars with surrounding nations, which reduced Bolivia's original land area by one-half. It was, therefore, fairly easy to stir up resentment against foreign "heretics."

At the time, South America was considered "the dumping ground of Spain" for outcasts. The priesthood included a number of undesirables from Spanish monasteries. While there were good men in the priesthood, priests were generally thought of as "grossly ignorant, lazy, gluttonous, heavy drinkers, and a byword for sensual immorality," as one historian wrote. Many would not record a marriage, a birth, or a burial without an exorbitant fee, more than the average Indian could afford. Valverde, the priest who accompanied the Spanish conquistador Pizarro, typified these undesirable qualities. One historian described "his hard, square face with pitiless eyes," a man "in whom every lineament of Christian character, except devotion to his faith, has been effaced."

This medieval corruption of Christianity, imposed on Indian spirit worship, continued to deteriorate in the isolation of Bolivia, cut off from the moderating influences that penetrated Catholicism in some nations. Bolivia's Catholicism was like a videotape that had been stopped and frozen on the screen for 400 years.

"That was the Bolivia my parents came to," Lola said. "They demonstrated a different Christianity--the love of Christ."

THE SILVER MOUNTAIN

One hundred miles to the south of San Pedro is the fabulous Cerro Rico (Rich Mountain), rising 15,827 feet above sea level. Almost a solid mass of ore laden with silver, tin, bismuth, and tungsten, it was the richest silver lode ever discovered, and it largely financed Spain's imperial adventures.

The Spaniards had been looking for gold when they stumbled on this "silver mountain" in 1545. At an altitude of 13,336 feet above sea level, they built the city of Potosi, which became the largest New World city in the 16th century, and even rivaled London and Paris for population.

The Spaniards sent Indians tunneling underground in swarms to haul out the silver, until the richest lodes were depleted. Potosi became a ghost town until a world demand for its tin developed early this century. It is still the highest city of its size in the world. In Spain, the phrase, "It's a Potosi!" is still used for anything superlatively valuable.

The Indian miners worked in appalling conditions--the high altitude, above ground the cold, underground the suffocating heat (up to 120° F)--all taking a toll in lives. They were considered as expendable as mules. Every daily shift, 4500 Indians had to climb down rawhide ladders into the foul air of the tunnels. Each miner had to carry as much as 100 pounds of ore back up the swaying ladders, and if he did not meet his quota, he was sent right back down, regardless of exhaustion. Some had to stay in the tunnels for a week at a time. Many died there.

Thousands more died from imported European diseases, to which the Indians had no immunity. It is estimated that the Quechua population in Bolivia and Peru was reduced to one-tenth in the first 300 years of Spanish rule. Spaniards who campaigned for better conditions were opposed by vested interests.

In the early forties, BIM missionaries Carl and Ellen Wintersteen ministered among the Indians around Potosi. Priests followed them, picking up and burning any literature they distributed. The priests tried to keep people from entering the services held indoors, and at open-air meetings they incited the people to throw rocks. However, it was not the opposition which eventually took the Wintersteens away from Potosi; it was the altitude, which affected Carl's heart.

I sensed the vision and burden of these Messengers of the Son in a hymn given me by veteran linguist, Minnie Myers. The words and music were by two BIM missionaries, and it was titled simply "Bolivia."

Bound with chains that Satan forged in darkest hell--
Overwhelmed with such dread woe, tongue could

never tell--
But, our God, by Thy great power, break the chains that
*   bind;*
Life eternal through Thy Son, God's rich gift so free;
Matchless love of God alone--Bolivia for Thee!

STRUGGLE TO SURVIVE

"Fasten your seatbelts," the Lloyd Aereo Boliviano flight attendant told us, jolting us back from the mule age to the jet age as we approached Cochabamba. Bolivia's third largest city, set in a fertile valley at an altitude of 8399 feet, with a semitropical climate, is sometimes called the Garden City. Our aircraft had to make a huge spiral approach down into the hill-ringed valley to line up for the airstrip.

In the terminal, Lorna and I were glad to see SIM Area Director Ron Wiebe and his wife Joan in the pressing crowd. Before they whisked us off to the guest house, we had to wait for a little ritual the baggage carriers went through. Half a dozen men wrestled the baggage from the plane onto a baggage cart. They pushed and pulled it to the terminal and off loaded the pieces into an enclosure.

We could see our bags sitting on the floor, but we were not allowed to have them until the crew had gone back to the plane to get further cartloads. When all baggage was assembled, we were allowed to point out our pieces. It was pandemonium as the baggage handlers scrambled over the bags, trying to follow the passengers' shouted descriptions ("That red one--and the plaid bag with the black straps!").

"They do it that way to make sure all the baggage handlers are on the scene together, so they have equal opportunity to pick up tips!" Ron explained."Maybe this melee's an illustration of Bolivia's struggle to survive. You'll see more of that struggle here in Cochabamba."

May they who love you be like the sun when it rises in its strength.

JUDGES 5:31

6

GROWTH

IN THE

GARDEN CITY

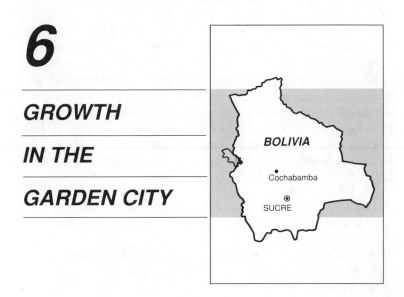

BOLIVIA

•Cochabamba

◎
SUCRE

I peeled a million-peso note off a wad of paper money and handed it to the market woman for a bunch of bananas. Two of the notes bought Lorna and me a Coca Cola each. At our feet were thousand-peso notes people had thrown away because they couldn't buy anything with them. Yet, just four years earlier when I first visited Bolivia, a thousand-peso note was worth US $40, and a million would have bought us a house in Cochabamba.

RECORD INFLATION

I couldn't grasp that kind of hyperinflation. I remembered reading a newspaper report of Bolivia's world record inflation rate of 3400 percent a year. Six months later the rate was 14,000 percent, and by the end of that year one report gave the annual inflation rate as 28,000 percent. The tragic reality was that a person could buy only a loaf of bread with savings which would have bought a new car only two years before. As a result, many people changed their Bolivian money into U.S. dollars as soon as possible. The Bolivian peso cost more to print than it was worth, so shortly after our visit the government knocked the last six zeros off the currency. One million pesos became one Boliviano. Under new control, inflation was reduced to 10 percent, and the exchange rate held fairly stable. But the situation we observed helped us realize the economic problems Latin American countries continue to face.

In Bolivia, the rich lost their savings and the poor became more hungry--unless they could grow their own food. Around the city, everyone seemed to hold more than one job. A teacher receiving about $60 would hold two other jobs, teaching at another school in the afternoon and taking private students at night. People turned their garages into little convenience stores, or set up stalls in front of their homes if they didn't have garages. Children were out on the streets, trying to sell everything from balloons to shoeshines.

"But people aren't dressed in rags," Lorna noted, thinking of the ragged poor in other continents we had visited. Once again, we heard that drug money kept the country's real poverty from showing. While Bolivia is known as one of the world's poorest countries, it is partly because the drug money doesn't go through official books. The government doesn't get the tax benefit of it, but the money does find its way through some extended families into the economy. So in spite of the country's poverty, the stores are well stocked with local and imported goods--some smuggled in, we heard.

CELEBRATION IN THE CITY

It was Bolivia's National Day, celebrating the Declaration

of Independence in 1825. The day has often been a time for strikes and government overthrow--the country has changed governments on an average of about one a year since General Sucre defeated the Spanish in 1825. That's when the country took on the name of the Venezuelan revolutionary, Bolivar, called the Father of South American Independence.

However, there was no coup on the holiday when we were there. Lorna and I strolled the streets and saw a whole cross section of Bolivian life. While government dignitaries took the salute on a flag-decked dais, groups marched by with banners representing almost every aspect of Bolivian life: factory workers, farmers, students, teachers, Boy Scouts, police, armed servicemen, meat packers, market women, and so on. They plodded patiently on, hour after hour, accompanied by the music of trumpets and drums.

Meanwhile, the spectators enjoyed themselves, buying fast food products made on the spot: bits of meat and potatoes on skewers, roasted over charcoal; sliced chicken on buns; colored sweet water in plastic bags, packaged by the side of the dusty road from an open tub of the mixture.

In contrast to the brightly attired city dwellers, a cluster of rural women, braided hair down their backs, gazed incredulously at the marvels of the city. They were oblivious to my taking a photograph of them, as their eyes were glued on a man making iced drinks. The procedure intrigued us also. The vendor turned a rusty crank to make a large block of ice rotate against a blade, shaving off the ice. He filled paper cups with ice shavings, poured on colored syrup from three bottles representing Bolivia's red, green, and yellow flag, and sold them to the excited children of a fashionable mother.

We crossed a bridge over a dry riverbed. A family had made a shack of salvaged cardboard and plastic draped over sticks, perched on a mound of gravel in the riverbed. Two laborers were digging sand to earn enough money to buy food for the day. An Indian woman, trailed by her rosy-cheeked daughter, carefully carried a cake baked in the shape of a llama, to sell in the market. At a streetside stall, flies crawled over cakes and pastries under a glass cover designed to keep out traffic dust.

A teenage mother had a child on her back and a cap on her head advertising Sprite. A prostitute in a slit skirt stood beside her pimp leaning against a doorway.

In Africa, Lorna and I had been used to greeting passing people with a wave or nod or smile. We learned that most Bolivians don't do that. People pass each other with a stony stare, because through the centuries the Indians learned not to show any emotion lest they be taken advantage of by the Spaniards. Yet, under the surface they are a humorous, affectionate people, we found.

On narrow streets in the heart of town, crossing an intersection was life-threatening. Most of them have blind corners with buildings blocking one's view. Motorists drive more by sound than sight, for the first car to honk when approaching a blind intersection has the right of way. The result is constant honking, with drivers zooming across intersections under the assumption that traffic coming the other way has heard them honk first. Amazingly, we didn't see any accidents.

In this Garden City, we could smell the blossoms of shrubs and trees hanging over the villa walls: red-blossomed oleander, yellow mimosa, orange tara, and yellow and red kantuta-- Bolivia's national flower. Some walls were covered with slogans, including a hammer and sickle under the words "Bolivia Socialista." Barking dogs guarded many of the houses. TV aerials poked above the walls. A Cochabambino can tune into five channels--four private ones in the city, and a government station broadcasting from La Paz. Films account for most of the programing, and gun-toting American Westerns are the big favorites. Churches and missions are financing some Christian programs, ranging from Bible stories using puppets to American electronic evangelists. Three of the four largest newspapers in Bolivia are computerized, using laser printers.

NATION WITHOUT A MEMORY

Walking down the streets of this city of 350,000 helped us feel its pulse--but what did a Bolivian think about this remarkable nation in the heart of the continent? No doubt I could get several different views, but a young member of the Bolivian

Congress, Luis (actual name withheld), helped answer my question with surprising frankness. His stylish wife set before us a tray of coffee in china demitasses as we talked in the privacy of his home. On the walls of the Spanish-style bungalow were huge antique oil paintings depicting the struggle for independence.

"In some ways, Bolivia is a stickler for detail," Congressman Luis began. "You could call it purist--in fact the most purist of the 'American' countries." He used the term "American" to refer to all countries in South and North America--not just to the United States of America.

"Bolivia is purist because it's isolated between mountains, desert, and jungles," he continued. "You'll find the Spanish here is a more pure form than in other countries around us, preserved from the language the Spanish brought with them. We call it *"Castellano"* from Castile, Spain, where it originated. The same thing occurred with the Catholic religion. It was a Spanish medieval form brought by the conquistadors, remaining uninfluenced by outside streams of thinking."

We talked about the economy and the home and the Bolivian world view. Then I asked the congressman why the government changed so frequently.

"Foreigners think it shows instability," he replied, "because they don't understand that the Constitution governs the country, regardless of who is in power. Whenever politicians don't adhere to the Constitution, the military feels it can step in as guardian of the Constitution. So even in their intervention, they feel the country is being run democratically."

The congressman said the Indian peoples had developed a subservient mindset over the centuries because they had to obey the Inca overlords in order to survive. During the Inca era as well as the Spanish era, any Quechua who showed leadership ability was killed off so he wouldn't be a threat to the state. The Catholic church strengthened the subservient attitude by imposing religious rites, Luis felt.

"The masses still believe what the priests say," he continued, "but they're increasingly wary of radical Catholic priests involved in politics. Many of these are political activists who use religion as an outlet for their views. We hear rumors that Communists have recruited radicals from Spain and sent them to seminary in order to infiltrate Catholic countries."

The congressman pointed out that the people quoting Marxist slogans are not the poor but the intellectuals, and that many of the intelligentsia have moved out of Bolivia.

"Bolivia is a strongly nationalistic country, but it doesn't really know its origins, like a child who doesn't know his father," Luis continued, toying with his coffee cup. "The Spanish rulers wiped out the history of the Incas, and then Bolivar's revolution wiped out 300 years of Spanish history. The nation has no collective memory.

"The Spanish conquistadors came with a sense of mission to overcome the devil's people. They looked on the Indians as the devil's people, yet they mated with Indian women. Their offspring hated their Spanish fathers because they knew they'd never be allowed to ride their fathers' horses, since they were Indians. So father and son could never accept each other, and that led to the struggle for independence.

"The 1952 Agrarian Reform was the turning point for the Indian peoples. Since then they have been called *campesinos* (people of the field, or farmers) instead of Indians. Politicians have to regard them because they are an important element in our nation."

As we set down our coffee cups and parted, I realized I'd received an unusually candid course in Bolivian history from a young nationalist with a burning concern for his own people. I thought back to the concern for the Quechuas which had brought George Allan to Bolivia. Although at first he concentrated on the rural Indians, he foresaw the day when nationals like the congressman would make their impact on the nation. Converts, plus many other restless Quechuas, would move into the cities, where they needed the Word of God to enable them to live as witnesses in the midst of urban vices. They also needed to be challenged and equipped to send the Word back into the villages and to provide Christian leadership.

Allan saw the need for an urban center for his work, and in 1934 moved BIM's headquarters into Cochabamba. When he died in 1941, he was succeeded by Verne D. Roberts. In 1956 Joseph S. McCullough became General Director. Under him the Mission began work in Peru and took on the name Andes Evangelical Mission. In 1974 Ronald Wiebe became General Director, and in 1982 AEM merged with SIM.

We discovered that BIM-AEM's impact on Bolivia included translation of the Bible into Quechua, formation of the *Union Cristiana Evangelica* (UCE), sponsorship of the first Conference of Evangelical Missions, and coorganizing of the National Conference of Theological Education, as well as Bolivia's National Association of Evangelicals (ANDEB). ANDEB was the first such group in Latin America to affiliate with World Evangelical Fellowship.

GROWING LEADERS

We saw Allan's vision for leadership training being fulfilled by Bolivian Daniel Ortiz, rector of UCE's seminary, as he prepared pastors and evangelists for both urban and rural ministries. His vice principal, SIMer Arden Steele, had just returned from a trek through the high valleys, visiting some of the graduates at work. Arden and two of his students, Lucio and Abundio, traveled over remote trails, catching fish for food and spending time in prayer and fellowship along the way. At night they slept in the simple homes of believers in seven different villages.

There were another seven villages the students wanted to visit, because each had one lonely believer. But there just wasn't time. The students pointed out other villages on distant ridges where there were no believers. When Lucio and Abundio had visited them six months previously, the villagers begged them to come back. Another village that had heard the gospel for the first time only six months previously, now had a little group of untaught believers. They would have continued asking questions through the night, but the team had to sleep and move on to the next town.

In Lucio and Abundio's own village, no one had been a believer more than three years. One had just died--the first death of a believer in the village. These new Christians knew they could not hold a traditional funeral service, which would have included incantations to the spirits over llama fetuses, a crucifix, and a lot of desperate wailing.

"Were those believers ever glad to see us!" Arden told us. "The first thing they asked was, 'How do we go about burying this man?' The students and I helped them plan an evangelical funeral service. The villagers were amazed. They had never seen anything like it.

"Then one of the dead man's sons threw himself onto the casket and wailed loudly. He was a believer, but he couldn't hold back his grief. The next day I spent time with him, showing him from the Scriptures the eternal hope which believers have in the face of death. It was amazing to see the effect of the Scriptures in this young man's life. His whole attitude changed as he rejoiced in the fact that his father was in the Lord's presence. He was comforted.

"It showed me afresh how much those new believers need the most basic teaching," Arden added, looking across the hills as if seeing a vision. He told me he had come out to evangelize, to plant churches. That was where his heart still was, but he now realized that church planting could end in shriveled fruit on the vine if pastors weren't trained to teach the Word and shepherd the little flocks of believers.

"That's why I got into training church leadership," Arden explained. "If we don't give the people a Bible basis, they can grow only to a certain point and then stagnate or fall apart spiritually. This is the biggest need I see in UCE, even in the areas of largest church growth. This is the most significant help the Mission can give right now. If we do this job properly, we'll see believers reaching out to unevangelized people in the mountains. There are still plenty to reach, and we missionaries can never do the job ourselves. We need to multiply ourselves through training others in the Word."

Arden Steele and Daniel Ortiz are doing exactly that. We saw Daniel in a different role when we attended worship service at the Calle Bolivar Church, the UCE "mother church" in Cochabamba. Daniel, a leading elder there, preached the Sunday morning message and his wife Sarvia played the organ. The auditorium was crowded with about 300 people, a cross section of old and young. Because there is no room for expansion on the property, the church has developed 10 daughter churches around the city over the past five years.

"We expect every congregation to be a mother," evangelist Julian Coronel told us. "Every mother should have at least one daughter, and every daughter should become a mother. That's how churches grow."

In its first 30 years, UCE averaged 21 new congregations per year. Now the number of UCE churches is doubling every six years, and the number of baptized believers every four years. Julian explained that the growth is largely a lay movement and that 80 percent of UCE churches are led by lay Christians. However, UCE has five Bible institutes as well as a degree-granting seminary, to help provide trained leadership.

A big factor in UCE's growth is the use of New Life For All (NLFA) methods, first developed by SIM's Jerry Swank in Africa. UCE churches invited Gerry to conduct NLFA seminars in which they studied how believers could be mobilized to witness systematically in every community, with a strong emphasis on prayer and Bible study. NLFA materials were translated into four languages.

Julian told us about 60 Christians who met to pray for a neighboring unreached village, White Fox. They studied the Scriptures and NLFA manuals. On an appointed day they set off for White Fox on foot, muleback, and oxcart. They entered the town singing, and two elders and a deacon gave gospel messages in the open air. Within three days 30 people had accepted Christ, and a little church was soon started in White Fox.

Another lay leader took a group of believers to a town which had no Christian witness. Thirty months later the town had five churches, one with 80 baptized members.

UCE's standard for recognizing a group of believers as a church is to have a minimum of 10 baptized believers from five different families meeting regularly, with their own elected leaders. "In practice, we aim for 20 baptized believers, with five or more married couples," Coronel explained.

This expansion was carried out in the midst of great poverty. Churches in one area had 20 evangelists ready to go to unreached villages, but no money for transport, whether by motor vehicle or muleback. The Mission made a contribution, UCE made up the difference, and the evangelists were able to get to remote areas. One was so isolated that the villagers, suspicious of strangers, at first chased the evangelists away with large knives. One year later, 18 of those villages had churches in them.

We'd been seeing spiritual growth in The Garden City. But not everything I'd see in this city would be pretty.

7

DISCIPLES

MAKING

DISCIPLES

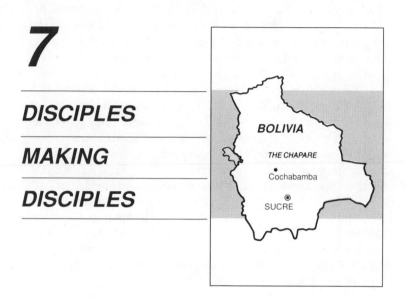

CHILD ADDICTS

I shed inward tears as I picked up the round-faced little boy and hugged him. Gonzales and two older brothers had been living in a cardboard shack, along with a baby brother. One of the older boys, crazed by drugs, killed the infant. The police took the remaining three to a rehabilitation center operated by a volunteer group in a village near Cochabamba. The two older boys had just escaped. They were both teenage homosexuals.

Four-year-old Gonzales and his brothers are typical of Cochabamba's one thousand street children. Some poverty-stricken parents put their children on the streets to help support the family. Other boys and girls run away from home to seek their own fortunes. They sell *pitillos,* a cigarette of tobacco mixed with cocaine, for the equivalent of 50 cents each. At first the children are paid with money, and then money and *pitillos.*

Once they are addicted, their employers give them only the drug-laced cigarettes. They have to steal their food. An estimated 66 percent of street children are addicts. Nationwide, an estimated 80,000 children are addicted.

Gonzales's older brothers earned a living as "stompers," trudging back and forth in vats of coca leaves disintegrating in kerosene, after which acid and lime are added. They earned as much in a ten-hour shift as the government minimum monthly wage. They smoked *pitillos* because the cigarettes kept them from feeling hungry and overcame their boredom. After a few months, their legs were acid-scarred and their minds shot.

Lorna and I talked with a teenager named Chino, who had lived on the streets for nine years. He left home in the lowland Beni area at the age of six because he feared his father's anger after he stole five pesos to buy candy. Finding his way to Santa Cruz, the major lowland city, he stayed alive by stealing, and slept on the streets.

Older boys got Chino started on drugs when he was ten. He had to steal more and more in order to pay for drugs, which he soon found he couldn't live without. The drugs kept him from feeling hungry, but they also made him nervous and so depressed that he became violent at times. He roamed from city to city, ending up in Cochabamba, where the police caught him and took him to the rehabilitation center which we were visiting. He couldn't handle much physical work at first because he was so malnourished, but the staff fed him well and showed him kindness. They also taught him reading and writing and handicraft.

Chino--that was his street nickname, because his eyes looked somewhat Chinese--ran away once, but he returned voluntarily. "I have to think about other things so I won't think about drugs," Chino told us. "The people here are teaching me good things, and I want to change."

Chino said he had known nothing about God before coming to the center, but now he was beginning to understand that God did love him. As we sat on a log under a tree, I prayed for Chino, that he would put his trust in Jesus Christ, who could free him not only from drugs, but also the power of the Devil.

Did not the Saviour say, "Let the little children come to me, . . . for the kingdom of God belongs to such as these"?

Coca, from which cocaine is made, is a mildly stimulating leaf. In its natural form it is no more harmful than tea or coffee, but it undergoes a chemical change and becomes the vicious drug cocaine when alkaloids are mixed with certain acids. The Andean people have grown the coca bush for thousands of years, using it for medicinal and religious concoctions. They considered it the favorite food of the gods.

Around Cochabamba we saw coca used in traditional ways: a market woman with leaves stuck to her forehead as a remedy for headache, a laborer with a wad in one cheek to ease hunger and fatigue, coca tea bags in cafes, and a poultice on an injured arm. It is perfectly legal to grow coca for these purposes. Trade unions oppose control, on the basis that coca-growing is a traditional right. However, only 10 percent of the crop is needed for traditional and modern medicinal use. Farmers sell 80 percent of their crop to dealers and turn 20 percent into cocaine on their own. It sells in Miami for 10,000 times what they receive for it, but they still earn more than they can from any other crop.

THE COCAINE JUNGLE

I recalled visiting the main coca-growing area on a previous trip to Bolivia. Bruce Anderson from New Zealand took me down to the Chapare ("Forest Wall"). A dusting of snow was on the rim of hills around Cochabamba as we left in Bruce's pickup truck and wound our way down toward the rainforest, where the foliage drips with humidity. At one point, Bruce stopped to change the ignition timing on the motor from high altitude to low altitude setting.

The first village we passed was in existence before the Spaniards arrived, a staging point for jungle Indians who carried coca leaves up to the high valleys to trade for salt produced by the Incas. Now, armed police at a barricade checked our documents and the contents of the pickup.

"The police are on the lookout for drug trafficking," Bruce explained. "A lot of vehicles on this road carry cocaine, but of course the drivers figure it's worth it simply to give the guards some money and carry on."

We saw lots of light green coca plants flourishing by the side of the road, and gray-green leaves drying on blankets or plastic sheets on the ground.

"The farmers don't see the bad results back in the city or overseas," Bruce explained. "They need money to send kids to school and buy clothes and food for them. Since growing coca is legal, they think it's insane not to plant it and get five times the money they could get from growing rice or some other crop. The coca bush thrives in poor soil and yields four harvests a year. Most farmers don't have transport, but they can easily carry a big bale of dried leaves out to the highway on their backs and make enough money to feed their families for a month!"

Even evangelicals struggle with the question of growing coca, similar to the question facing Christians in tobacco-growing countries. When we reached the forest floor, we found one community which had withstood the pressure to grow coca. Aurelio Chavez and his wife, Vasilia, welcomed us to New Canaan, a village they had helped establish. Aurelio was now lay leader of the local church and superintendent of the 18 UCE churches in the district.

A group of UCE families had moved down from the highlands as part of a government resettlement plan offering free lowland plots to farmers who could hardly subsist on the poor soil of their highland farms. An evangelical relief agency, World Concern, put up a building for the group, and now about one hundred families grow produce and run a health clinic, an agricultural nursery for oil palms, and banana and tea plantations.

Vasilia picked a huge papaya from a tree by their simple bungalow and passed refreshing chunks around. Then Bruce, Aurelio and several elders discussed the Theological Education by Extension (TEE) classes in the area. They also talked about a current problem: The community's banana crop was ready to ship into the city, but a transport strike was on. The transport drivers demanded that the government allow them to put up their rates, because with the peso's devaluation they couldn't earn enough to pay for imported spare parts for their trucks. The government refused, knowing the farmers would immediately block all roads in protest against the price hike.

"We'd rather give the bananas to some of the poorer churches in Cochabamba and to the Bible school than have them rot here," Aurelio told Bruce. "Can you take a load back to the city?"

Bruce readily agreed and we drove farther into the forest on a rough trail, at times sliding along logs thrown across patches of bog. Mammoth mosquitoes attacked my sticky skin as I helped load 4000 bananas into the covered pickup. Word had come that strikers were stopping all transport vehicles from entering Cochabamba, so the New Canaan church provided us with a letter declaring that the bananas were a gift to other churches, and that we weren't paid to transport them. Before nightfall, we prayed with the little group of believers and started up the mountain road to Cochabamba.

"I hope we won't have trouble getting past the strikers' barricade," Bruce said as we arrived outside the city and saw a long line of trucks stranded in the darkness. Drivers and passengers huddled under tarpaulins to shelter from a cold drizzle.

Just before reaching a barrier of oil drums, Bruce pulled up to the adobe house of a church elder. The elder helped us unload half the bananas, to be distributed to local churches. We carted them through his bedroom to a rear shed. Four small children were asleep on one bed. A stranded family slept soundly on the floor--father, mother, and three children. They looked like sardines in a tin, lying head to foot, so they could all squeeze under one blanket.

We offered a silent prayer before driving over to the barricade with the remaining 2000 bananas. Ahead of us was a pickup similar to ours. The strikers yelled at the driver to turn back. Obviously they'd been drinking and were in a belligerent mood. Bruce rolled down his window to talk to the guards.

A rough looking strike leader strode over and pushed the guards aside. I couldn't understand what he said to Bruce, but I could smell the alcohol on his breath. Bruce kept calm and pointed to the back of the pickup. The union leader shouted orders and someone started opening the rear of the truck. Bruce got out.

"Guess we're in for trouble now!" I thought. "They'll see the bananas!" Then several strikers carried a limp form out of the darkness and dumped it into the truck on top of the bananas.

"What's happening?" I asked Bruce as he got back in behind the wheel.

"Oh, the union leader asked if we'd take an injured striker to the hospital," he explained. "Two motorcycles collided a few minutes ago. The other man is dead. Been drinking, I suspect."

We felt concern for the accident victims, but we were thankful to be waved past the barrier without further delay.

When Bruce later died of cancer, Don and Doreen Nelson took up the work in the Chapare. It wasn't an easy assignment, especially when coca farmers were angry at Americans for pressuring the government to eliminate cocaine production. But every month the Nelsons piled into their van and spent two weeks teaching Bible in the villages. Sometimes their vehicle was checked at gunpoint, because everyone was suspect in the drug war.

However, the Nelson children begged to go on a trip whenever they had time off from school. For them it was an adventure to swim in the jungle river, play with village children, eat roasted yucca root, and sleep in the back of a church on beds made of poles, under mosquito nets.

Besides teaching Bible through TEE methods, Don and Doreen taught Spanish and reading, and tried to help farmers find alternative crops. Bolivia, assisted by other nations, has encouraged agricultural projects, including rice, tea, rubber, beans, and fruit. "Fifty-four substitutes have been tried, but nothing can compete with coca for cash income," Don said. "It's discouraging, but we keep trying--and we keep teaching the Word of God in the midst of vice and drugs. We're seeing people saved, and renewal among Christians."

COURAGEOUS WOMEN

Back in Cochabamba, Lorna and I noticed how the city honored its women. On a hill is an imposing monument commemorating the defence of the city by the heroines of Cochabamba when the men were away fighting in the War of Independence.

The city, like most in Bolivia, has retained a distinctive feminine custom. Traditionally attired Bolivian women wear hats in styles introduced by the Spaniards. There are probably over a hundred hat styles in Bolivia, each representing a community or culture. Most common is the English bowler, named after the English hatter who began shipping hats to South America in the 19th century. One factory in Sucre turns out half a million felt hat casings a year.

The same factory also produces 60,000 rabbit-hair hats, which are considered very stylish.

A white top hat with a black ribbon indentifies a native of the Cochabamba valley. We stopped by the roadside to watch a man making one. He was sanding the plastered straw stovepipe top. Adding a ribbon band, he had a chic hat ready for the next customer. Lorna turned it down!

Lesley Kayser from Canada is one of several missionary women who have great rapport with Bolivian women. "I often come here with a Bolivian teacher to have fellowship," she told us as we sipped a spicy drink at a cafe. "Her husband won't allow us to meet in her home."

Lesley had opened a hostel for young women who were working or studying in the city. At one time she had 15 girls living with her. When the hostel became too much to manage, Lesley moved into an apartment with extra rooms, where needy young women could stay temporarily. Some had been deserted by their husbands. Grateful for her help, at least ten have named their babies "Lesley." Most have since happily married Christian men.

"If desertion by husbands is so common, how do single

mothers manage in this economy?" Lorna asked as Lesley passed her a chicken turnover.

"One of my close friends is a teacher with 27 years' experience," Lesley replied, "but she has to work at three jobs in order to make ends meet. Her take-home pay for teaching at one school is $65 a month. A second school pays her $60 a month. Then she packages drinks and makes desserts for her daughter to sell in the market after school. That's how she manages."

In spite of such poverty, Lesley is always amazed at her friends' generosity. When she was coordinator for UCE Women's Fellowship, she helped develop teams to work among women. Once, when members learned that Lesley had a financial need, they secretly collected money and presented it to her.

"There was no way I could take that money!" Lesley said. "But the more I refused, the more they insisted. Then I realized they'd received a blessing from doing this, and they were trusting the Lord to meet their own needs as well as mine."

The UCE Women's Fellowship asked Lesley to continue as a consultant. She told us of one conference held at an altitude of 14,000 feet. "After walking for three hours and facing a steep climb, I wondered if I could make it," she recalled. "Then I remembered I'd been teaching the women about the Lord giving strength in times of need. I made it!"

"THE VIRGIN GAVE ME WHAT I ASKED FOR"

Joan Wiebe was another missionary tackling the special needs of Cochabamba's women, especially the educated wives of men in business and the professions. Joan asked Lorna if she'd like to attend a Bible study for them. Occasionally a husband was allowed in, and so I could go too.

"Can we have special prayer before we set off?" Joan asked when she picked us up in the mission van. "One of the women phoned as I was leaving the house. She'd just received a call from the hospital to say her father-in-law had been admitted with a brain hemorrhage. She was crying because she hadn't witnessed to him, and she asked me to pray for his recovery so she could show him the way of salvation. She herself is a new believer."

After praying for the woman and her father-in-law, we set off for the Bible study. It was held in a hotel owned by Marietta, a woman who had grown spiritually through participating in the study group. She places a Bible in every guest room and witnesses to guests. A man from Chile stayed at the hotel while taking radiation treatment for cancer. For three months he refused to listen to Marietta's witness, but finally, ten days before he died, he gave his heart to Christ and told everybody he saw.

Marietta welcomed us into a room where a couple of dozen women sat around a long table sipping tea. I tried to make myself, the only male, as inconspicuous as possible by sitting in a corner behind Lorna. Everyone seemed to accept one another. Two of the women were smoking, and most wore casual clothes, including jeans. A couple of the women had Indian features, while others could have come straight from Madrid. The expensive jewelry and fashionable dress of several indicated their social status, but they had no problem mixing with the poorer women present.

"The women often take turns leading the Bible study," Joan whispered as one woman started to read the Scriptures. "This week we're studying 1Corinthians 8, about meat offered to idols. It's especially relevant, because this is the week of the Festival of Urkupiña. Thousands will make a pilgrimage to a shrine outside the city and pour out an oblation on the rocks."

It was not difficult to involve members in discussion, because the women all chimed in, and at times everybody talked at once.

"I've been praying to the Virgin Mary and images of the saints for years," one woman stated. "This chapter we're study-ing says there is only one God--does this mean I've been wrong all this time?"

Several of the other women answered her question, point-ing out that Jesus, the Son of God, is the only mediator, and that believers don't need to pray through the saints or the Virgin. Then someone asked about offering sacrifices to idols, and what this meant to the celebration of Urkupiña. That started a noisy discussion.

"I don't think it's bad to worship at the shrine of the Virgin," one woman said. "The only wrong thing is picking up rocks that have been blessed--that's idolatry."

"No, the whole thing is idolatrous!" exclaimed the group leader, a Bolivian.

"It's all one thing--whether the Virgin or the rocks!" chimed in the daughter of the woman who raised the question.

When the debate calmed down, there was a time of prayer, and one woman asked God to make her sweeter so she could help her daughter and her grandchildren. Joan explained to us afterward that when this woman started coming to the Bible study she was so deeply troubled that several of the other women didn't want her around. Personal tragedy had left scars. But the gospel dramatically changed her life. Now everyone loved her.

The group leader asked Joan to close in prayer. "Lord," she prayed, "this chapter of your Word has shown us you are the only God, and that you are capable of providing all our needs without our offering to the idols. During this week of Urkupiña keep us true to yourself and free from idolatry."

Several of the women were new to the group and stayed to ask more questions after the study.

"I'm sure it's all right to pray to the Virgin of Urkupiña," a young woman told Joan. "I did last year, and she gave me exactly what I asked for--a child!" She listened hungrily as Joan explained the Scriptures.

"DO YOU PLAY BASKETBALL?"

Ron and Joan Wiebe arrived in Bolivia in 1960 as youth workers. During his college years in U.S.A., Ron had become interested in SIM through meeting several missionaries. However, SIM was not working in South America at the time; therefore when Ron and Joan became concerned for Latin America, they joined the Bolivian Indian Mission, which became Andes Evangelical Mission. When Ron became General

Director in 1974, he little thought that in eight years he would be helping to lead AEM into SIM.

"Do you play basketball?" asked the UCE youth group when six-footer Ron first arrived in Cochabamba. From then on, the Wiebes found themselves heavily involved with youth. They had instant rapport, making good use of a keen sense of humor. Ron developed the Cochabamba Youth Center basketball team, which toured the country challenging other teams. The players witnessed to the other teams, and at night they set up projectors and showed gospel films.

"Many people came to Christ, and we all had a great time!" Ron told us. One of the young fellows in the youth center was Tito Montero, who exchanged practical jokes with Ron--like the time Ron found a bag of marshmallows Tito had taken on one of the team's trips. Ron passed them around for the whole team to enjoy before Tito realized they were his own. Tito got back at Ron by hiding Ron's lunch.

Tito went on to become president of UCE for 10 years before directing the work of World Vision in Bolivia. Tito was also a member of a musical group the Wiebes developed, the Andinos. Recently an Australian accepted Christ as Saviour after listening to a recording the Andinos made 17 years before. When the Australian asked World Vision if he could sponsor a Bolivian child, he didn't realize that their Bolivian director was one of those singers--Tito Montero!

Bolivia has the highest infant mortality rate in the Western hemisphere: statistics range from 11 to 23 percent. One out of two children dies before the age of ten. Ron and Joan could empathize with Bolivians parents facing these problems, for sorrow had touched their own lives when their first children, twins, died at birth. They subsequently had three boys, and they adopted a Bolivian girl, Reyna, after a landslide killed her mother and three other children. Reyna obviously picked up Ron's sense of humor, because later when she was a student at Biola University in U.S.A., she introduced him as chapel speaker this way: "Some of you may wonder why he is so white and I am so dark. That is because I was born at night!"

Ron and Joan became concerned for the many street

children they saw around the city, trying to make a living either by selling or stealing whatever they could. The Wiebes saw a dream come to reality when they developed Camp Candelaria on an old mining estate 40 miles outside Cochabamba. But the camp was left without a director when Ron became the Mission's leader.

Five years later a young couple, Jake and Sarah Wetzel, applied to SIM for camp work. They had met as staff at a camp in U.S.A. and after marriage directed another youth camp. Then a visiting SIM missionary mentioned youth work. Overseas mission work was a new idea to the Wetzels, so they applied rather hesitantly.

"Don't worry," Jake remembers saying to Sarah. "They won't have any openings for camp work. But at least we will have tried."

SIM did have openings, and one was in Bolivia. They ended up directing the work at Camp Candelaria.

Jake is built like a woodsman from Michigan, his home state, and Sarah is a southern belle from a cultured Texan background. They make a perfect pair running children's camp, family conferences, and church retreats. Although a week at camp costs only $10 for a child, including food and transportation, many can't afford that, since the average family breadwinner receives only $50 to $100 a month. So the Wetzels use donations to make up the amount whenever they can.

"The work is really developing!" Jake and Sarah told us excitedly. "Recently we had three firsts: a family camp, a leadership training camp, and an outdoor school camp. A number of kids and parents found Christ as Saviour and grew spiritually."

"One couple, even though they were Christians, said they'd never heard anything like this about family life," said Ron and Joan Wiebe, who were the guest speakers at the family retreat. "One man was converted, and four families were reconciled. One had been on the verge of divorce."

THE TEACHER FROM AFRICA

Around the Cochabamba area we saw several needs being met through evangelism and discipling. A special ministry was going on at SIM's Carachipampa Christian School, attended by missionary and local children. We arrived just in time to see the principal, Richard Edlin, help a Bolivian couple remove a five-foot cardboard tree from their car.

"We're curious to know about the tree," we said to Richard when we sat in his office. "It looked like a stage prop."

"It is," he explained. "Each class has a turn leading the chapel service for a week. Often they'll act out a Bible story. The tree is for the story of Zaccheus. The Bolivian parents won't miss coming for the chapel services their kids are involved in, if they can possibly be here. The kids and their parents really get involved!"

Richard and his wife, Annette, knew God had led them to "Carachi." Back home in New Zealand, they had wanted to get into Christian service and assumed it would be in a Christian school. Nothing opened up. However, one Friday night they asked God to show them if they should consider a mission school overseas. The very next day they read a newspaper announcement that SIM's Murray Dunn would be in town on Monday. They weren't free on Monday and concluded they wouldn't see him. Sunday morning at their church they were surprised to find that the speaker was Murray Dunn! He and his wife accepted the Edlins' invitation to stay overnight with them--and Richard and Annette ended up in Bolivia.

I liked Richard's outlook on education: developing a whole world view from a scriptural perspective. The students didn't live in isolation, but played and studied with Bolivian students, some of them unsaved. Richard showed us around the classes. In a science lab, Lorna was interested to see students using microscopes which her friends had donated in memory of her mother. In another class, students were using computers. We dropped into Dianne Guta's grade two class and counted students from eight different countries.

Dianne was born in Cape Town, South Africa, and her dark skin gave her instant acceptance in Bolivia. But getting there was a difficult pilgrimage. The family had depended on her to help with payments for the family house. When Dianne decided to give up her teaching job to go to Bible college, that meant a loss of income. Her father pled with her to change her mind, accusing her of disobedience. He was very upset and told her that if she went, she should not even phone or write.

Dianne packed her bag with a heavy heart and went to the train station with a Scripture ringing in her ears, "Though my father and mother forsake me, the Lord will receive me." Just as the train was about to leave, her father turned up. He embraced her and they both wept. Dianne felt as though she were cutting herself off from her family, although they were also Christians. When she arrived at the Bible college, she telephoned home, but as soon as her father heard her voice, he slammed down the handset. Dianne tried to send as much of her salary as possible back to her father to help with the house, but it wasn't much.

While she was at Bible college, a mission asked her to be matron at their girls' school in Swaziland. When she returned home, she was afraid to tell her father. Finally she burst into his room and announced, "The Lord has called me to Swaziland!" Her father was stunned, but let her go.

Dianne worked in Swaziland for three years, until the nation's immigration policy required Swazi citizenship. After three more years of teaching back home, she attended a missions conference and that night dreamed she should go to Bolivia. Had it been an African country, Dianne could have set aside the dream because, at the time, most African countries would not accept her, a South African, even though she was not white. But Bolivia was in South America and would give her a visa. She further found that SIM needed a teacher there.

Dianne remembered that one of her Sunday school teachers, Mavis Stuart, had become a missionary with SIM. When Dianne applied to the Mission, she didn't know SIM had been praying specifically for recruits from South Africa, and that she was the first one from there to apply in 10 years.

"Would you mind if I served the Lord overseas?" Dianne asked her father hesitantly.

"Don't be stupid!" he replied. "I'm a pensioner, and we're depending on you to help us buy the house!"

There was a weekly prayer meeting in her father's home. At each session he prayed, "Lord, help my daughter to be obedient!" She asked SIM to explain to her father that she really wanted his blessing on her going. SIM sent him a copy of their pictorial, *The Ends of the Earth,* along with a personal letter. Her father was fascinated with the photographs and began to realize the part which his daughter could play as a missionary in Bolivia.

At the next prayer meeting, Dianne was amazed to hear her father pray, "Lord, I'm willing to let you have my daughter for missionary service." The prayer meeting exploded in hugging, clapping, and shouts of "Praise the Lord!"

Dianne's next test of faith came when she sought God's provision of financial support. She was amazed when the entire amount was faith-pledged within two weeks. After Dianne gave her testimony at her farewell service, her father stood up. Everyone wondered what he was going to say.

"When Dianne was a little girl, she used to sing 'A Volunteer for Jesus,'" he told the gathering. "I thought then that someday she'd be a missionary, and now she's become one!" Dianne's heart skipped a beat. Her father joyously joined in the farewell when she left for Bolivia. And 26 teacher friends, most of them unsaved, including two Muslims, came to see her off.

At Carachipampa, Dianne found a place in everyone's heart. Bolivians especially identified with her, and the UCE youth committee asked her to be their adviser. On her birthday, the youth group gave her a traditional serenade, bringing their own refreshments and games. It was 3 a.m. before they left!

Dianne broke into tears as she finished telling us about the difference in her father's attitude. Lorna put her arm around her. We knew she was in the right place, especially when we saw the warm embraces which Bolivians gave her wherever she went.

Before we left the school grounds, Richard showed us the site of the new Ruby Miller Building, providing a much needed gymnasium, auditorium, library, music suite, and other facilities. The building was named for the school's beloved Bible teacher, "Aunt Ruby."

"WE LOVE YOU, AUNT RUBY"

I'll never forget talking with Ruby. She was dying. She knew it. I knew it. Everyone who knew Ruby knew it. And yet it didn't seem as if she were dying. She had just received test results confirming she had two inoperable tumors. But as I sat and talked with her in her little apartment, there was no fear or anger in her eyes--only peace.

SIM was going to fly Ruby back to her relatives in California, but she asked to stay in Bolivia, where she felt at home. The Mission agreed after consulting with her relatives and pastor, who traveled to Bolivia to visit Ruby before she died.

I was surprised at my own reaction as I sat talking with her. I didn't feel I was speaking with a dying woman, even though Ruby was failing quickly. You'd think she was preparing to leave for her home in another land--and she was!

Ruby spoke lovingly of her students and showed me a card from one of them:

> *I want to tell you something really special that I wanted to tell you before. I have come to love you as if you were my real grandma. I really have had great times with you, and by you I have come to know Christ. You were a great teacher. Thanks for your love and friendship toward all of us.*

Each day a member of one class was allowed to come and visit Ruby, since she could not stand having a large group. The other missionary women took turns sitting with her. Ruby's ability to face death as a believer was a witness to everyone. She was making disciples by example, and the students would never forget.

Before I said farewell to Ruby, I read Psalm 90:16,17 to her:

May your deeds be shown to your servants,
your splendor to your children.
May the favor of the Lord our God rest upon us;
establish the work of our hands for us--
yes, establish the work of our hands.

Ruby squeezed my hand as we prayed together. A month later she was with the Lord. I like to think of her as holding God's hand now.

All the gods of the nations are idols, but the Lord made the heavens.

1 CHRONICLES 16:26

8

PILGRIMS

AND

SAINTS

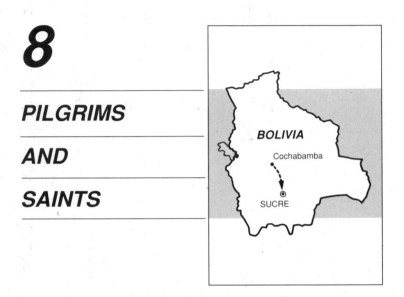

MAGIC ROCKS

Be careful when you go to Urkupiña," Julian Coronel told us. "It's a very explosive time!"

This was the festival we had heard discussed at the women's Bible study. Urkupiña is a hillside shrine eight miles outside Cochabamba. It attracted nationwide attention after children playing there claimed they had seen the Virgin. As the story went, they found a baby in the grass. When they picked him up, the Virgin appeared and helped them care for the child, who turned out to be an apparition of the Christ-child, they said.

Word of the "miracle" spread quickly, starting a stampede of pilgrims on each anniversary of the finding. A larger shrine was built, and as many as 30,000 pilgrims came from all over Bolivia and other countries. A newspaper report compared the pilgrimage to that of Lourdes in France, or Fatima in Portugal.

A few weeks before our visit, an evangelical pastor stirred up a hornet's nest by declaring that Bolivia's problems stemmed from such things as the worship of the Virgin of Urkupiña. Townspeople were incensed over this and vowed to stop the work of evangelicals. But the new mayor of Urkupiña, himself an evangelical, announced over the radio that he would not lead the Festival parade, as was expected of the mayor. He told his friends there was no way he was going to take part in carrying a pagan image through the streets. Feelings ran high.

Lorna and I witnessed that opening parade. Every fraternity, union, or agency of any note coveted a place in it. There were 73 groups, and sponsors spent between $2000 and $3000 (the equivalent of two years' wages for some teachers) on each group of performers. They passed us in waves, the patrons solemnly marching with banners announcing their organization, followed by colorfully attired whirling dancers, flute players, singers, and marching bands.

Interspersed were traditional spirit figures. Ekeko was first. A god of prosperity and fortune orginating before the Inca era, he looked like a rotund Santa Claus covered with miniatures of goods representing prosperity: a car, doll baby, house, furniture, various foods. Pilgrims believed that sacrifices to Ekeko would ensure that the owner would acquire these goods.

Then followed the Devil and his wife, surrounded by scantily clad girls representing Satan's temptations. Marchers carried figures of the saints. A mother preceded one group, carrying her own child in her arms to represent the baby Jesus.

Some of the dragon heads could have been straight from China, and many of the local people could have come from Mongolia. But there were also very Spanish-looking *caballeros* straight out of a bullfight scene, along with flamenco dancers. It was a mixture of Orient and Occident in the crucible of Bolivia.

Then the Virgin herself entered the parade, standing on a dais on the back of a pickup truck. Although only a mannequin, it was considered so sacred that a woman stood beside it, holding a large umbrella to shade the Madonna from the heat of the blazing sun.

Soon the pilgrimage itself was in progress at the shrine's site. I suggested to Pastor Julian Coronel that the four-day festival would provide a good opportunity to distribute an appropriately worded tract with a positive message.

"That might be all right at other times," replied Julian. "But during Urkupiña? People are very emotional, and many are drunk. Handing out tracts to a crowd could produce a riot!"

"If I go tomorrow to see the pilgrimage, will it be safe to take photos?" I ventured.

"That's probably O.K. People are proud of the pilgrimage. Just be careful!" warned Julian. He felt he shouldn't be my guide, because people might misunderstand why he was there. However, he said there would be no problem in my going with one of our missionaries--we would be looked upon only as curious foreigners. So I set off in tow of David McLeod-Jones, a lanky Bible teacher from New Zealand.

Before dawn the main highway out of Cochabamba was choked with vehicles piled with pilgrims. Somehow we squeezed inside a minibus that was already too full. Everyone got off at the roadside village and started the mile-and-a-half trek to the sacred hill behind the village. Men carried children on their shoulders. Women had babies tied on their backs, and teenagers carted picnic baskets.

Along the dusty route vendors did well selling refreshments. A woman had a wheelbarrow full of Bolivian pretzels, and other vendors sold locally made candy bars, yogurt, spicy turnovers, biscuits, Jello in plastic glasses, and chewing gum. One enterprising man was selling candy floss made on a hand-cranked machine with a kerosene burner melting the sugar! Dirty white cloths hanging from long poles indicated where pilgrims could buy local corn beer.

As we neared the hill, vendors were selling miniatures of everything imaginable, including dolls, toy cars, houses, and

U.S. dollars. I could buy a miniature diploma for a degree in any subject. People bought the miniatures to have them blessed at the shrine, believing they'd get the real things within a year. We even could have bought used fiberglass sacks to take sacred rocks back home, as some were already doing. The sacks had originally held powdered chemicals for making cocaine.

"Look at that hillside!" Dave exclaimed. It was covered with tents, awnings, and people milling around like ants. "It's going to be difficult getting there, because there's only one bridge across the river."

True enough, the streams of people, some trying to reach the shrine and others returning from it, converged on a narrow bridge. As we were pushed along in the crowd, I nearly had my jacket ripped off my back. I was amazed to see a mother holding a baby, trying to keep it from being crushed to death. Apparently she felt it was worth the risk, in order to have her baby blessed at Urkupiña.

Armed soldiers tried to channel the human flow across the bridge into two separate lanes, one coming and one going. Their cause was hopeless. The turbulent mass flowing in from opposite ends of the bridge formed two fronts that pressed against each other, trying to find a way through. The police were caught in the middle of this, their submachine guns pressed flat against their bodies.

"Mind your camera bag!" Dave shouted in my ear above the din. I had the strap around my neck and the bag under one arm, trying to protect it from being ripped off by the pressing crowd. Dave and I could only go with the flow, slowly inching forward.

Suddenly something struck me on the head. I looked up to find a huge bass drum high in the air. A poncho-draped Indian was holding it above the crowd, to get it to the other side to play in the festivities. Another man was holding a model truck in the air to avoid having it torn out of his hands. At one point I was pushed toward the edge of the bridge and noticed that some enterprising young men were making good money carrying people across the river on their backs.

Eventually we struggled through to the other end of the

bridge and found the place in a festive mood. Families pic-
nicked. Food and drink sellers set up blankets and tarpaulins
on poles to provide shelter for the customers. Tape recorders
and radios blared; firecrackers exploded. A military plane
zoomed overhead and dropped parachutists as part of the show.

Armed police kept open a wide path leading to the shrine
at the foot of the hill, allowing within the enclosure only the
lineup of those who were waiting to be blessed. I was interested
to see what went on, but I wasn't about to become number 1001
moving at a snail's pace. I held my camera with its long lens
up on my shoulder and walked up to a guard, who immediately
pointed his machine gun at my navel. *"Jornalisto!"*

I said to the guard, thinking that adding "o" to "journalist"
would change the English word into Spanish. That was the case
with a number of words derived from Latin, I'd noticed. But
this time I was wrong. "Jornalisto" sounds like "day laborer"
in Spanish, and the guard looked puzzled. *"Periodista!"* cor-
rected Dave, using the word for a person who writes for a
periodical or newspaper. *"Si, si! Periodista!"* nodded the
guard.

The burly soldier swung his gun away from my navel,
pointing with it over the rope barrier and into the cleared
pathway. Dave and I stepped over the rope and followed the
guard alongside the line of people. He called a Boy Scout, who
escorted us up to the shrine.

We watched as each pilgrim came before the figure of the
Madonna, knelt, and prayed. Then the pilgrim held out the
article he or she wanted blessed, while a Catholic priest
sprinkled it with holy water from an oleander branch dipped in
a basin. The pilgrims then left the shrine to head up the hillside
to get a piece of rock. Some of them crawled on their knees,
doing penance.

Urkupiña is a Quechua word meaning "already it is in the
hillside." The pagan shamans had long ago divined that this
was a sacred spot because of a crystal spring bubbling from the
hillside over a rocky projection. This was probably why the
Catholics placed a small Madonna shrine at the site back in the
forties. Since the miraculous apparition was reported ten

years ago, the original protruding rocks have been broken up and carted away by pilgrims and now the entire hillside was scarred, as professional rock busters swung mallets and picks to break off pieces of stone to sell to pilgrims.

Dave and I tried to get up the hillside to see what was happening. Again we found ourselves being pushed along in a stream of people. The problem was that there were several streams crisscrossing the hillside, and when one stream met another, the stronger pushers won the day.

We eventually found ourselves in a circle of people around a man with a mallet. He was selling pieces of rock. A businessman bought a large chunk and handed it with a wad of money to a Quechua priest, who was dressed in poncho and floppy-eared cap, with dried llama fetuses hanging from his neck. The priest held a crucifix in one hand and a can of beer in the other. As he touched the rock with the crucifix and poured a beer libation over it, he chanted incantations to invoke the blessing of the spirit supposedly within the rock.

Pressing my way through the crowd, I followed the purchaser to another circle, where he added his rock to others that were piled over a small fire, to ensure that the full blessing of the earth mother passed into the stones. Several women lit votive candles, propping them between stones around the fire. People also threw their miniature money and confetti on the flames. The man eventually picked up his rock, paid a million pesos to the woman attending the fire, and headed back down the hill.

Making our way between the piles of rocks was hazardous. I saw one woman lose her balance and fall onto a burning pyre, but people pulled her off. The same thing nearly happened to me as the crowd pressed from behind. I quickly stuck out a foot to balance myself on a rock protruding from the flames. Pilgrims saw me having trouble, grabbed my arm, and pulled me back.

On the way back to the bridge, Dave talked with a friendly Bolivian who had completed his pilgrimage. On a string around his neck were some miniature dollar bills and a little wallet with a picture of the Virgin on it.

"What you see here shows how Christian our country is!" he told us, noting we were visitors. "You won't find this in Europe. Europe is very pagan now, but here we still adore God."

"What will you do with that rock and the miniature truck you're carrying?" Dave asked.

"Ah, that shows the power of God!" the pilgrim replied. "Last year when I came to Urkupiña I had no possessions, but now I own a house. So this time I brought this truck to be blessed, so I'll get a real one."

The crowd parted as a Bolivian Red Cross team, complete with stretcher and battery-operated siren, carried out a woman who had fainted. From our elevation on the hillside, we could see a solid stream of pilgrims all the way back to the highway a mile and a half away. High winds were blowing billows of dust through the valley, turning the distant range into a gray outline.

"Now we have to negotiate that bridge again!" I said to Dave. It was high noon, and the crush was worse than before. My arms were pinned to my sides, and at times I could not turn my head because my chin was pressed against someone's back. I felt something wet with one hand, and when I could look down was amazed to find a little child squeezed between the adults, there being more space below our hipline than above. My fingers had entered the child's mouth. I was glad it wasn't his eye.

Further in, a bagful of rocks on the back of a woman in front of me pressed into my chest, and everyone else was stepping on my big feet--except, it seemed, myself, for at times I was almost off my feet, borne along by the crowd. Children on parents' shoulders were crying and women were screaming. One father held his jacket aloft on a stick so the rest of the family could see where he was. I could easily understand how people could be trampled to death in such a crowd. I tried to push back in order to relieve the pressure of the rocks on my chest, but it was impossible. A thousand other people were pressing from behind.

At the far end of the bridge, the police had taken to flailing with their batons at the heads of pilgrims. However, the people could do nothing but keep coming. There was no turning back.

Finally Dave and I were jettisoned from the end of the bridge as if disgorged by a giant, writhing dragon. We drew deep breaths and checked our cameras. We had left our wallets and other valuables at home.

We felt that if there were any merit to the pilgrimage, we certainly deserved it after enduring its rigors. But it was really with a sense of sadness that we trekked back to the highway, past the oncoming stream of zealous pilgrims caught up in a tragic mix of religious superstition and profane materialism. It was their way to "tie down the sun"--to try to control their world.

I couldn't help thinking of Jesus' conversation with the pagan Samaritan woman who told him, "Our fathers worshiped on this mountain, but you Jews claim that the place where we must worship is in Jerusalem."

Jesus directed her thoughts away from the pagan mountain shrine as well as from the ritual temple worship and told her, "God is spirit, and his worshipers must worship in spirit and in truth."

I also remembered that Jesus, seeing the white-robed villagers streaming across the fields toward him, challenged his disciples: "Open your eyes and look at the fields! They are ripe for harvest."

THE IDOL SMASHER

At Urkupiña I saw pilgrims worshiping at the shrine of a dead saint. Back in Cochabamba Lorna and I met a Bolivian who used to make images of saints. He and his wife had an amazing life pilgrimage.

Short, stocky, and as bald as the Altiplano, Arturo Arana had the bearing of a general and the smile of a pastor. Hilda was a gracious hostess. We admired the antique clocks and bronze pots in their living room, as well as original oils painted by Arturo's mother and grandfather.

"Here is a picture of the only Bolivians ever crowned prince and princess by the Catholic Church and King of Spain,"

Hilda said, showing us a book of steel engravings published in 1904. "Princess de la Glorieta was Arturo's great-aunt. Here's a picture of her and her husband being presented to the Pope in Rome, and this one shows them being presented to the King and Queen of Spain."

As we sat down to lunch, Hilda commented that she'd learned to cook after becoming a believer. "I'd never had to do a scrap of housework before that!" she explained. "The maids did it all."

"How did you and Arturo become Christians?" we asked.

"My husband should start, because he came to the Lord first, and that made me very angry!" Hilda said.

As we enjoyed a salad of palm hearts, Arturo started at the beginning. His great-grandfather was a Spanish merchant who lived in Antofagasta, Bolivia's seaport before it was taken over by Chile. The family later settled in Bolivia's constitutional capital, Sucre, in the high valleys. They maintained the best of connections in church and state. Arturo's parents and grandparents spent vacations in Paris, as upper class Bolivians often did. They gave property to the church and founded orphanages. The Pope recognized this benevolence by bestowing the titles of Prince and Princess of the Church on Arturo's grandmother's sister and her husband, who lived in Glorieta, on the outskirts of Sucre. There the family built a castle.

Arturo's father, also a merchant, raised his son to take over the family import business, strongly opposing the suggestion of friends that the brilliant boy be sent to Rome to study for the priesthood.

Hilda was born into a wealthy society family in Santa Cruz on the lowland plain at the foot of the Andes. After her marriage to Arturo, she spent most of her time playing cards, smoking, and drinking imported wine with other society women, to make the time pass more quickly while Arturo was managing his businesses. These included a men's clothing shop, a pharmaceutical import company, and a religious figurine shop.

Arturo got into the latter business because he noticed the high demand for Catholic images in Sucre, the nation's most devout Catholic city. He had inherited his mother's artistic ability and produced clay models that surpassed anything available in the country. From these he turned out plaster statues of the Madonna, Christ of the Bleeding Heart, crucifixes, and the saints. His display window was the most attractive in the capital city.

Arturo and Hilda were themselves devout Catholics. Arturo studied at the College of the Sacred Heart and became a member of the executive board of the Congregation of Worshipers of Mary.

"I thought that even if I failed to win favor with Christ, I would win Mary's favor," Arturo explained. "She seemed more attainable and loving. Of course, like most Catholic young men, I was gambling and drinking, and we fellows would boast about our affairs with women."

As for Hilda, every morning she kissed the feet of a crucifix in their bedroom, which they had set up under an autographed portrait of the Pope, given them by Arturo's mother.

"My lipstick made the feet turn red!" Hilda laughed as she got up to bring the next course in from the kitchen.

When a Eucharistic Congress was held in Sucre, the Aranas were anxious to hear the lectures. Hilda became ill, so they sat at home and listened by radio. One night a Jesuit professor lectured on prophecy in the Bible, stating that it was the Word of God revealed to mankind.

Arturo had never heard such a statement, and as he listened to the list of fulfilled prophecies, he decided he had to read this marvelous Book for himself. He went to the Catholic college and asked the prefect priest if he would lend him a Bible.

"He wasn't very willing to do so at first," Arturo said, "but I guess he figured it was safe to lend one to such a strong church member as I. He warned me that only the church could interpret what was in it."

The prefect had only a Protestant version, not the Catholic. The priest explained that he used the Protestant version because it had useful cross references in the margin for study.

Reading the Bible raised many questions in Arturo's mind, so he returned to ask the Jesuit about them. The priest confessed he had the same questions and doubts, but he simply accepted the church's interpretations, and Arturo should do the same. This bothered Arturo because he thought the priest should believe what he was teaching others. Arturo returned the Bible to him and went out in search of one for himself, finally finding one at the Seventh Day Adventist bookshop.

Arturo then went to the other Roman Catholic order in Sucre, the Franciscans. "Son, I confess I do not know a potato about these things," the head priest replied. "I have the faith of a coal miner: I believe because I believe."

Although Catholics taught that Protestants were Satan's servants condemned to hell, Arturo eventually got up courage to visit a Brethren Assembly missionary in town. Gordon Turner showed Arturo Ephesians 2:8: "It is by grace you have been saved, through faith--and this is not from yourselves, it is the gift of God."

Suddenly the truth dawned! Arturo accepted God's gift by faith. He was walking on air when he arrived home from Turner's house. But when he announced he'd found the way of salvation, Hilda was shocked.

"You're crazy!" she cried. "You've become a Protestant!"

Arturo's father and brothers were also upset and didn't want him to continue working with them. So he ran his pharmacy business and added a small bookshop.

"That bookshop became my Bible institute," Arturo told us. "As I sat waiting for customers, I read the Bible and other Christian books. The bookshop was my ministry, and my pharmacy business supported me."

One of the main things that bothered Arturo was the commandment not to make graven images or to worship them. After reading this in Exodus 20 in the Protestant Bible, he was surprised not to find it in the Scripture quoted in the Catholic catechism. That commandment had been left out entirely, and another one was split into two in order to restore the total of 10. That discrepancy began to shake his faith in Catholic teaching, especially when the priests had no explanation for it.

At first Arturo rationalized his religious statue business by telling himself that the purchasers really weren't worshiping them, but using them only as aids in worshiping God. But he

In Peru, the author and his wife were awestruck by the ruins of Machu Picchu. Was it the secret hideout of the last Inca's survivors? **Right:** The deified Inca, portrayed here during a celebration of the Festival of the Sun, presided over sacrifices designed to "tie down the sun" in its drift away from the equator.

CULTURE

Photos by W. Harold Fuller unless otherwise noted.

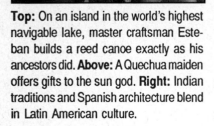

Top: On an island in the world's highest navigable lake, master craftsman Esteban builds a reed canoe exactly as his ancestors did. **Above:** A Quechua maiden offers gifts to the sun god. **Right:** Indian traditions and Spanish architecture blend in Latin American culture.

A lowland Indian Christian is proud of his traditional attire.

A Bolivian shows visitor Lorna Fuller one way to wear a locally woven shawl.

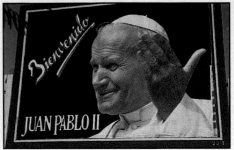

A billboard welcomes Pope John Paul II on one of several visits to Latin America.

Right: Pilgrims line up to be sprinkled with holy water at a Catholic shrine.

Above left: One of the pilgrims pays a pagan priest (middle, in cap) to bless the rocks he has picked up in the belief these will bring him good fortune. **Below:** Incense is burned to the crucifix and to the spirits in the rocks, in Christopagan syncretism.

RELIGION

Above: A Chilean businesswoman clutches her transistor radio and cross while waiting for the Pope to pass along her street. **Left:** A nun shelters a figure of the Virgin Mary from the sun during a parade.

Liz Major photo

A figure of the crucified Jesus is carried on the shoulders of mourners through the streets of Lima.

One of Latin America's restive street children strives to break his cocaine habit at a rehabilitation center. Drug cartels fight to control communities and governments.

Outside a Catholic church on which guerrillas have drawn a Communist symbol, a poor woman buys potions and prayers from pagan spiritists.

UNREST

Left: In Cuzco, soldiers investigate the rail car blown up by terrorists the morning the author and his wife had planned to travel by train. **Below:** A political agitator organizes an anti-government demonstration.

Cuba's Fidel Castro sought to further his revolutionary aims throughout Latin America by espousing liberation theology in this book by a Catholic priest. **Below:** Revolutionary slogans confronted the author during his extensive tour of Cuba.

Fidel and Religion

Conversations with Frei Betto

EL ENEMIGO NO NOS ENCONTRARA DESORGANIZADOS, DESARMADOS NI DESPREVENIDOS

knew that to many Bolivians, figures of Jesus, Mary, and the saints simply had taken the place of pre-Catholic idols. So he eased his conscience by taping a note on the bottom of the figures:

I am an image without a soul, the work of man's hands.
Therefore I do not merit any worship or homage.

On the bottom of the figures of Christ, he taped:

I may represent God, but I am not He.
God is Spirit, and they that worship Him must worship
Him in spirit and in truth.

When customers read the notes, they hurriedly left without making a purchase. This confirmed to Arturo that most people had been buying images because they thought they had supernatural power. What to do? He couldn't sell the images; yet to destroy them openly would incite a riot. Besides, he was still haunted by the superstition that anyone destroying an idol would be damned.

The more he read the Scriptures, however, he knew he must get rid of those images. He took the entire lot--over two hundred--into the back of his shop and smashed them, storing the pieces in boxes. The next problem was how to get rid of the boxes, because he knew no one would lend or rent him a car for the purpose. He finally looked up a missionary of the Evangelical Union of South America working in a nearby village, and made two trips with him to toss the debris in the river. Arturo also traveled to Cochabamba, where he had another stock of images. He took them to the edge of a cliff, smashed them, and threw them over.

Meanwhile Hilda's fury mounted.

"You can do whatever you want with the images in your shops," she raged, "but the ones in our house are mine, and you can't touch them!"

Arturo told Hilda he'd leave them alone, but he would pray for her until she'd want to smash them herself. Arturo's mother ranted at Hilda for allowing Arturo to do these desperate things.

She said that the teaching of Protestants was just for Indians, not for cultured people like their family.

In order to find arguments to turn Arturo from his heresy, Hilda began reading his Bible when he was at work. Upon his return she'd ask him questions to try to trip him up, but these only served to show him that she was reading the Bible for herself. She vehemently denied this without a twinge of conscience, because lying was not a sin--just a part of her culture.

Arturo continued witnessing to Hilda. "Without Christ you are going to hell!" he told her sorrowfully one day.

"I have Christ around my neck!" she retorted. "I worship Him every day. I haven't committed any great sin, so God won't send me to hell."

Arturo asked her to read the Gospel of John. That convicted her of her need of salvation. To forget what she read, she spent more time playing cards, but one day she became ill with fever during a party and had to return home. She picked up Arturo's Bible, which opened at the third chapter of Romans: "There is no one righteous, not even one."

Hilda came under such conviction that Arturo's mother asked him why she looked so sad. When Arturo asked Hilda, she burst into tears.

"Because I'm going to hell!" she wept.

"You don't have to if you find the Saviour," he replied lovingly. Through reading John 3:16 and other Scriptures with him, Hilda accepted Christ as her personal Saviour that day.

Meanwhile, opposition to Arturo's evangelical faith was mounting in town. People boycotted his businesses, until he had to sell his stock at a loss. He even received death threats.

One night when Arturo was staying at his father's house, he heard an angry mob outside, demanding he come out or they would burn down the place. The family tried to keep him from going out, but he insisted on going rather than risk damage to his father's property. He kissed his wife goodby, prayed for God's protection, and boldly walked out the front door, expecting to be beaten up. To his surprise, he suddenly found himself surrounded by friendly students and others who respected his convictions. They had heard the commotion and had come to protect him from the drunken mob.

THE EARTHQUAKE

The incident showed Arturo and Hilda that their lives were in danger. They left town for a family cottage, where they could read the Scriptures and pray together, seeking God's direction for their lives. One day the quietness of the cottage was disturbed by a loud rumbling.

"At first I thought that pumas in the hills were roaring in hunger!" Arturo recalled. "Then the house shook. I rushed to the door to look out, and realized that a major earthquake had struck the area. Cracks opened in the ground and water ran out of burst pipes."

It was Good Friday, 1945. The city of Sucre had been commemorating the day in the usual way, in deep mourning for Jesus. They believed that Jesus actually had died again, and would be dead for the three days of the Easter weekend. They were terrified when the earthquake brought down buildings all over the city. Arturo hurried into Sucre and found the people most alarmed by the number of churches damaged, especially the plaster figures of saints, Madonnas, and crucifixes that toppled from their niches in churches and houses, smashing to pieces. Surely this was an evil omen, especially on Good Friday!

"What are you going to do with me now?" Arturo challenged the people as he went from place to place assessing the damage. "I destroyed only two hundred images, but God has destroyed thousands through the earthquake!"

The people had no answer, and from then on they didn't openly oppose the Aranas in case more trouble would come upon the city.

BIM missionaries who had come to know the Aranas invited them to a village near Cochabamba for a few months, to give them a complete change while gaining some rest and Bible study. In the village, Arturo found that the few believers were very afraid of the local priest.

"I guess I had more hot pepper in my soul in those days!"

Arturo told us with a laugh. "I went right into the village square and started preaching. That made the believers bolder."

In nearby Cochabamba, a Christian barber was emboldened by Arturo's witness and hung two Scripture verses on his barbershop walls. When the priest came in and saw them, he tore them off the wall and was about to rip them up.

"Watch out if you tear up my signs!" the barber warned him. "Your head and hands and feet may be sanctified, but I'm not afraid to hit the rest of your body!" The startled priest dropped the Scripture posters.

LEARNING TO LIVE BY FAITH

Word of Arturo's fearless witness got around, and evangelicals invited him to preach in a number of places. Before leaving Sucre, he had given his father all the family assets that had been under his care so the family wouldn't accuse him of absconding with the money. This left the Aranas without financial resources. Arturo took work in a bank to help meet expenses, but became convinced that God wanted him to spend full time in evangelism. He talked with Verne Roberts, then General Director of BIM. "Do you think my wife and I could live by faith like the missionaries do, and serve the Lord full time?" he asked.

Verne encouraged Arturo with Scripture promises of God's provision. Later, perceiving Arturo's gift of evangelism, Roberts invited him and Hilda to become associate missionaries. From that time on they lived entirely by faith.

"This was a new kind of life for me," Hilda chuckled. "I had never had to wash clothes, but when I saw missionary women scrubbing their clothes by hand, I figured I could do the same. My hands got red and the skin peeled. The first time we were invited out to dinner after that, I kept my hands under the table because I was embarrassed by their appearance. When the hostess asked if I didn't like the food, I had to take some-- and she saw my red hands! So I sold the diamond necklace Arturo had given me as a wedding present, and bought a wringer washing machine. Most of all, I felt sorry for Arturo, because he had to suffer while I learned to cook!"

"Do you think she learned well?" Arturo asked, with a mischievous look. *"Delicioso!"*

Lorna and I both replied. "You learned well, Hilda."

As we finished lunch with grapes and black coffee, Arturo told us something about his subsequent ministry. He planted and pastored a church in La Paz, maintained a weekly radio broadcast, and published an evangelical magazine. Military barracks and schools opened to him as he showed Spanish versions of Moody Science films. He preached in 21 Latin American countries and in North America and Spain.

Eventually, the Aranas were able to fulfill their vision to have a Practical Institute for Evangelism. A staff of 12, mostly volunteer, conducted youth meetings, evangelistic campaigns, and follow-up Bible study courses.

Later in my travels to other parts of Bolivia and neighboring countries, I was impressed with the number of people who told me they had come to Christ through Arturo's ministry. The sessions with the soldiers at the training camp in Cochabamba were especially fruitful. Constantly there was a new audience as soldiers completed their basic training for compulsory service and new recruits came in. Arturo estimated that 70 percent of one contingent made a profession of faith before leaving the camp. Some of these young men were from remote parts of the country. Arturo once received a call to preach in a village he had never heard of. One of the converted soldiers had returned to his home there and witnessed to his people.

Arturo survived death threats and stoning, but he knew he had a disease that could kill him at any time--*chagas*. Arturo probably picked it up during his ministry in warmer parts of the country, where the disease is endemic. It affects half the country's population. The carrier is the *vinchuca* beetle, which tends to bite the tender spots of the face while people are sleeping at night. There is no known cure, and the disease may lie dormant for several years without observable symptoms. Attacking the walls of the heart, it can cause sudden paralysis and death.

"I've had chagas for 16 years," Arturo said when Ron Wiebe once expressed concern about his health. "I know the

Lord can keep me alive as long as He wants me to minister. Then I'm ready to go home to be with Him."

That day came in December 1986. At the memorial service, UCE President Remigio Ancalle, told how he had trusted in Christ as Saviour while a boy, through Arturo's preaching.

"Arturo is probably the spiritual father of more Bolivians than any other person," Ron Wiebe stated at the service. "BIM-AEM, and now SIM, have been enriched through 35 years of close association with Arturo and Hilda Arana."

Lorna and I included ourselves in those whose lives had been blessed through personally knowing the Aranas. We were thankful for that time in their home shortly before Arturo went to receive his accolade from the Lord: "Well done, faithful servant!"

NO TIME FOR SWINGING FROM VINES!

We saw antiques from Arturo's relatives' castle when we visited Sucre. The city of about 85,000 is the judicial capital of the country and one of its most important centers. It was established in 1538 by Spaniards who worked their way along the river system from the east coast through what is now Paraguay, rather than over the Andes from the west. It was from Sucre's San Miguel monastery that Jesuit missionaries later went south to convert Paraguay, Uruguay, and Argentina. From the university went forth the first call for Bolivia's independence, in 1809, and the new nation's Declaration of Independence and the Constitution were signed there in 1825.

In the historic city's main square was a monument of General Sucre, after whom the city was named. A national hero of the War of Independence, he was killed by robbers at the age of 32. Sucre served under the revolutionary patriot who gave his name to Bolivia--Simon Bolivar. Born in Venezuela in 1783 and educated in Europe, Bolivar was influenced by the philosophies of Voltaire and the example of the French Revolution. He returned to South America and led in the liberation of six nations from Spanish rule, becoming known as "the greatest genius the Hispanic-American world has produced." Bolivar's statue now appears in 60 capitals around the world. His fellow revolutionary, Jose de San Martin, is a national hero in Argentina, Chile, and Peru, which he liberated.

Sucre's history was fascinating, but we really wanted to see what was happening in the work of the gospel today. Paul and Lucinda Bentley, both from U.S.A., were on hand to show us. A young couple with two active boys, the Bentleys had their hands full with a team of American teenagers who arrived to construct three dormitory rooms at the Quechua Bible School where the Bentleys taught.

I had often wondered how valuable teen summer projects were in terms of the expense and also possible cultural reactions from the local people. However, seeing Monroe and Corinne Hughbanks of TEEN Missions with 21 teenagers in action convinced me it was a great idea.

"A lot of teens have a romanticized idea of missionary work and want to be off in exotic jungle settings," Monroe told us. "We usually fit in a visit to the wilds, but they come to realize that a lot of strategic missionary work is done in places like the Quechua Bible Institute in Sucre. They soon see that missionaries and national Christian leaders don't spend their time swinging from vines, but they plod away under many pressures. These weeks are a great education for them."

"And they're a great help to us!" added Paul and Lucinda. "See those walls going up? We prayed for that for a long time, and now it's happening. We'll be able to take in more students next school year."

The Quechua Bible Institute graduates go back to the villages and work under difficult conditions with little financial support. Lacking transportation (a bicycle would be useless on the mountain trails), they travel long distances on foot. They have no money to buy study materials for their own growth and preaching, so Paul visits them to encourage and instruct them. The school also has a one-month refresher course for pastors and evangelists.

PADLOCKED CHURCH

Two of the pastors arrived for breakfast in the Bentleys' simple home one morning while we were there. Atiliano was one of them. He itinerates from village to village, living by faith.

Atiliano told us that there is still occasional violence, as when a priest incited the farmers to throw dynamite at an UCE church. But most opposition these days is subtle. For instance, the government finances public schools operated by the Catholic church under the name Schools of Christ. The priests threaten to remove the teacher if the people do not become Catholic church members. They also use food and medicine to influence the people, the pastor said.

Paul told us about a village he had visited where the priest was making problems for the evangelicals. The local soccer team, which had a number of believers on it, had removed a tumbledown hut to enlarge the community soccer field. The hut actually belonged to one of the evangelicals, and was used only as a sheep shelter. However, since the Catholics had at one time used it for a chapel, the priest told the evangelicals they must rebuild it elsewhere for use as a chapel or he would remove the village teacher.

The Christians did rebuild it and even thatched it, but that did not satisfy the priest. He wanted them to take the new aluminum roof off the UCE church and put it on the chapel. The Christians refused; so the priest removed the teacher, declaring he would return the teacher only when the evangelicals had all signed a statement they would become Catholics. The untaught believers didn't understand what they were agreeing to, and signed the statement so the village would get its teacher back. Paul encouraged them to stand up for their rights as citizens, and not be pushed around.

Epifanio was the other pastor we met. He was UCE's district superintendent for Potosi, the once rich silver area but now a ghost town. He told us that a priest in Potosi had padlocked the UCE church door because the believers held a gospel meeting in a schoolhouse. The believers felt they had the right to do this since the school was owned by the government (although operated by the Catholics), and the Catholics were allowed to hold their meetings there.

Some of the believers felt they should saw off the padlock,

but their elders counseled them to commit the matter to the Lord and wait until He caused the priest to remove the lock. Meanwhile, the believers met in one of their homes.

"We need you to send us a missionary couple to disciple and counsel the pastors and evangelists," Epifanio told us. "There are 75 churches in the area, but they lack leaders. In one district of nine churches, there are only two trained pastors, and besides those nine, there are seven other groups that are just forming into churches. The people are so poor they feel they can't support pastors. We need a spiritual revival."

We prayed together with these men--simple *campesinos* in appearance, but really spiritual giants. Or maybe living saints!

The rest of my travelogue research would have to be without Lorna's companionship. As she headed back to Canada, I missed not only my wife but my secretary, for in the two months with me she typed up all my notes from dictation tapes and wrote over one hundred letters. Her own diary of events included braving (by herself, for I was away) a market full of pickpockets, in search of stolen items, surviving altitude sickness, sampling exotic foods she had never seen before, shivering through a four-hour country baptismal service beside an icy stream, encouraging many with her presence, plus play-ing the part of Visiting Grandma to several MKs and many BKs (Bolivian Kids). Believe me, she could write her own travelogue!

As for myself, there was one more place I needed to visit before leaving the Andes for the lowlands to the east. I must see Oruro, a city of significance to the work of the gospel. It was where BIM pioneer George Allan met Baptist pioneer Archibald Reekie. It was where Bolivia's first Protestant martyr was killed. And it was a city I'd often heard Lorna's mother mention as she prayed for missions.

Our struggle is . . . against the spiritual forces of evil in the heavenly realms.

EPHESIANS 6:12

9

OF DEMONS

AND

ANGELS

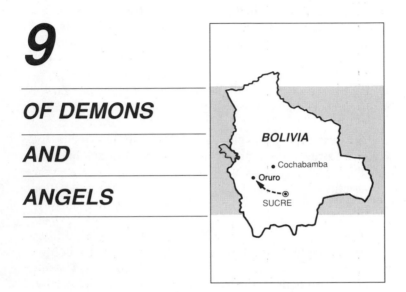

Astring of empty ore carts rattled past us and disappeared into a black hole in the face of the hillside. UCE evangelist Julian Coronel was showing Ron Wiebe and me around one of the mines that Oruro has been famous for. Silver mining built this city (12,160 feet altitude) which once was Bolivia's capital. By the time the Reekies and Allans reached it, the city had degenerated into one of the dirtiest they had seen. Later, the world tin market temporarily rejuvenated the mines, but now Oruro is dusty and derelict.

We followed a group of hard-hatted miners into the mouth of the shaft. Darkness enveloped us, with only an occasional dim light bulb casting shadows along the rock face. I shuffled cautiously to avoid tripping over the ore train tracks.

Mining today is a far cry from the appalling conditions under the Spaniards. Now there are safety regulations, miners' unions, and modern equipment. As our eyes adjusted to the dim lighting, we watched heavy cables lower an elevator down eight levels to 1400 feet below the surface.

Beside the elevator Julian pointed out a shrine with a figure of the Virgin del Socavon, the patroness of miners. With their traditional beliefs linking the spirit world and the earth, the miners believe that Lucifer lives inside the mines. Most miners say they have seen the Devil walking in the mines, and they ban females from the mines so the women will not become infertile.

Traditionally, before an Indian started mining on his own, he sacrificed a white llama and spread its blood over the rock face. This was supposed to placate the Devil and help the miner find precious metal. However, Quechuas also believe the Devil seeks revenge for the disturbance caused by mining. Miners keep an image of the Virgin inside the mine to protect them from illness and injury. At the annual carnival, the people of Oruro stage the *Diablada* (Devil Dance) Festival, involving Satan and a separate Lucifer wearing scarlet cloaks. Each carries a serpent and a miner's trident. St. Michael the archangel and the Devil's wife are also represented, along with hundreds of dancers in diabolical costumes. After licentious revelry, everybody ends up in the chapel of the Virgin, where they chant an ancient pagan hymn and pray for pardon.

CAVE-IN!

This was the context Julian worked in when he was a mining superintendent. As we felt our way along a tunnel, Julian told us the mines can still be dangerous, in spite of safety devices. One day as he was working in a tunnel, a cave-in started. Julian's first instinct was to run. Then he noticed that the miner working with him was trapped to the waist. Praying for strength and time, he clawed the rocks away and freed the other man. They both raced to safety before the mine tunnel collapsed completely.

Julian also vividly remembers when an elevator went out of control and plummeted to the bottom of the shaft, crushing its 12 occupants to death. The safety claws failed to operate. Only a month after that accident, Julian was returning to the surface in an elevator when it suddenly reversed direction and started to fall. "Santa Maria!" his companions screamed in terror, calling on the Virgin Mary to save them. Julian felt assurance that God would protect them, and called out to the men that they would be all right. All at once the elevator shuddered and jolted as the safety claws began to dig into the sides of the shaft, breaking its fall. Julian and the others were badly shaken but not seriously injured.

These experiences gave Julian many opportunities to witness to the miners. Noting the good influence of this, one boss sometimes told him to go and talk to the men, even during working hours.

Now Julian was back as a visitor, but he used the opportunity to witness to one of the miners, Augustin, who guided us with the light of his helmet lamp back to the tunnel entrance. Outside, we squinted in the sunlight. I took a photo of the miner and offered to send him a print. He asked me to send it care of Julian, "so he can come and tell me more about the gospel!"

If there were demons in the mines, God also had His angels there.

A CASE OF GRACE, A WALK OF FAITH

When Julian told me his own background story, I marveled at God's grace. He never knew who his father was, and his mother abandoned him when he was eight. From childhood he wanted to train as a priest but became disillusioned by the immoral lives of the priests he'd looked up to. As a teenager Julian drifted into village vices and was planning a robbery when an event changed the course of his life.

Julian and other members of a gang sat in on gospel meetings held by two visiting Pentecostal missionaries. Their aim was to break up the meetings. Instead, Julian became convicted of sin and ended up responding to an invitation to repent and trust in Jesus. His relatives were furious when they heard this. His mother, who had taken Julian back into her house, called the priest to cast out the demon of false teaching from her son. She seized his Bible and burned it, but Julian bought another and studied in secret. He served in the army several years but eventually left his home town permanently, in the face of continued persecution.

While visiting La Paz, Julian heard a Latin American evangelist preach. This reawakened his childhood desire to serve God. But how could he prepare? Then a friend told him about the UCE Bible Institute in Cochabamba. He enrolled, attending classes half days, working half days to pay his fees, and studying into the night. After graduation Julian married and became a part-time pastor with UCE, working as a mine superintendent in Oruro to support his family.

Julian still had the urge to spend full time in Christian service, however.

Although his wife and children encouraged him to quit his mining job, he was worried about providing for them. While working for the mine, he at least could buy groceries at a discount, and he had a regular salary.

"Why don't you quit the mining work, Daddy?" his five-year old daughter challenged him. "God will probably give us more to eat than we have now."

Julian did quit, and from then on it was a life of faith. Up to that time he had never had a vacation or taken his family back to his own village, Sopachuy (Devil's Island), near Sucre. The family prayed for the money to travel. The day Julian had to buy the train tickets, a believer said he had some extra money he'd like to give him. It was just enough to get the family halfway to Potosi. They went that far, and the churches there asked Julian to preach. The offering they gave him covered the rest of the trip to Sucre, where he also preached. An offering there covered the return trip to Oruro.

As Julian told me his story, I sat looking at this man of slight build with piercing eyes, unruly black hair, and boyish grin.

With his childhood background, he could have become an alcoholic or a drug addict involved in crime. Instead, he'd become a faithful father and a responsible pastor--president of UCE for several years.

"Your story makes me believe in God's sovereign grace," I said at last.

"It *is* God's grace!" Julian agreed.

"I went with Julian back to his village last March," Ron joined in. "The first person we met was the town clerk, who asked if Julian would like to preach in the town hall. He said he had the key, and the priest was out of town. Over three hundred people came nightly for three nights. Five accepted Christ, including Julian's aunt. The community now respects Julian as a man of God."

That's not all that happened back in Julian's village. His mother was converted when missionaries from Gospel Missionary Union visited her town several years ago. She later told Julian she turned to Christ because Julian never abandoned her through the years when she abused him and left him. He even sent her money from his meager earnings when she was ill. After her conversion, she sent for Julian and asked for his advice on the best way to get rid of the images and sacred paintings in which she had previously trusted. They prayed together, and then threw the items on a bonfire.

"BURN HIM!"

We stayed overnight in the stone house Julian had built while working at the mine. It was squeezed between other houses perched on a hillside overlooking the town.

"I'll take you to the village where my father-in-law, Braulio, came from," Julian said. "You'll meet people who once wanted to kill him!"

Early the next morning we set off for Choro, 40 miles out from Oruro on the high plain. Braulio went with us.

Before we left the city, we stopped in the open market for a stand-up breakfast. Water in the gutters was frozen, but steam rose from big tubs of boiling corn gruel. A glass of the hot gruel and a fistful of deep-fried flat bread warmed us for the trip to

Choro. As we drove out of town, we passed Braulio's youngest daughter and several other women climbing the mountainside to fast and pray for the day. Tucked in their Quechua shawls was Bible study material to read.

Normally the drive would have taken us an hour, but we had to detour for another hour because the road had been washed out by flooding from far-off Lake Titicaca. In places we had to crawl cautiously along the detour trail where it also had been washed out. The expanse of water accentuated the flatness of the plain. Harvested bundles of grain formed little islands. Blue-billed ducks, migrating geese, and pink flamingos protested our noisy passage. A fox ran across our trail. On higher ground, boys shepherded their llamas and sheep. The stone huts of farmers blended in with the gray-brown earth. There was not a tree in sight all the way to the horizon. Only sagebrush covered the ground where there wasn't water.

As we traveled, Braulio, a quiet man, told me that years ago his wife, Anna Maria, had hovered near death for three years. She and Braulio spent their savings and even sold their truck to pay physicians and witch doctors for treatment. When their money ran out, there was nothing left but to wait for death. Then two Salvation Army officers, a Bolivian and a German, visited the couple and showed them the way of salvation. Anna Maria believed, and within a month was feeling better. Amazed at this miraculous recovery, Braulio also accepted Christ as Saviour.

They had been staunch Catholics until then, and had planned to donate a large statue of Christ to the village of Choro, where Braulio was a teacher. The villagers were outraged when they heard that Braulio and Anna Maria had instead become evangelicals. The priest stirred up the people, and someone dynamited the house of the little couple.

"Heretic!" the people shouted. "We'll drive you out of town!"

Someone started the rumor that Braulio had nailed shut the doors of the Catholic church. The town leaders called a community court meeting, and sat Braulio on a platform in the middle of the village square.

"See--there's the platform over there still!" Braulio exclaimed as we drove into the village. "I called out to the crowd, "What have I done wrong? I have only believed in the Lord Jesus Christ!"

"Burn him! Burn him!" the people screamed.

Finally a visiting official calmed the crowd, and the hearing continued. Farmers from a radius of 30 miles had come in for the case. They heard the gospel for the first time as Braulio defended his new faith.

"Listen to me, listen to me!" the official said to the people after everyone had had his say. "Aren't you practicing your witchcraft along with your Catholic faith? Our nation's Constitution guarantees religious liberty, and so Braulio and Anna Maria should be allowed to practice their faith."

They were released, but Braulio found it impossible to continue teaching. He was constantly accused of diverting the children from the true faith. The school superintendent wanted to transfer him to the Chilean border, but Braulio resigned so he could give his full time to strengthen the believers in town. He supported himself by ranching.

And so the gospel came to stay in Choro.

Anna Maria later discovered that one of her relatives was a main troublemaker, but he and others eventually turned to Christ. Braulio's brother, Max, didn't give in as quickly. He would come to their house and kick on the door, shouting obscenities. "We're Catholics here!" he'd yell. "Get out of town!"

Braulio returned good for evil, and Max finally went off to Santa Cruz. Ten years later he returned and again banged on their door, making such a row that police came and locked him up. Braulio took him food and a mattress, and the next day posted bail for him. Max again disappeared, but two years later turned up with a smile instead of a scowl. He had found Christ as Saviour.

One of the things which enraged the villagers was construction of a tiny church. To reduce the reaction, the believers built it at night, carrying the building materials in the darkness ten miles from another village.

Braulio had done much to help the little village of 200 people. He organized them to dig a canal 45 miles long, ensuring a year-round supply of water for irrigation. The villagers elected him as president of the agricultural cooperative, and eventually made him village mayor. A number of evangelicals have become village elders, and the priest comes to the village only once a year. There are now five other evangelical churches on the surrounding plain.

Braulio took us to the edge of the village, where a large new UCE church stood. At the back of the church, through a gateway in a stone wall, we found a church district meeting in progress, out in the open air. The church district chairman had cycled from Oruro the night before to meet with the elders to plan an evangelism campaign. One of the elders was a man who once tried to chase Braulio out of town.

Upon our arrival, the elders and a dozen women sitting in the shadow of the wall burst into a welcome song, and the chairman offered a prayer of thanksgiving for our safe arrival. Braulio's wife, Anna Maria, was there, organizing a welcoming feast. The women squatted on the ground, cutting up piles of vegetables while Julian brought a Bible message. With an open Quechua Bible in his hand, Julian shed his typically sheepish look. I couldn't understand the words, but I sat spellbound as he let loose his gift of evangelism and Bible teaching. Ron whispered that he was speaking about the change which Christ makes in the home.

After the Bible study, Anna Maria motioned to Braulio to take us into a small room at the side of the church. There they served us spiced sheep's milk.

"Don't eat too much," Julian warned as Anna Maria put a basket of flat rolls on the table. "This is just a snack--the meal is yet to come!"

QUECHUA POTATO ROAST

We followed Anna Maria out to the field to see the traditional way of baking potatoes. The men had lit a fire of grass and sticks inside a mound of clay chunks and rocks. When this improvised oven was hot enough, they doused the fire, opened up the top, and poured in potatoes. Then they crushed the glowing clay and rocks down on top of the potatoes.

While we were waiting for the potatoes to bake, Ron told me more about this group of believers. The chairman gives full time to the church district but lives by faith, without salary. During the last rainy season, the villagers became worried about the heavy rainfall; so the believers prayed that the rain would stop--and it hadn't rained since. Now that flooding from Lake Titicaca was again threatening the community, the churches had taken up an offering to purchase food to give to flood victims. Throughout the border area, an estimated 50,000 Bolivians and 30,000 Peruvians had lost their homes in the worst flooding of the century. The villagers asked the believers to have a day of fasting and prayer that God would stop the flood.

The evangelism plan the UCE elders were discussing was based on SIM's New Life For All program. Julian's vision was to see believers take the gospel into every village and city street across the nation. The task is enormous, because 60 percent of Bolivia's 6.5 million population still has not heard the gospel.

Back in the little room we sat down to the traditional bowl of vegetable soup. Then we had a main course of potatoes, chunks of mutton, and pounded millet topped with onion sauce. We washed everything down with a Bolivian soft drink.

The believers asked me to tell them how God was working in other parts of the world. They nodded with empathy as I told about Christians in lands such as Ethiopia, Cuba, and China, where there has been persecution, and they were happy to hear that Asian missionaries are serving with SIM in South America.

While I was talking, the women listened as they raked through dried potatoes--a process invented by Quechuas long before the era of freeze-dried foods. The potatoes are spread out, jackets and all, until they shrivel from being frozen. Periodically the women thaw the potatoes and stamp out the moisture with their feet. Women sometimes soak the potatoes and clean them, keeping the good pulp to freeze and dehydrate further. The people live off dried potatoes until the next harvest.

We said it was time to leave, but our hosts insisted that we sit down again for another plate of food. The potatoes in the field oven had finished baking. We ate them with chunks of freshly roasted lamb.

Then these believers, struggling to subsist in one of the poorest countries in the world, presented Ron and me, the two foreigners, with two live sheep! I was stunned. I should be giving to them instead of receiving from them. But it was impossible to refuse, and Ron and I later passed the sheep on to Julian's family. I was glad I had some money from friends at home, and I left it to help with the evangelism fund.

As we said goodby, each man and woman embraced us and gave us "a holy kiss." In the world's eyes they were simple Indian *campesinos,* short, wiry, bronzed from the rigors of farming on the high plains, cheeks ruddy from the altitude. They'd weathered more than the harshness of nature. They had come through tribulation. They were God's children. They were beautiful people.

As we drove off across the plain, that little group of Indians in ponchos and shawls was transformed on the screen of my mind into part of the crowd John saw in The Revelation, "arrayed in white robes." And I thought I could hear a voice saying:

These are they who have come out of the tribulation; they have washed their robes and made them white in the blood of the Lamb. . . . Never again will they hunger, never again will they thirst. The sun will not beat upon them, nor any scorching heat. For the Lamb at the center of the throne will be their shepherd; he will lead them to springs of living water. And God will wipe away every tear from their eyes.

The sun was setting over a range of hills. A bank of clouds captured its rays and turned them into layers of burnished gold. Then only darkness. There was not a light anywhere, except our headlights, until we reached the main road.

MARTYR'S MEMORIAL

We got back to Oruro in time to meet with a group of university students crammed into Braulio's living room. The next morning was Sunday, and we headed off to the New Jerusalem church, which Julian at one time pastored.

En route we stopped in at the Norman Dabbs Memorial Church, where a memorial plaque states: "Evangelical Baptist Church built in memory of Norman Dabbs, martyr for Christianity, Oruro." Dabbs, a Canadian Baptist missionary, was stoned to death August 8, 1949, along with seven Bolivian Christians. A mob attacked them during an evangelistic meeting in a village outside Oruro. Dabbs preached his last message from the text, "If anyone would come after me, he must deny himself and take up his cross and follow me." As a result of this martyrdom, several young people committed their lives to Christian service. (BIM's Arturo Arana was helping Dabbs in this outreach, but that night Arana preached in another village and so escaped the attack.)

At UCE's New Jerusalem church in town, we came upon a different scene from the quiet village we had been in the day before. A musical group played guitars and sang hymns over massive loudspeakers, nine electric cords trailing across the platform. On one wall of the church was a poster listing the dates for fasting and all-night prayer through the year. The church grew from 60 to 100 members in a year and has a goal of 300. Modern young people filled the auditorium. One of the members introduced a couple who had come to the Lord just two days before in one of the 18 Bible study groups held in homes. Then seven new converts were baptized.

UCE's current President, Remigio Ancalle, a striking figure with a black goatee, played the organ and then preached a message on forgiveness. I was able to follow the Scripture reading, and could tell he was preaching with great power. Eleven people came forward when he gave an invitation to those who had sinned and wanted forgiveness.

A communion service followed. Before passing the bread portions around, the leader asked if anyone had a word of testimony or anything to confess. One of the elders who had been sitting on the platform slowly stood and said he had held a grievance against his two sons-in-law. One was the songleader. The father went over and embraced him and the other son-in-law, asking both for their forgiveness.

A woman who had been baptized just that morning asked people to pray that she might overcome her habit of arguing with her family. A young man tearfully confessed adultery and asked prayer that his wife would forgive him and come to the Lord also. Another member said he had held something in his heart against a man, and he went over and embraced him.

After the communion service there were many embraces and tears. The elder who had asked his sons-in-law to forgive him was surrounded by other members of the family expressing their joy.

GROWTH STRATEGY

Remigio and his brother, Casiano, took us to lunch at Oruro's new hotel. They shared something of the vision they had for the work. At the beginning of the year the UCE churches in Oruro set a goal to win 100 people that year. They achieved that goal in six months. They divided the entire city into sections for visitation. Training groups prepare members to disciple the new believers. Now they face the need for a larger church.

"We Bolivian Christians say we're poor, but when we want to buy something, be it a radio or a new chair, we're able to save up and get it," Remigio told us. "It's true people don't have much money, but if we challenge them, we believe they will rise to the challenge so we can build a larger church as a base to reach many more people."

Two months earlier the elders had challenged the people, who went back to their homes and brought money or furnishings to give to the building fund. Casiano, a businessman, gave a dining room set. In a week the church had $1500, a large sum in terms of local wages. The elders asked the people not to bring more items until the church could dispose of those already collected, because there wasn't room to store anything more.

"Most pastors don't encourage their people to tithe, because they feel sorry for the poverty of the people," Casiano said. "But that's not scriptural. God has promised to bless those who honor Him; so we teach tithing. Now our church doesn't have an economic crisis."

(We had also seen one of the new little churches, called "God Is Love," where most of the members are young, unemployed people, and the average offering is only $12 a month. Braulio was giving a lot of his time to them because they could not afford a full-time pastor.)

Both Remigio and Casiano studied at American universities. Remigio, an agricultural engineer, lectured at the university in Oruro, and for several years Casiano headed up the Oruro Development Corporation. It was while he was in Puerto Rico as civil engineer that he met the daughter of a Presbyterian minister and took her back to Bolivia as his wife. Ten years later his wife went to visit her people in Puerto Rico. Tragically, as she returned to Bolivia, her heart was not able to stand the sudden change from sea level to the altitude of La Paz, and she dropped dead at the airport. That made Casiano think about his goals and his commitment to the Lord.

"Until then I had been seeking status for myself," Casiano told us. "I saw that I needed to give everything to God and do whatever He wanted me to."

He and Ron laughed as they remembered how Casiano, at the age of 13, came to one of Ron's youth meetings to cause trouble. Ron recognized young Casiano's potential and assigned him the job of writing a script for the group to dramatize the story of the prodigal son. Casiano rose to the challenge. Later, in the university, he became an activist in student politics and was imprisoned several times by the right wing military government. However, Casiano said he was never a Marxist-- he only felt strongly that Quechuas should be given the opportunity to develop within their culture. He had grown up in a Quechua village and he wanted to show the world that Quechuas deserved respect.

"I owe a lot to Ron Wiebe," Casiano told me. "He was our family's pastor in the sixties, and he helped me and many others follow the Lord. Ron taught us everything--attitudes to life, practical things and spiritual things. We emulated him. Now it's time for us Bolivian Christians to take up the torch and pass it on to others."

The Oruro church's strategy is to divide the members into 12 groups for Bible study, prayer, and evangelistic outreach. Although the church has a wide cross section of culture and society, the groups are made up of people of similar background so they can understand each other's problems and work on them together. After a group develops to 15 families, it subdivides.

The group meetings are in addition to the Sunday services and midweek prayer and Bible study. The leaders of the groups meet weekly to discuss problems and plan their strategy. Rather than seeing a pyramid structure in the church, with a pastor at the top and everyone else doing nothing, they want every Christian to be involved in the growth of the church.

At Oruro and Choro we had seen two different facets of the church: work among educated city dwellers, and work among rural peasants. In both cases, God was using the particular gifts of His people to build His church.

Until now I'd been traveling in the Andes. The time had come to descend more than 11,000 feet to the plains of the east. After all I'd seen God doing among the people of the mountains, I knew I'd also see His power in the lives of lowlanders.

The rising sun will come to us from heaven, to shine on those living in darkness.

LUKE 1:78,79

10

THE LOWLANDS:

COWBOY

COUNTRY

We're in a different world!" I exclaimed to Ron Wiebe as we stepped off the aircraft at the town of Trinidad in Bolivia's lowlands. I could tell we were at a much lower altitude (in fact, under 800 feet) because my lungs had no trouble breathing. We were only half an hour's flight from Cochabamba, yet the Andes were nowhere to be seen. A well-watered plain stretched in every direction. We were in the Beni, one-fifth of Bolivia's area, named after a river which drains into the Amazon basin.

Travel by air or by water was the only practical way to get

into Trinidad, although there is a jolting bus service that would take a day from Cochabamba. The capital of the Beni, Trinidad, has a population of about 36,000, and until the drug trade escalated, it was a sleepy staging post on a river.

"See all those light planes parked out there?" Ron pointed out. "They're the Beni ranchers' pickup trucks. Every ranch of any size has one, and who knows how many are used for flying drugs!"

Trinidad is the hub of the vast drug enterprise in the lowlands. Raw coca paste from areas like the Chapare flows through the town to processing plants hidden on remote ranches. The finished product, cocaine powder, is flown back to Trinidad and exchanged for American dollars by drug lords who send it on to Bolivia's cities and other countries, mostly U.S.A. At the time we were there, Bolivia was producing one half of the world's cocaine base. A good percentage was shipped to Colombia for refining, adding to that country's reputation as the world's major processor of cocaine.

I was traveling with Ron to visit one of UCE's outstanding evangelists, Rodolfo Leigue, at Desengaño, a remote village with a population of 500. Rodolfo's son-in-law, Bruno, picked us up in his Cessna. To make room for cargo, there was no third seat. Ron, being heavier than I (there are advantages!) had to sit up front, and I sat in the rear of the plane on a carton of Spanish New Testaments we brought with us for Rodolfo.

The sun reflected up at us from water lying on the plain below. It was a vast wilderness of green grass pocked by blue ponds. There were very few trees, except those which lined the meandering rivers. Cattle, some of the Beni's one million head, grazed along trails leading to the ranchers' corrals. A flock of flamingoes started up in alarm at the sound of our plane overhead.

OXCART TO AIRPLANE

As we flew so easily across those threatening wastes, I thought of Wally Herron's ordeal nearly 50 years before, traveling by oxcart with his infant son after burying his wife.

Wally, from Australia, and Violet, from New Zealand, had

pioneered for the Bolivian Indian Mission in the isolated village of San Ramon. Violet had complications in childbirth, and there was no medical help within call. Violet died, but the baby survived. With a heavy heart, Wally piled supplies on an oxcart and climbed on with baby Robert. For five days the wooden-wheeled cart creaked and bounced across the pampas and splashed through swamps. The sun was merciless during the day, and the mosquitoes were vicious at night.

Once Wally heard the drone of a motor--an airplane passing high overhead. It was an unusual sight in 1939, when there were very few aircraft in the country. But that glimpse was enough to make Wally realize his infant son might not have been motherless if the Mission had had an aircraft. That tortuous five-day trek to the nearest airport would have taken only 30 minutes by light plane. That was it! He would ask God to enable him to get a plane for the Mission.

After leaving his son with Violet's parents in New Zealand, Wally traveled to U.S.A., earned his pilot's license, and returned to Bolivia to await the arrival of a Piper aircraft that friends provided. In 1941 Wally became the founder of South America's first missionary flying service. At the time, there were only two other airplanes in Protestant missionary service worldwide, one in Borneo and one in Alaska.

Wally remarried and, with his second wife, Emily, developed a leprosy settlement in the Beni, at the town of Tane, which became the government treatment center for the entire District of Trinidad. In 1961 the government recognized Wally's outstanding service to the people of the Beni, present-ing him with the nation's highest civilian award, The Condor of the Andes. But Wally's greatest joy came when his son Robert joined him in Bolivia as a pilot. Ironically, that which helped save lives caused Wally's death in 1964, when he died in an air accident.

MECHANIC, DOCTOR, EVANGELIST!

"There's Desengaño ahead!" shouted Bruno over the Cessna's roar. We circled a cluster of buildings by a river bend, zoomed over a grassy landing strip to scare off 15 cattle, and landed. Rodolfo had heard the plane coming and was at the strip to welcome us. Bruno took off for his ranch, another 15 minutes away, while we walked through the little village toward Rodolfo's house.

It was a pleasant little village, with boys playing soccer in a grassy square surrounded by palm-thatched huts. Horses, tied to hitching posts by the houses, nibbled lush grass. Little children played on an oxcart sitting under a mango tree. The wheels, 36 inches in diameter, were each carved out of one solid piece of hardwood. Across our path lay a six-foot-long snake, just killed by the boys on their way back from watching the airplane take off.

As we walked through the village, Rodolfo pointed out the houses of believers where he holds Bible studies.

"But that's the home of a drug dealer," Rodolfo said as we passed a building that looked in better shape than most. "Recently he called me to treat his wife for an illness. I was able to witness to her about Christ."

"Rodolfo is the unofficial village doctor," Ron explained.

Rodolfo said he became interested in medicine when he developed high blood pressure. He read up on the condition so he could look after himself. A doctor friend in Santa Ana also gave him some first aid tips, including how to help a mother in childbirth. When a woman with severe abdominal pain called him, he correctly diagnosed her condition as peritonitis, and got her flown out to Trinidad just in time to save her life. Rodolfo diagnosed a man with enlarged lymph glands as having septicemia, which a doctor later confirmed.

"I don't have a lot of medical knowledge," Rodolfo said. "I just read my medical manuals and try to come to a logical conclusion."

An obviously pregnant girl greeted us as we passed.

"She's only 15," Rodolfo explained. "That happens with a lot of village children. They start out well, memorizing Scripture and attending Sunday school. When they reach puberty they give in to immorality. It's everywhere around them. Their models seem to be the animal world rather than the spiritual."

Pigs, chickens, and ducks foraged for food around the huts,

while scrawny dogs scratched incessantly. We had to watch our step to avoid horse and cattle manure. There were no paved roads and no cars. Barefoot children lugged buckets of water up from the river a quarter of a mile away.

Rodolfo's house was a rancher's aging homestead. Weathered by the years, it was slowly settling into the damp ground. Rodolfo's wife, Irma, welcomed us with glasses of refreshing *chicha*--the unfermented version made from ground corn and spices. As we sat on the porch, it was sometimes difficult to hear conversation because of the shrill cries of tropical birds in the fruit trees outside. In the summer Desengaño is very hot and sticky, but now we were glad to put on sweaters as the sun set, for a wintery south wind was blowing. Rodolfo turned on the diesel generator, which he kept in perfect working condition to provide electricity for the house. Irma, a pleasant matron, bustled about and soon set before us a delicious meal of fried turnovers, banana chips, and salty homemade cheese. More chicha washed everything down.

"Whatever do young people do here for a living?" I asked as we finished the meal with dark, syrupy coffee.

"That's the big problem," Rodolfo replied, wiping his moustache and looking at me intensely from under shaggy eyebrows. "The people here have nothing to motivate them. Their lifestyle is laziness. I wanted to start a carpenter shop to make furniture, but no one was interested in working. Maybe leatherwork is a possibility. I'd like to organize a farming cooperative. There just aren't any jobs for young people, except a little work at the slaughter house."

I'd noticed a slaughter shed beside the airstrip. Ranchers could slaughter their cattle right there and ship the quarters out by aircraft.

"Most young people move away to Trinidad or other towns when they reach their midteens," Rodolfo continued. "In the nine years I've pastored here, probably four hundred people have come to the Lord, and I've baptized about two hundred of them. But very few are here now because they've moved out to continue their studies or to find work. I can't blame them."

Rodolfo had written the names of many of his converts in his Bible so he could continue praying for them. One of them was a 70-year-old woman from the Movima tribe. She told Rodolfo she'd like to believe the gospel, but couldn't.

"When I asked why, she replied she was a Movima," Rodolfo recalled. "She didn't think God understood the Movima language. But thank the Lord, she eventually believed."

As we chatted, Rodolfo touched on topics from American politics to Canadian salmon fishing, all in faultless English. He also speaks French, German, and Portuguese, apart from his native Spanish. There seemed nothing he wouldn't put his hand to, including building a light trailer for his motorbike, made from the parts of a rancher's wrecked plane.

Rodolfo's background was typical of the people of the Beni. Most came from Europe and settled on the well-watered plains. The Indians of the lowland were farther east in the thick forests near the Brazilian border, or southward toward Paraguay and Argentina. Rodolfo's grandparents came from France, first of all to Argentina, and then on to Bolivia. His father was French, hence the surname Leigue. Rodolfo worked at several things as a young man, including road surveying, mechanics, and cattle ranching.

In spite of Rodolfo's early education in a prestigious Catholic boys school, he became very resentful of the Catholic Church. After reading an account of the Spanish Inquisition, he was angry at the way the church had treated Protestant believers and Jews. He would shake with rage whenever he saw a priest on the street. After Rodolfo became a Christian, he asked the Lord to give him love for Catholics, even though he disagreed with their doctrine and actions.

When Rodolfo was dating Irma, he heard that a Spanish priest was telling Irma not to go with him because he wasn't a Catholic. Discovering that the priest was living immorally, Rodolfo rebuked the Spaniard for coming to interfere in the country while messing around with homosexuals.

"THE HAIR STOOD UP ON MY NECK!"

"I'm curious to know how you first heard the gospel," I said to this remarkable Bolivian.

"The first time I heard the gospel was in 1951, in Santa Ana, downriver," Rodolfo recalled. "I saw boys throwing stones at a foreigner preaching in the town square. I asked why they were doing this, and they said the priest had told them to because the missionary was of the Devil. I stopped them from throwing stones and listened to the message. Later I found that the missionary was Frank Trotman of Bolivian Indian Mission. When he left Santa Ana, other BIM missionaries came: William and Margaret Searle. I was really impressed by all these missionaries, and also by Wycliffe missionaries I met. But I wasn't a Christian.

"I tried to stop smoking, but couldn't. Although I didn't think of smoking as a sin, I didn't like to feel it was my master. So I thought it would be a good test of whether God was real, to ask him for a miracle. I prayed: 'Oh God, if you are in heaven, show me your power by taking away the smoking habit!'"

The next day Rodolfo gave away his cigarettes and his lighter. During the following two weeks, the rancher he worked for offered him cigarettes, but he simply didn't care for them. One day the rancher congratulated him for stopping smoking.

"It was then I realized God had done a miracle and broken the habit," Rodolfo exclaimed. "The hair stood up on my arms and the back of my neck! It was an experience something like Paul's. God had made himself real to me!"

The experience so shook Rodolfo that he asked William Searle if he thought God had done this. Searle could see that God was speaking to Rodolfo and asked if he had accepted Christ as his Saviour yet. Rodolfo admitted he hadn't. When Searle told him he should do so right then, Rodolfo prayed for forgiveness on the spot. He was so happy that he raced home to tell his wife the good news.

"Irma was so angry with me she wouldn't let me sleep in the same bed with her that night!" said Rodolfo, while Irma laughed with him at the recollection. "So I had to sleep in a hammock with the mosquitoes. That night I prayed God would save Irma, and a few months later she came to the Lord through hearing Arturo Arana preach. That made me very happy, because then we had a united Christian home. I hadn't known a stable home as a child, because my father had lived with several women."

Rodolfo operated a river barge for five years, earning around $1000 a month--a princely sum. Then a rancher in Desengaño asked him to install a motor, and he became burdened for the handful of believers he found there without any pastor. Two BIM missionaries who had started the work had moved on. Rodolfo studied briefly at BIM's Bible institute in Cochabamba, and when the Desengaño believers asked him to be their pastor, he left his $1000 job and became pastor for around $250 a month. He has since used the village as a base for traveling up and down the river, preaching the gospel.

"There's hardly a ranch or community for a couple of hundred miles along the river where Rodolfo hasn't ministered," Ron told me. "He has an open door among ranchers, as he stays with them while repairing their equipment."

"Just when I was beginning my ministry in Desengaño," Rodolfo continued, "Verne Roberts of AEM said something to me I'll never forget. He told me, 'Remember that the Lord Jesus is a person who is in your life. This is not a religion but a Person, the Holy Spirit in your heart. The Lord is with you always.'"

It was time for all of us to get to bed. Rodolfo and Irma's bedroom was on the upper floor, and the lower floor was given over to storage, equipment, chickens, and the guest room. After chasing out a clucking hen, Ron and I tucked ourselves in under mosquito nets.

"Don't let your feet touch the net," Rodolfo warned. One morning he had awakened to find blood on his foot because it had rested against his net, enabling a vampire bat to enjoy a nightcap of his blood.

Ron forewarned me that he snored, but I said that wouldn't bother me because I used earplugs. Notwithstanding, I was later awakened from deep sleep by guitar playing and loud singing. I couldn't imagine what was happening. Had some automatic radio been set for the wrong time? I reached for my flashlight and saw that my watch read 1 a.m. The singing and guitar playing continued outside our shuttered window for about five minutes, ending with a loud chorus: "Happy birthday, pastor Rodolfo!"

So that was it! Sunday was Rodolfo's birthday, and his church members had come to serenade him in proper Bolivian fashion. I could hear Rodolfo get out of bed in the room above, shuffle along the floor boards to the window, and acknowledge the serenaders.

I wondered why Ron didn't make any comment. Instead, his snoring grew louder, as if to compete with the sound outside.

"What music?" Ron asked in the morning. "I didn't hear anything." Then he explained that in Cochabamba his house had a beer tavern on one side and a wedding party hall on the other. As loudspeakers blasted at maximum volume well into the night, he and Joan had learned to sleep right through the noise. That I could believe!

It was Sunday morning, and Rodolfo was sitting on the upper veranda, playing on his flute, "When We All Get to Heaven." Then we walked over to the little church. It was about 30 feet long by 16 feet wide, built of adobe brick. Spiders and mud dauber wasps added their decorations to the peeling plaster inside.

The congregation of about 40 adults and children sang a welcome for us. Like most Bolivians, they sang in a high, thin voice that seemed to come out of the tops of their heads. It was plaintive, innocent, childlike.

Ron preached in fluent Spanish on the topic of temptation, from James 1. As he warmed to his subject with typical Latin gestures, I could sense his heart for evangelism. Afterward, the people begged for another meeting the next night. A backslidden woman asked Ron to pray for her. Two teenage fellows asked Ron to play basketball with them. They were still talking about the fun they had playing with him on a previous visit. A barefoot woman brought a chicken as a welcome gift, and another woman presented us with three grapefruit tied in a cloth. A young horseman gave me a leather whip he had braided, as a keepsake.

THE DRUG BARON

Sitting on Rodolfo's porch afterward, I learned more about the Beni.

"Can you explain how this whole area's become involved in the drug trade?" I asked as we sucked the juice from sweet grapefruit Irma had just picked.

"There was no drug trade when I started working in the Beni," Rodolfo replied. "The main economy was in cattle. Although the government taxed ranchers for their cattle, it didn't do anything to encourage better production or prices. There were no veterinary services, no roads, and no price controls. The government hasn't encouraged agriculture either. The Beni could produce enough rice for the entire nation and for export, but the country imports rice. Rubber is grown in the north of the Beni, but instead of encouraging production and employment locally, one of the regimes built a factory in the highlands.

"The result was that when the drug trade began, people saw it as a quick way of making money in comparison to the discouraging cattle and agricultural business. I know people who look upon it simply as business. They can buy $1000 worth of cocaine, package it, and retail it for $3000. The Beni people appreciate luxury, and they can enjoy it by being involved in the drug trade. Even in rural villages like Santa Ana you'll find young families living in houses with marble flooring and expensive mirrors and lamps imported from U.S.A. or Europe—things they could never afford with normal earnings."

I asked how the government was combating the drug trade.

"The previous government had to appear to fight the drug trade or it wouldn't get overseas assistance. But you could buy cocaine right under the eyes of the soldiers or police without any problem--you just paid them a bribe. High officials of government regimes regularly visited ranches for cocaine."

Rodolfo told me about a prominent drug baron with whom he played when they were boys. "We met again recently,"

Rodolfo said. "I told him that though he now has millions, he can't spend it as he'd like to, because he's a marked man. I said, 'You need something you can always keep: eternal life!'" Once Bolivia's biggest drug lord, this man has since been imprisoned.

MONKEYS AND COWBOYS

"We're heading upriver at 6 a.m.," Ron informed me that night. "Rodolfo is going to take us by river to Bruno's ranch, and then Bruno will fly us back to Trinidad."

Early the next morning, mist blanketed the muddy brown Aperes (Banana) River. We climbed down the 25-foot mud bank to Rodolfo's canoe, which was carved from one log. Rodolfo manned the outboard motor in the stern, Ron provided ballast amidships, and I sat in the bow, where I could keep an eye open for exotic wildlife.

"The last time I was on the river with Rodolfo, we came upon a 21-foot boa constrictor lying on a log," Ron shouted over the roar of the outboard motor. "The boa was sleeping while he digested his dinner. We could see a large bulge-- probably a monkey."

The river was only 700 feet above sea level at this point; the sluggish water meandered for another 2000 miles through the Amazon basin before reaching the sea, averaging a drop of about only four inches a mile. Right now it was at its lowest, but along the high banks we could see where it had flooded. Large sections of the bank had washed away, leaving uprooted trees lying in the water like fallen giants. Rodolfo had to lift the motor quickly at times as the canoe shuddered over a submerged trunk. Fortunately, our pilot knew the river well.

As the morning sun rolled back the mist, long-legged insects scurried along the surface of the water ahead of our dugout. Black and white swallows dived to scoop them up. A handsome heron rested from diving to catch its breakfast, while three macaw parrots flew screaming across the river, displaying their magnificent red, blue, and yellow feathers. A stork, startled by the sound of the outboard, lifted off from a log in the river and lighted silently on top of a giant cottonwood tree.

A large fish broke the surface of the river ahead of us.

"Could be an inland dolphin!" Ron shouted. "There are a lot of fish in the river, including catfish, electric eels, and vicious piranhas. Look--there are two dolphins now, playing alongside us!" Just then they rose out of the water in a graceful arch, venting air with a sneezing sound.

"That's where I saw the boa constrictor!" Ron exclaimed as we rounded a bend. This time there was none on the log, but a long alligator slithered off a mud bank and sank from sight. Around another bend, six turtles perched on a log, sunning themselves.

The green forest lining the river was full of life, from brilliantly-hued butterflies to monkeys swinging from vine to limb. A flock of wild turkeys chattered noisily, but a large toucan clamped his orange bill shut, refusing to be drawn into their argument.

We could tell how serpentine the river was from the way the sun changed its position (or we changed ours!), first in front, then to one side and to the other side, and at times completely astern of us. After five hours we arrived at Bruno's ranch. Ruggedly handsome, Bruno and his raven-haired wife, Adele, had built their home around their aircraft--literally. It was essentially an airplane hangar, open at both ends, with living accommodation along the sides.

Rodolfo was proud of his daughter and her husband, who, unlike many of the Beni people he had described, were industrious. Bruno took us for a quick tour around his ranch. He certainly was making full use of the land. He used the clay to make bricks and roofing tile, cut firewood to burn bricks and tiles in a kiln, sawed planks from his own timber, and had carpentry done on the spot. He made his own lassos from cowhide, and soap from the fat of slaughtered cattle. To provide an alternative to roast beef, he made a fish pond and also raised ducks on it. Bruno grew his own rice, which was washed, dried, and husked on a huge machine he and Rodolfo had built from looking at a sales catalog drawing.

Bruno and Adele cared for their employees well, providing housing, a schoolhouse, and a full-time teacher for the children of their staff.

After we sipped lime juice, sitting on the floor of the hangar, Bruno sent me off with two of his cowhands for an impromptu rodeo demonstration. They were experts with their lassos, quickly throwing two over the neck of a steer, holding him to a post with a cinch, then releasing the bucking animal as one of the men jumped on his back and rode him.

Just when I was getting some action photos, they yelled at me to get out of the way. As they released the steer, I climbed the corral fence just in time. The furious bull took after the two cowboys, who nimbly leaped to safety.

When I got back to the house, I told Bruno his cowboys were as good as I'd seen anywhere. He laughed and pulled up his pant leg to show me where a bull had gored him a few months before. A long gash had been opened right to the bone, and Bruno had to call on another rancher to fly him to Trinidad to have it sewn up.

The cowboys had to be on the lookout for another danger —this time a threat to their 2000 cattle. The Beni is jaguar country, and ranchers are constantly losing cattle to them. Jaguars aren't easy to shoot. They have very tough heads, and bullets tend to slide along the skull without piercing it.

"Mules smell jaguars very quickly," Rodolfo said. "I was riding a mule when it suddenly shied and nearly threw me. I couldn't get the mule to go back on the path. Then I noticed jaguar tracks on the path. A boy coming along the trail confirmed that a jaguar was in the area and had killed two sheep the night before."

All the food Adele put on the table that night came from the ranch, with the exception of the salt and flour. The couple could have milled their own wheat for flour if they had wanted to. Even the coffee was prepared from beans grown on the ranch. Before dinner, I watched Adele's aunt prepare it Bolivian style. She roasted the beans mixed with sugar until they looked like charcoal. Then she ground up the black mass and added water to make Bolivian coffee syrup. Typically, the syrup is put on the table in a small pitcher and diners mix their own brew, pouring as much syrup as they want in a cup of hot water.

During my travels I endured this strongly aromatic coffee at first, but after a while found myself positively reaching for it.

After dinner Bruno rolled his plane out of the hangar and set up chairs and benches for a Bible study led by Rodolfo and Ron. Afterward I walked out into the darkness and looked up at the southern sky. The moon was upside down from the way I was used to looking at it in Canada. The Southern Cross was high in the sky, pointing to the South Pole.

Early the next morning as the east began to glow with dawn, the air was filled with a strange noise.

"Sounds like killer bees swarming," Ron said.

Was it coming from the tops of the trees or from the distant river? At breakfast we asked Bruno, who explained that it was the sound of male brown monkeys, the kind we had seen from the river. Surrounded by their harems, they declare their lordship by setting up a loud buzzing sound. Other males respond, until the whole jungle seems to vibrate.

HELP WANTED

On the radio we heard that the Bolivian airline, LAB, was on strike. We decided to head for Trinidad anyway, praying that God would help us get a flight out so we could keep our onward travel schedules.

"How can SIM help nowadays?" I asked Rodolfo before climbing into Bruno's plane. The veteran evangelist rubbed his broad forehead and ticked off the following on his fingers:

• Help provide literature and films.

• Encourage Bible studies over the radio. Cassette tapes of Bible studies would be useful.

• Send more dedicated missionaries like Ron Wiebe and another missionary who works in the Beni, Ingo Manhold. They are important examples to the young people, displaying spiritual maturity, dedication, and reverence for the Lord. UCE has evangelists, but needs teachers of the Word to bring about spiritual depth.

• Send missionaries with practical skills. Ingo knows how to repair equipment and he can organize relief when floods come. These skills are essential in rugged areas like the Beni.

We lifted off toward the sun, Bruno dipping a wing of his Cessna in salute to his father-in-law. Rodolfo deserved a salute, but he wouldn't have accepted it. In business or politics he would have been at the top. In the work of the gospel, he'd taken the lowliest place. He was John the Baptist in the wilderness of the Beni.

The Lord God is a sun and shield.

PSALM 84:11

11

BOAS

AND

ARROWS

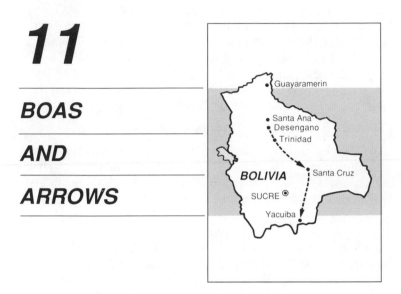

$\mathbf{A}$s we flew back to Trinidad, I thought of Ingo Manhold, whom Rodolfo had mentioned. Ingo and his wife, Christel, were based farther north in the Beni, in Santa Ana, and had helped Rodolfo and Irma grow spiritually when the Bolivian couple lived in Santa Ana.

A rugged, hardworking German, Ingo was certainly built for the work. Christel was just as dedicated, but not strong physically. However, her commitment and spiritual gifts helped make the team. "It takes a special sense of call and a lot of grace and humility to work in the Beni," they told me.

Ingo's abilities shone in 1982 when rivers reached their highest recorded level and flooded 80 percent of the Beni. Twenty-five thousand people were made homeless throughout the Beni, and thousands of cattle drowned. Santa Ana's community appointed Ingo as executive secretary of the Civil Defence Committee, and the Red Cross made him their local agent. Later, the state appointed him director for rebuilding the town. SIM relief and other evangelical agencies supplied food and medicines, provided shelter for 8500 people, and helped rebuild 27 homes. The result was not only rehabilitation of the area, but an open door for the gospel.

THE PYTHON PLAINS

When I was with the Manholds on a previous trip, Ingo told me some of the most amazing snake and crocodile stories I've ever heard. One was about a Bolivian friend who was on his way to meet Ingo and Christel in a remote village.

Luis was wading through a swamp, knife in one hand and gun slung over his shoulder, when an anaconda boa ("King of the Water") bit him on the buttocks and dragged him down so he was sitting with water up to his neck. Luis next saw the huge snake's coils rise to the surface, to wrap around his head. He instinctively threw up his hands to keep them free, and realized that although his gun had fallen into the water, he still had his knife in his hand. In panic he stabbed repeatedly at the boa's body, causing it to recoil. Luis beat a retreat.

When the Bolivian reached the village, Ingo treated the man's wounds, as large as a big dog's bite. If Luis had not had his knife in hand, he probably would have been swallowed by the snake. Boas can unhinge their jaws to swallow objects the size of a man, Ingo told me.

Pablo was a rancher who encountered another boa. After driving his cattle across a river one day, Pablo dismounted from his horse to bathe by the river. He put his clothes and revolver by a tree trunk and was washing himself when suddenly an anaconda grabbed him by an ankle, causing him to fall in the water. As his hands flew out, he felt a tree root in the water and held on to it for dear life while the anaconda kept pulling on his ankle. The reptile alternately pulled and then rested awhile, at which times Pablo inched himself toward the tree trunk. Grabbing his pistol, he shot into the water, frightening off the snake. Ingo said it must not have been a full-grown anaconda, or it would have pulled him right into the river.

Mario's story was even more astounding. He was known around town as an alcoholic. One day when he was asleep on the riverbank in a drunken stupor, a crocodile seized him around the chest, like a stick in a dog's mouth. As the crocodile swam off with him, Mario came to his senses and realized that at least he was face up and had one arm free.

Terrified, he plunged his fingers into one of the crocodile's eyes before the reptile could dive and drown him. The crocodile snapped open his jaws in pain, and Mario found himself by the trunk of a dead tree sticking out of the water. He quickly climbed it as the crocodile angrily circled the trunk, thrashing the water.

Mario pulled off his trousers, rolled them into a ball, and threw them as far as he could into the middle of the river. When the crocodile darted after the trousers, Mario jumped down and swam to shore, just inches away from the jaws of the hungry crocodile. Unfortunately, Mario's escape did not turn him to the Lord; he showed off the scars on his chest and back to anyone who would buy him a drink at the bar.

Ingo and Christel witnessed to people like Luis, Pablo, and Mario as they toured up and down the river system on a launch named *The King's Messenger*.

"The Beni is the size of West Germany," Ingo told me. "But the one million people in this whole area are isolated in little communities and ranches. Many have not heard the gospel. Believers need instruction. Under the government's relocation plan, more highlanders are moving down here. We need other missionaries to help us. But remember, it takes a special sense of call to work here!"

That's what brought Ingo and Christel to the Beni in the first place.

CLASH WITH EVIL SPIRITS

As we landed in Trinidad town, the good news was that the airline, LAB, had returned to work. The bad news was that the National Fuel Agency had just gone on strike, so the planes still couldn't fly. We tried phoning into town to get further information from the office, but the telephone didn't work.

Trinidad is a frontier town, full of motorcycles rather than cars. Ron and I rode two motorcycle taxis into town. Rows of one-storey shops with roofs extended over the sidewalks and supported by posts lined the brick-paved streets. This is where the ranchers come to bank their money, and their wives come to buy trinkets in the many jewelry shops. A lot of products are labeled in Portuguese, imported from Brazil.

The LAB office in town confirmed that the 9 a.m. flight had been canceled, and the next information would not be available until 10. At 10 o'clock the agent told us to come back at noon for an update. At noon we were informed that a plane had come and gone!

Ron finally got through on the telephone to Cochabamba and asked Joan to see if New Tribes Mission would fly their plane down to pick us up. Joan called back later to say the plane had developed trouble and was under repair.

"Lord, if you want us to keep to our schedule, you're going to have to provide some way to get us out of here!" we prayed. We hadn't eaten since 6 a.m. at the ranch; so we headed for a restaurant.

"There's Pastor Alfredo Eggers!" Ron exclaimed. "I tried to get him to meet us in Cochabamba so you could interview him, but he's based in a town away up on the Brazilian border and just couldn't make it. But here he is! Looks as if the Lord's arranged for us to meet!"

Surprised to see us, Pastor Alfredo explained he was on his way to a conference but was stranded in Trinidad by the strike. We all went to lunch together.

Alfredo told us he was converted in his teens after receiving a gospel tract from an AEM missionary. Alfredo wanted to study the Bible, but didn't have the money to go to Cochabamba. When Beni Bible Institute opened, he was able to study right in town. Later he spent two years at the seminary in Cochabamba, returning to his town, Guayaramerin, to head up a youth center opened by AEM missionaries.

Meanwhile, the Bible Institute had closed because of lack of local interest. Alfredo wanted to reopen it, but the churches didn't share his vision. AEM missionaries Eunice Wellings and Penny Ball, who were based in Guayaramerin, encouraged him, and in 1982 he was able to reopen the school, becoming its principal.

"You'd be surprised at the number of unreached people in the Beni," this sharp-looking young pastor added. "It's not easy to reach them, because many are isolated. My vision is to train the Bible students in practical evangelism so they will become itinerant preachers rather than settle down in comfortable situations. We could really use several missionaries in the youth work and Bible teaching to help train these evangelists. Our Bible Institute facilities are very simple, and that prepares the students to sacrifice when going out to reach others."

It was good the students were prepared for hardship. Just the previous week, five were returning from witnessing in villages when the river launch they were on sank. Fortunately, all made it to shore.

Alfredo had seen the forces of light and darkness clash. He told us about Elma, a spirit medium. When she began to have seizures several times a day, she started attending the UCE church and one day went to the front of the church to accept Christ as Saviour. Pastor and elders explained the way of salvation and invited her to ask Christ to come into her life if she were ready. Just then she went dumb and lost consciousness. They got her home, and later that evening when she became normal, they prayed with her. She asked Christ to save her.

The woman continued to be troubled, and Alfredo and the elders perceived she still had not been delivered from evil spirits. They demanded that the spirits confess their names and commanded them in Jesus' name to come out. The woman listed 19 of them and confessed she had made a blood pact with Satan. She brought out articles that had been consecrated to

Satan, including a crystal ball, an occult book, and a red cloth. The elders destroyed them all.

When the woman continued to have attacks, they asked if she had anything else dedicated to Satan. At last she brought them the dress she had always worn in her work as a medium. They destroyed that, too, and committed Elma to the Lord. The seizures ceased and the woman found peace.

"GOD HAS SENT YOU!"

When Alfredo said that the two missionaries who had encouraged him were Penny Ball and Eunice Wellings, my mind went back to their retirement farewell, which I had attended in Cochabamba. Alfredo had been one of their students in the earlier days of the Bible School, and more recently he'd become their principal--a relationship they thought was just great!

They were a most interesting team. Penny, erect as an army sergeant, came to Bolivia from Britain, while Eunice arrived from the opposite side of the earth--Australia. God must have put these two remarkable women together, for they formed an effective team in reaching the northern Beni.

Perhaps I should have used the word "crew" instead of team, for they spent six weeks at a time living on a riverboat, *The King's Herald,* plying the waterways along the border between Bolivia and Brazil. Penny was usually the teacher and speaker, while Eunice used her nursing skills and ran the launch. But they could reverse the roles. The two women and their Bolivian crew members had many scary experiences, especially when squalls hit their vessel before they could make it to port. But they saw the gospel produce exciting results.

One instance was along an unevangelized section of the river. After two days without seeing any other living soul, they had about given up, when their Bolivian pilot cut the engine and swung the launch toward the shore. He had spotted a hut in the forest. As they stepped onto a rotting dock, an elderly woman bent with arthritis hobbled to the edge of the bank and glared down at them.

"Who are you?" she demanded.

"We are evangelical missionaries!" Eunice and Penny called back.

The woman raised her hands in the air. "Oh! God has sent you! We have six people in our house who are ill, and we've been praying to the saints to send someone to help."

The two missionaries climbed the sandy bank and found a bamboo shack, with only a grass roof to shelter the family. There was a crucifix on one of the supporting poles. The woman's husband was prone on a reed mat, almost white from anemia with bleeding ulcers. Another couple and three children in dirty rags huddled in a corner, their feet so badly infected they couldn't walk. Chickens, ducks, and pigs wandered in and out, and dogs scratched their fleas. It was a piteous sight.

Eunice got out her medicine box and Penny shared some food from the launch. When darkness fell, they sat with the family around a rough-hewn table and read the Scriptures with the light of a wick set in a can of kerosene.

It was the first time any in the family had ever heard the Bible read. They listened in awe as the two missionaries talked about salvation and prayed. The elderly woman, Margarita, wanted to know more about prayer because God had answered her prayer for help. When the missionaries had to continue their trip upriver, the family begged them to return on their way downriver. None of the family could read, so the missionaries used a gospel poster called "The Heart of Man."

When Penny and Eunice did return, they were happy to see Manuel, the man with the ulcers, come down to the dock, feeling much stronger.

"You told us how to know God," were the words with which he greeted the two missionaries. "I want Jesus in my heart!"

Margarita couldn't walk as fast, but when she came hobbling down the bank, she demanded, "What is he saying to you? Did he tell you he wants the Lord here?" And she placed her hand over her heart. "Did he tell you I want Jesus here too?" she continued.

The missionaries stayed several days to instruct these new believers in the Scriptures and teach them choruses and pray with them. When the women did move on, they left behind them a little group of believers. They couldn't return for nearly a year, but when they did, they were met with great rejoicing.

"There are many others who want to know the Lord!" Margarita said excitedly. That evening 15 neighbors from huts farther back in the forest gathered in Margarita and Manuel's hut, and that night all 15 said they wanted to follow Christ. They had already been prepared through the witness of the elderly couple.

Later, on Independence Day, the adults went to an army outpost for the usual celebrations. Formerly they had joined in the drinking and lustful dancing. Now Margarita pushed her way to the middle of the floor, called for the music to stop, and told everyone she couldn't join in the dancing because of her new life in Christ.

The missionaries were amazed when they heard about this, because they had not said anything about dancing, and the family couldn't read the Scriptures for themselves. The army captain later became a Christian, and his son has since graduated from the Beni Bible Institute.

The people in the area move across the border freely. Manuel and Margarita moved to the Brazilian side for a while and found the villagers very hostile to their witness.

"So we just opened our window and doors and sang hymns and recited Scriptures," Margarita later told Eunice. "The neighbors could all hear." She knew of at least one family that came to the Lord as a result.

"SPECIAL CONNECTIONS"

My reminiscences about Penny and Eunice, and our lunch with Alfredo, came to an abrupt end when our waiter rushed over to say he'd just heard a rumor that a special flight was coming into Trinidad, but he didn't know if it was going back out. We paid our bill and hurried to the airport by motorcycle taxis. Yes, the ticket agent had heard that a plane was on its way. No, he wouldn't book us until the plane landed and he found out more details. The plane did land, with almost no one on it. The agent eventually gave us boarding passes, and we found ourselves to be three out of 10 passengers on a plane which could seat 110. The other seven may have thought the flight was laid on in order to get people with special connections home before the strike closed down everything. But Ron, Alfredo, and I accepted it as God's provision -*our* special connection.

A week later Trinidad was crawling with narcotic agents, Bolivian troops, and 160 American soldiers. They fanned out over the Beni in military helicopters, with orders to burn cocaine labs, confiscate airplanes, guns, and money used by drug dealers, and to blast craters in the airstrips. It was a grand plan, but on most of the ranches with labs, the soldiers found nobody home. The drug traffickers had received advance information.

We were glad we got out when we did.

INDIAN ARROWS

Farther south, in the lowland city of Santa Cruz, I came across two statements that told me something about the area. I read the first item in the daily newspaper: 30,000 CHINESE TO SETTLE IN SANTA CRUZ.

I heard the second item over the shortwave radio network used by ranchers: "Please get me medical help for two of my staff who have been shot by forest Indians with bows and arrows." The cowboys had been looking for new pasture land on the forested tropical plain that stretches from the base of the Andes eastward to the Brazilian border.

Santa Cruz, founded in 1561 by Spaniards who came in from Paraguay, lay 250 miles by air south of Trinidad. It is Bolivia's boom town, the center of its economic future. As I flew over the city, I could see burn-off flares from oil and gas wells. Stretching back from the river were fields of cotton, sugar, rice, and other crops. Mennonites from U.S.A. and Canada and businessmen from Japan run agricultural projects; Chinese immigration was part of the government's plan to develop the fertile lowlands. Although this booming city, now second largest in Bolivia, has become the new economic frontier, sloths still sleep in the trees of its central plaza, and off toward the eastern horizon there are suspicious forest Indians, like the ones who had put arrows through the two cowboys.

I had met members of the New Tribes Mission who work among these Indians. In the forties, NTM's founder, Paul Fleming, had become concerned about the many smaller Indian groups, ranging from 50 to 50,000 members, living in the lowland rain forests of Bolivia. To evangelize each isolated group means learning a new language. Sometimes it has involved danger and death.

In 1956 the world was shocked to hear that five missionaries working independently in Ecuador had been killed by Auca Indians. But few people knew that 13 years earlier, five NTM missionaries had given their lives in Bolivia, attempting to reach a small Indian tribe, the Ayores. The story was not published at the time because one of the widows believed her husband was still living. Also, it was during wartime, when many widows worldwide were grieving for their husbands lost in battle. Finally, one of the widows, Jean Dye, wrote the story under the title, *God Planted Five Seeds.*

Jean was daughter of one of SIM's pioneers, Guy Playfair.

SIM General Director Emeritus Albert Helser wrote in the Foreword: "As I read, I cried, prayed, smiled, and longed for the fullness of the presence of Christ as experienced by these missionaries and Ayore Christians in Bolivia."

The NTM members I met were thanking God for the recent escape of three missionaries, one a Bolivian, from attack by members of another tribe, the Yuquis (about three hundred population). Dick Wyma, NTM Field Chairman, and Alan Foster, one of the missionaries involved, told us how it all happened. The Yuquis are nomadic, making them difficult to contact. The three missionaries planted gardens while learning the language. Rapport seemed to be developing. A village elder and his servant overcame their fear of the ancestral spirits in the sky and agreed to fly in a New Tribes aircraft from a jungle strip to a settlement. They wanted to observe other Indians caring for crops, and to see children learning to read and write.

Upon returning to the jungle, the Indians were confused. Flying through the sky, they had seen the sun in place, and the spirits had not attacked them. But they should have been able to see the spirits in the sky, they reasoned. What had happened to the spirits? Had they gone away angry?

Eventually a group of Yuquis agreed to go on a monkey hunt with the missionary team. The three missionaries camped near a tribal burial ground, and the Yuquis set up camp about three hundred yards away. The Indians were not hostile, but apparently they felt this was a prime opportunity to dispatch one of these helpful missionaries to placate the ancestors in the sky. After all, human sacrifice was necessary from time to time to accomplish this.

A Yuqui brave took aim and shot an arrow at one of the missionaries, Steve Parker. It passed right through his back and protruded from his upper right side. His companion, the Bolivian missionary, was only slightly injured. The Indians then looted items from the missionaries' camp, but miraculously overlooked the radio, which Steve had left out on a log after contacting their base that morning.

The uninjured missionary ran back to the camp and made radio contact with the base. Thirty hours later a pilot flew in with a helicopter, lifting Steve out in a sling. As the helicopter rose from the forest, one blade struck a tree branch. The machine shuddered, but was able to maintain flight. Steve's life was saved, and by the time we visited Santa Cruz he was back contacting the same Yuquis.

New Tribes Mission had had their problems with some anthropologists. One of them, after visiting a New Tribes camp, wrote a book viciously attacking the mission. He accused NTM of violently arresting old Indians from the jungle and regimenting them in virtual concentration camps. These attacks on NTM were syndicated in other publications around the world. A radical group charged that the missionaries were committing "gradual ethnocide, extortion, and economic exploitation against the indigenous forest dwellers with whom they work."

"We know that some of our missionaries have not always been wise in their enthusiasm--they've sometimes given visitors the wrong impression by the things they've said," Dick explained. "However, many anthropologists would like to keep the forest people as clinical museum pieces, whereas they are in danger of being killed off by disease or encroaching settlers.

"When one Indian believer heard the translation of what a visiting anthropologist was saying, he said to the missionary, 'Tell him he can go and live in the jungle if he wants, but I don't want to. In there I was constantly afraid of evil spirits and I was suspicious of everybody. I didn't have enough food or clean water, or medical help. I didn't know there was any other way of life--but now I would never go back!'"

One jungle dweller had killed her first three babies so she could flee more quickly if her people were raided by other Indians or settlers.

Both the New Tribes Mission and the Swiss Evangelical Mission had been attacked with false reports by anthropologists. The government set up a commission to investigate the work. UCE's Casiano Ancalle, then executive secretary of the Bolivian National Association of Evangelicals, was a member of the Commission, which completely absolved the missions of all the charges and commended them for their service to the people. The government renewed the contracts of the missions and granted NTM a large tract of land in the Chapare to help teach Yuqui Indians farming methods.

"The missions are to be complimented for their accomplishment," stated one member of the Commission, an anthropologist from the University of New Mexico. "As far as the charge of ethnocide is concerned, I think if these people had not been contacted by missionaries, they would be much closer to extinction than they are now. I can see that the missionaries have helped preserve the ethnicity of these groups."

In fact, one tribe, the Araonas, about to die out with only 45 members 20 years ago, now numbers over 70. Since NTM first started, the missionaries had learned much about cultural needs. Even though their work was still criticized, I was thankful they were willing to endure privation and risk danger in order to help people whose very existence is being threatened.

BORDER POST

Hugging the base of the Andes 300 air miles south of Santa

Cruz is the little town of Yacuiba on the Argentine border. I arrived there with SIMer Myron Loss. The local missionaries, George and Fidelia Beckford, didn't know when to expect us because the telephones didn't work and the Beckfords' radio had broken down. They couldn't hear the regular SIM radio transmission.

We hitched a ride from the airport, lurching along the muddy road into this border town of about twenty thousand population. The streets were not paved and there were no sidewalks. Every house seemed to be equipped with a barking dog sitting on the front steps. Our breath turned into white vapor in the early morning south wind. At the Beckfords' bungalow, we soon warmed up with welcoming embraces from George and Fidelia, and a hot breakfast. Myron then hooked up a spare radio he'd brought, to put the Beckfords back in touch with the outside world.

Fidelia was the daughter of a Bolivian soldier who was taken prisoner by Paraguay during the border war of the thirties. He heard the gospel there from a German settler, and upon release moved to Yacuiba to farm. Pioneer Canadian missionaries of the Evangelical Union of South America were there at the time and encouraged the family, who became foundation members of the UCE church in Yacuiba.

Fidelia became an outstanding Child Evangelism Fellowship missionary. While attending a World Vision conference in Cochabamba, she met a black missionary from Jamaica called George Beckford.

"Bolivians believe it's good luck to pinch a black person," Fidelia laughed. "So when George asked me to marry him, my friends thought I was the luckiest person in the world. I'd be able to pinch him anytime!"

Another member of SIM's international team in Yacuiba dropped in and tucked into the scrambled eggs. Henry Cheah, a Malaysian, had become concerned for South America while traveling with Operation Mobilization. Back in Malaysia, he applied to SIM's Singapore office and was accepted for Bolivia. His Chinese home church didn't support missions, but he prayed about his finances and was encouraged when within a few months faith pledges made up the entire amount needed.

Henry had just made the four-and-a-half-day road trip from Cochabamba to Yacuiba, bringing a green Toyota four-wheel-drive vehicle. That was another answer to prayer. An Indonesian Christian had sent him a third of the vehicle's cost, a church in Singapore donated another third, and Henry's home church in Malaysia took up a special offering to pay off the rest. "My green mule," Henry called it, patting a muddy fender.

The SIM team members in Yacuiba were concerned as they saw Mormons, Jehovah's Witnesses, Seventh Day Adventists, Hare Krishna, and Baha'i missionaries moving into Yacuiba. The Mormons had a large church. However, SIMers were thankful for openness to the gospel. When a visiting Campus Crusade for Christ team showed the film, *Jesus,* over nine hundred people stood in the rain for two hours to watch it.

We attended a service in the UCE church, which could seat 200. We also sat in on another embryonic church: a Bible study in the one-room shack of a 50-year-old woman whose husband had left her. She put a partition across the 12-by-20-foot room so that half could be used as a chapel. On the rough wooden door she had chalked in Spanish: GOD IS LOVE. The dozen people who gathered that evening under a gas lantern sang more heartily than some churches of 100 people back in my home country.

Henry drove us across the border into Argentina. Ahead of us was a man driving a pickup truck with 10 girls in the back. George, who seemed to know everybody on both sides of the border, explained that the man was a hotel owner, bringing his maids over so each one could carry back the maximum 25 pounds of goods allowed into Bolivia duty free. Under the bridge, traders divided up large sacks of flour into smaller bags which were then carried by women wading across the river back into Bolivia. A policeman didn't like my taking a photo of this customs evasion. In Pocitos, on the Argentine side, we found the stores well stocked with manufactured items, and also large stocks of chemicals used in making coca paste and cocaine.

Our main purpose in visiting Pocitos was to meet Dr. Moises Darrull--businessman, management instructor, lay evangelist, and mission director. Moises' grandparents had immigrated from Syria in 1925, after his grandmother nearly died at the hands of Muslims who had imprisoned her for her faith. Moises' grandfather had preached the gospel all across the Argentine plains, Bible in one hand and rifle in the other to protect himself.

"The Catholic Church has established a model of a professional priesthood doing the work of the church," Moises told us as we sipped black coffee together in the office of his trading business. "That makes it difficult to get lay people actively involved, but they're beginning to get the vision."

Moises certainly had a strong vision himself. He had formed a mission board to send Argentines to North Africa to work among Muslims, and he was interested in tying in with our SIM radio broadcasts to North Africa from Liberia. Moises and his wife, Beatriz, are coordinators of Child Evangelism Fellowship for Argentina and Bolivia, with George Beckford as a board member.

"Our greatest need is discipling new believers," Moises told us. "Evangelism is not our biggest need--people are turning to the Lord everywhere. Last week 350 people made a decision during a week's campaign in a nearby village, using Campus Crusade's *Jesus* film. But the village church has only 25 members. How can 25 people counsel and teach those new converts before they fall away?

"This happens all the time. People are excited about the big numbers of decisions, but they don't realize that within a few months the majority can't be found, simply because of lack of follow-up. If SIM could provide a couple to train disciplers, we could use them right away!"

My mind went back to discussions with Bill Bright, Campus Crusade's founder, who was developing a network of discipleship training centers to help meet this need, not only in South America, but worldwide.

Moises was respected by both the community and the government. The latter commissioned him to do a study of the potential of Pocitos as a free trade zone with an international airport. This would mean tremendous population growth and social change in the area, as well as unlimited opportunity for the gospel.

It was 1 o'clock, and suddenly life in Pocitos came to a halt. Shutters rolled down over storefronts, traffic stopped, and people disappeared from the streets for a siesta. We headed back to Yacuiba in Bolivia.

ON ALLAN'S TRAIL

As we headed back to Yacuiba, I thought of George Allan's 1902 crossing of the Argentine-Bolivian border further to the west, where the high valleys cross the border. I wondered how he felt as he entered Bolivia in pursuit of his vision to reach the Quechuas. I could never recapture that moment because today there is no death penalty for preaching the gospel. Instead there are hundreds of thousands of believers. Today, travel is relatively easy, even if uncertain at times.

Nevertheless, in a nostalgic moment I wanted to ride horseback into the foothills. We found a farmer who rented us his horse, and off I rode up the trail into the hills behind the town. George and Henry were better off on foot, for part way up the hillside my saddle began to slide to the rear of the horse. It finally slipped sideways and nearly catapulted me over a cliff. After adjusting the saddle, we continued, the horse's hooves sliding over damp rocks. Tangled vines hung down from the trees. Two Indian farmers were coming down the narrow trail, driving a pig to market. Pig and horse confronted each other for a moment, and then the pig, prodded from behind, squeezed by with a squeal. By now the horse was sweating and trembling from the steep ascent; so I got off and climbed the rest of the way on foot.

Eventually we found ourselves in a clearing ringed with thorn shrubs covered with pink, yellow, and white blossoms. At our feet lay Yacuiba, already in shadow. George Beckford pointed out the spot where he hoped to build a youth camp. He and Henry returned down the hill with the horse, but I couldn't tear myself away.

I stood in the clearing, trying to relive the drama of George Allan's venture. The inhospitable Chaco plains lay between his base in Buenos Aires, Argentina, and the Bolivian border. For centuries, east coast Indians had crossed the plains to trade peppers for salt from the Quechuas. Spanish invaders braved the Chaco in search of fabled Inca gold. To them, Indian lives were expendable in their quest. Allan was driven by a different motive: to reach the Quechua people with the message that would bring them eternal life. He and Mary had long prayed for the Quechuas. Argentina was fairly well known outside South America because of its ties and trade with Europe. But what would the Allans find in the hidden valleys of Bolivia's interior? In faith they hung on to the promise Mary had received in her time of prayer: *multitudes of Quechuas would turn to Christ.*

The flat horizon of Argentina lay behind me as I faced Bolivia's interior. The sun was slipping behind a formidable range of hills ahead of me. Myriad insects danced in the blazing rays backlighting white tassels of pampas grass. I could see and hear no one, but I knew there were still millions of unreached men, women, and children in the deep shadows between those jagged ranges. I bowed my head and prayed for them as the sun set on the altar of the Andean hills. Through faith, courage, and determination, George and Mary Allan did their part to reach the unevangelized of their day. I prayed for the same resolve for all who follow their trail in this generation.

The darkness is passing and the true light is already shining.
1 JOHN 1:8

12

LAND

OF BIG

WATER

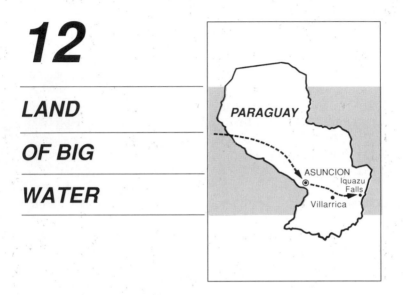

The "Green Hell" of the Chaco plains spread out below as I flew southeast from the Bolivian foothills to Asuncion, capital of Paraguay. The Chaco had become a graveyard for 135,000 Bolivians and Paraguayans in the Chaco War of 1932-1935. BIM-AEM's Verne Roberts, who later became general director, had been in the thick of that conflict as he sought to help the wounded and dying.

The erstwhile battlefield is still an inhospitable waste, semidesert in the north and a swamp in the south. Mennonites from Russia, Germany, and Canada have had the most success in taming the wilds to any degree, establishing a town called Filadelfia and a network of communities in the less hostile Middle Chaco. Mennonites now number over 11,000, and their ranches and farms ship food into the capital.

East of the Paraguay River lie jungle-clad hills and a fertile plain. Vast stretches of tropical forest have been replaced with a patchwork quilt of cultivated fields extending southward to the Argentine border. Prospecting lines of oil companies crisscross the landscape. It is in the south of this landlocked nation, the size of California, that most of its 3.7 million people live--45 percent in towns. Possibly another .75 million citizens live outside Paraguay, mostly in Argentina.

OLDEST SURVIVING CITY

As we prepared to land, I noticed several Korean passengers having difficulty filling in their immigration forms because they spoke neither Spanish nor English. I completed their forms from the information I could glean in their passports, and guessed at the rest. I had to include their mothers' maiden names, a significant detail in the Spanish-speaking world, for a person adds his mother's family name at the end of his father's name. It is essential for identification.

In the airport terminal, local Indians, colorfully garbed in ponchos and green parrot feathers, pestered passengers to buy their handicraft. Ninety percent of the population has Indian blood; as a result the population is much more homogenous than in some countries of Latin America. The aboriginal Guarani language and Spanish are both official languages. In fact, I heard Guarani spoken more than Spanish. "The language of poetry," Paraguayans proudly call it.

I traveled into Asuncion on a bus locally built on an imported Mercedes chassis. The driver peered through a windshield decorated with a Madonna and two palm leaves. He sat on a seat of stretched plastic cord, the kind you find on patio chairs. The rough, angle iron frame was bolted to the hardwood floor planks. The bus doors didn't close properly, but the company went to great pains to ensure that passengers paid their fare. Laden with baggage, I struggled through a narrow turnstyle. There was one for boarding and one for alighting. Then a supervisor got on and checked the driver's unsold ticket numbers and each passenger's ticket. However, the five-mile trip into town cost only 15 cents, so I couldn't complain.

Ron Wiebe and I teamed up again in Paraguay, where Ron followed up on plans for SIM outreach. As we walked down the main street, we had the feeling of being in an old city.

"Asuncion is actually older than Buenos Aires as a permanent settlement," Ron explained. "The Spanish were looking for a passage to the Inca's legendary city of gold. They came upriver, and in 1537 built a fort here called Our Lady, Holy Mary of the Ascension. That became the town of Ascension, or Asuncion in Spanish. In contrast, Buenos Aires was abandoned several times before pioneers from Asuncion established a permanent settlement in 1580."

Asuncion dwellers boast that theirs is the oldest surviving city on the continent. In fact, it was founded before either Spain or Britain established settlements in North America. Yet, few people overseas have ever heard of it, let alone visited it. Ron and I savored its Old World charm as we sauntered across plazas ringed with colonial-style buildings snuggling among red bougainvillaea bushes and purple jacaranda trees. Over the venerable post office fluttered the nation's red, white, and blue flag, the only one in the world to have a different emblem on each side. On one side is the treasury seal; the other carries the national coat of arms.

I gaped as an ancient yellow trolley, the only streetcar I saw in all South America, labored by on its five-mile circuit around the city. A luxurious Mercedes passed a horse-drawn load of plywood and a pickup truck carrying large milk cans.

"I met someone who counted 50 new Mercedes within 30 minutes," Ron said.

Some of the cars we saw were part of a local phenomenon at the time. Hundreds of stolen cars were brought into Paraguay and sold at bargain prices. Gangsters even seized trucks from Brazilian drivers as they crossed the border, in several cases shooting the drivers. Finally Brazilian truck drivers barricaded the border in protest.

Stolen cars were just part of the problem. Goods of every description were smuggled across the border and sold on the black market. At the time we were there, half of Paraguay's trade was illegal, according to one estimate. It didn't help the government's economy, but it and a liberal import policy kept shops full of inexpensive goods. Brazilian and Argentine shoppers knew that Asuncion was the place for bargains, and Asians obviously thought that Paraguay was a good place to do some selling. I remembered the Koreans on my flight, as we saw Korean shops along the streets. Some were only shelves set up in stairwells or narrow passages between buildings, but that was a start for new immigrants with a mind to work. There are 4000 Koreans, 4000 Chinese, 8000 Japanese, 28,000 Russians, and more Germans (60,000) than pure-blooded Indians of all tribes (50,000). Unlike Brazil next door, there are no blacks.

I was fascinated to learn more of Paraguay's history. When Spanish explorers encountered hostile Indians along the east coast, they followed the Paraguay River until they met the peaceful Guarani. In contrast to what happened in other areas, the conquistadors did not massacre the native people. The Spanish made this their base for the southeastern part of the continent. From here they founded settlements in what are now Bolivia, Brazil, and Argentina.

In Bolivia and Peru I noticed most of the towns had Indian names. In Paraguay there were a lot of Spanish religious names. In English they'd be Ascension, Incarnation, Conception, and Trinity, plus names of saints. That arose from southern Paraguay's being the center of work by Jesuit Catholic missionaries. They arrived in 1609 and gathered some 100,000 Guaranis into settlements called "reductions." The Jesuits educated many of the Indians and used their skills to build huge churches. The most famous is at Trinidad (Paraguay). It has a large carved statue depicting God. A priest could hide in a hollow at the back and speak so that worshipers would think it was the voice of God.

The Jesuit Order became a commercial power rivaling the

Spanish government until the King of Spain expelled it from Paraguay and all Spanish domains in 1767. The Indian settlements quickly fell apart because they had depended on the Roman Catholic patron system. Today, in spite of continuing tension between the church and state, Catholicism is still the state religion. Not only is the church tax-exempt; it also receives contributions from the state budget. The constitution requires that the president be a Catholic and ensures a seat on the Council of State for the archbishop of Asuncion.

"Why hasn't the rest of the world heard more about Paraguay?" I asked Ron. "Everyone's heard about Peru and Bolivia--but Paraguay?"

"That's because the nation really has been isolated," Ron replied. "In fact, complete isolation was the policy of one government for a quarter of a century. It was a kind of paranoia because the neighboring nations either blockaded it or tried to annex it."

The national anthem begins with the rousing words: "Paraguayans--the Republic or death!" In the 1860s this feisty nation took on Brazil, Argentina, and Uruguay in a war that killed off three-quarters of her 800,000 population. Only 2100 men over the age of 20 survived, leaving a total of 14,000 males of all ages out of a population of 194,000. That meant there was one male for every 13 females. For years after that, women had to provide the community leadership. With the shortage of husbands, men were expected to have extramarital affairs to repopulate the nation.

Remarkably, until 1989 Paraguay had had the same government for 34 years, the longest rule on record in the Western Hemisphere. Perhaps that was another reason it didn't attract international attention--there weren't any revolutions!

BIG WATER

Paraguay is a Guarani name with at least two possible interpretations: "The waters of the Paraguayes," an ancient Indian tribe, and "river which originates a sea."

The Guarani believed their rivers had great spirit power, but they couldn't have imagined the industrial power of those waters. Ron and I took time to visit the new pride of the nation, the hydroelectric complex at Itaipu, Guarani for "stones that sing," referring to the rapids on the river before the dam was built. It straddles the Parana River on the border between Paraguay and Brazil. A joint project of the two countries, Itaipu is the largest hydroelectric plant in the world. Its 18 turbine and generator units can produce six times more power than Aswan Dam in Egypt, and a quarter more than Grand Coulee Dam in U.S.A. An even larger hydroelectric dam is under construction on the border with Argentina.

We watched the placid brown water from Itaipu Lake suddenly turn white as it plunged from the top of the dam, 60 storeys tall, thundering down the spillway and leaping up in a gigantic rooster tail of foam. Paraguay uses only 10 percent of the electricity, but earns foreign currency by selling the rest to Brazil and Argentina.

Paraguay has become a tourist route to one of the world's most spectacular waterfalls, Iguazu, just across the border in Brazil. Although spelled differently in Portuguese and in Spanish, in both languages it is pronounced "ee-gwah-soo," a Guarani word meaning "much water coming down," or "big water."

That's an understatement. Every second, about half a million gallons of water, nine times Niagara's controlled volume, thunders out of The Devil's Throat and other basalt formations on the edge of the Parana precipice. At high water 275 separate cataracts spill over the two-and-a-half-mile-wide brink, plunging as much as 274 feet into the jungle-lined gorge below.

Iguazu Falls are higher than Niagara and twice as long as Victoria Falls in East Africa. The world's largest-volume falls, Guaira, were also in Paraguay but are now covered by Itaipu's dammed-up waters. South America also boasts the highest falls in the world: Angel Falls--19 times higher than Niagara--on the border between Venezuela and Guyana.

Ron and I trekked along the escarpment for an hour, awed by the primeval scene. High over our heads, giant hardwoods spread an umbrella for shorter palms and shrubs, adorned with necklaces of vines. The leafy walls of our jungle path flashed with hues of red, blue, green, black, and yellow, as exotic butterflies fluttered between wild orchid blossoms. The thunder of the falls increased until their dazzling foam blazed before us. Swifts played tag through the spray that shot up 500 feet into a perpetual rainbow, while, higher still, reeling vultures kept an eye open for any carrion spewed out by the falls.

Edging along a slippery observation walkway on a ledge that split the fall of one cataract, we felt consumed by the awesome thunder above, below, and around us. Downstream the turgid river pulled itself together, exhausted, spent. No doubt it congratulated itself on its spectacular leap, captured by hundreds of camera-toting spectators from around the world (96,000 come in both January and February when the water is at its highest).

"I'M REPEATING THE MACEDONIAN CALL!"

"Brothers, we've made a serious commitment to God, to the evangelical churches, and to the people of Paraguay, that we're going to change the spiritual history of this country. To do this, we need help. So I'm repeating the Macedonian call: 'Come over and help us!'"

The little, energetic man who challenged Ron and me with this call was Pastor Francisco Veron, general secretary of the Bible Society of Paraguay. He was active in a number of evangelical projects, including COMIBAM '87, the continent-wide missions conference I'd be attending later in Brazil.

We had asked Pastor Veron if he felt SIM should consider sending missionaries to Paraguay. We explained that we were already more than busy in other countries, and we certainly didn't wish to duplicate the work of others.

"Of course we need your help!" the 40-year-old Paraguayan responded vigorously. "Look, four years ago I was in a conference where we reviewed the status of evangelicals in each country. I was shocked to find that Paraguay had one of the lowest percentages of evangelicals--1.8 percent at the time. I began to challenge our pastors, missionaries, and other evangelical leaders. That's when we made our commitment to the Lord to begin more aggressive evangelism at a national level on a continuing basis."

I had heard that the percentage termed "evangelical" now stood at 2.5 or even 2.8 percent. Half of that would be charismatic Catholics and large immigrant communities like the Mennonites and Koreans. Many of them are isolated from the country's mainstream, especially because of language differences.

"We praise God for the sacrificial work missions have done in evangelizing the Indian peoples," Veron continued, thumbing through a survey report. "They are 25 percent Christian, although there are still small unreached groups.

"But how about the more than three million unreached Paraguayans? They represent over 90 percent of the population. They are neither Indian nor Spanish--they are a new race resulting from the two. Most of them live in the south of the country in cities and towns. If you're looking for unreached people groups, these are unreached. How are they going to hear the gospel?"

"Aren't there a number of fine evangelical churches and missions already here?" we interrupted, wanting to be sure we understood him. "Can't they do the job?"

"Half of the missionaries are working among the five percent living in the Chaco," Veron replied. "The other half can't hope to reach the remaining 95 percent by themselves. They are calling for help to fulfill the commitment they've made to evangelize the whole nation.

"I'm a Paraguayan. I love my nation. I also love the Lord. So I repeat to you the Macedonian call. We have a wide-open door now, but we don't know how long it will stay open. So don't lose time! Come and preach the gospel!"

Veron told us about that wide-open door--like the 200,000 Bible portions and one-and-a-half-million Scripture selections the Bible Society had distributed that year. These went to schools, universities, prisons, hospitals, and military bases. Many Catholic churches received Bible study courses.

"Now I'm constantly invited to preach the gospel in Catholic churches," Veron said. "And we can't keep up with the demand for Bibles. Catholics are reading the Bible massively and accepting Christ as Lord and Saviour."

We left the Bible Society office with the general secretary's words ringing in our ears: "Don't lose time!"

INDIAN VENDETTA

Over at the office of the New Tribes Mission, we found Norman Fry sipping herbal tea from a cowhorn through a silver straw, in good Paraguayan fashion. He confirmed the Indian responsiveness Pastor Veron had told us about.

"We understand there are still tribes that haven't heard the gospel," we said.

"Yes," replied Norm. "Some ethnic groups now have strong churches, thank the Lord. But there are still a few that must be given the opportunity to hear the gospel. Most are small in population, but each one takes the same kind of patient work that a large tribe would take--learning their language, establishing friendships, and telling them about the Saviour. It takes time, love, and hard work."

"I know you've faced criticism of your work. How does that affect you?" we asked.

"The Indians welcome us because we help them develop their farming and fishing and cattle raising," Norm said. "But sometimes outsiders misunderstand what's going on--like the incident last December when five Christian Ayoreos were killed."

"Five? Killed? Only four months ago?" I asked. "What happened?"

"A group of Indian believers came to the conclusion, from their Bible studies, that it was their responsibility to take the gospel to the unreached," Norm said, poking in the cowhorn to stir up a wad of tea leaves. "For them, that first meant a related group of Ayoreos in the Chaco. They're part of the same tribe who killed five of our pioneer missionaries over in Bolivia in 1943.

"So 30 believers trekked away up to the northwest and found an Ayoreo encampment. The Christians carried no weapons. They told the Ayoreos they had come to be friends.

As the Christians were telling where they were from and why they had come, an Ayoreo brave suddenly jumped up and drove his spear through one of the believers. Other Ayoreos joined in the attack. The believers quickly retreated, leaving five of their companions dead.

"The pastor who led the group had a spear thrust through his face. He pulled it out and walked back into the village. The Ayoreos gaped as they saw this unarmed man standing there, with blood streaming down his face. He must have lost half his blood. The other believers didn't try to retaliate. That convinced the Chaco Ayoreos that these intruders really did want to be friends. So they listened to their message about a God-man who gave His life for them."

"Why would they attack the believers like that?" I asked.

"Well, there's an understandable reason," Norm replied. "The Christians found out that, decades before, one of their tribe's pagan chiefs had warred against the Chaco Ayoreo camps. He'd go in as if he were their friend, then signal his warriors to slaughter the people.

"One of the surviving Chaco men told his son, 'If you ever see this chief's people, kill them!' That's why the brave jumped up and threw his spear when he heard where the Christians came from."

It was half a century since the five New Tribes pioneers had also laid down their lives. The day of Christian martyrs is not over, I mused.

"Our own New Tribes mandate in Paraguay is to concentrate on isolated linguistic groups," Norm explained when we told him SIM's goals. "But we encourage other missions and churches to evangelize those who can be reached through Spanish and Guarani. They all need Christ, whether they're rural or urban. Illiterate and educated groups both need special approaches, and if SIM can get the gospel to the city dwellers, we'll rejoice."

As we talked, an Indian loomed in the office doorway. Bedecked in a headdress of green and red feathers, he held a bow and arrow. "Don't be alarmed!" Norm smiled. "He's a believer who's come to the city to sell bows and arrows and other handicraft."

THE TASK FORCE

Ron had made an earlier survey with SIMer Myron Loss from Bolivia. They had found the same warm welcome among other missions and church groups. South America Mission, which actually originated in Paraguay, had just conducted a survey which confirmed the urgent need for urban evangelism.

With this kind of encouragement, on top of a conviction of God's leading, SIM appointed Myron and Alice Loss to spearhead the Mission's entrance to Paraguay in 1988.

"That was a thrill to me," Myron said, "because I had visited Paraguay three times while in the U.S. Air Force. It was here the Lord spoke to me about spiritual needs in Latin America, and 18 years later I'm back here as a missionary!"

That represented quite a pilgrimage--from military service to missionary service. While he was still in the Air Force, his first wife was killed by a drunk driver. Myron resigned himself to a single life, until the promise, "Ask and you shall receive," seemed to jump out at him in his Bible reading. He was stationed in U.S.A. and planning to attend Moody Bible Institute's Founder's Week conference; so he prayed that God would lead him to the right woman on the first day--and that she'd be willing to be a missionary.

"I learned to be specific in praying!" Myron said. "I met Alice the day I arrived at the conference, and a year later we married in Saigon, Viet Nam."

I had seen Alice in action, leading the singing with her guitar at a Bible study for professional women, and then opening the Scriptures. Seeing her in a ruffled blouse and upswept hair style, I would never have guessed she could beat many a male racquet ball player.

Now Myron and Alice are using their experience and gifts to build bridges of friendship to communicate the gospel in Paraguay. "These are lovable people, carefree and full of humor," they say. "Paraguayans seem to have a healthier self-image than some other South Americans we've met."

Myron wrote about a healthy self-image in his book, *Culture Shock: Dealing with Stress in Cross-cultural Living.*

It contains some of the lessons he and Alice learned through their own missionary work, and now a number of missions are using it for orientation. One couple whose missionary daughter had just committed suicide wrote to thank Myron for writing the book. "Our daughter suffered from the very symptoms you describe," they wrote.

Joining the SIM team in Paraguay later were Filomeno and Leonila Belen, Filipinos supported by Chinese churches in Singapore and Indonesia. The Belens came from Asia's only country with a Catholic majority, to witness in an officially Catholic South American nation. Once while participating in showing Campus Crusade's *Jesus* film, they were startled when a Catholic mother superior stood up and told the viewers that the film showed what they'd been missing--a personal faith in Jesus Christ as living Saviour. That night and in subsequent meetings, she invited the people to trust Christ.

Mike and Sara Coss from U.S.A. were another addition. Shortly after they arrived, Asuncion made an unlooked-for "impact" on Mike when he was struck by a vehicle as he crossed a street with gospel tracts to hand out. He apparently achieved his purpose, for when he regained consciousness, all the 100 tracts he had been carrying were gone.

"We've identified one area of several towns totaling 110,000 population without any evangelical church," the Losses reported. "There are at least 40 towns in the east with no evangelical church. We hope to reach them through films, Bible correspondence courses, and Theological Education by Extension methods. And right here in Asuncion there's a great need among the unreached educated class."

"How do you plan to plant churches?" I asked.

"As people come to the Lord, we'll form local groups of believers and disciple them into churches. We'll also disciple Bible school students by involving them in outreach. Although there hasn't been time for much response from city folk, I'm convinced we're on the verge of a major breakthrough. Groups like the Mormons have built magnificent temples that attract people dissatisfied with the past. One of our great needs, apart from missionaries, is for finance to rent or build places for young churches to meet in during their early years."

"Come over and help us!" Pastor Veron's Macedonian call kept ringing through my head as Ron and I took off from Asuncion for Uruguay, entrance to the continent's Southern Cone.

You are the light of the world. A city on a hill cannot be hidden.

MATTHEW 5:14

13

THE

SECULAR

NATION

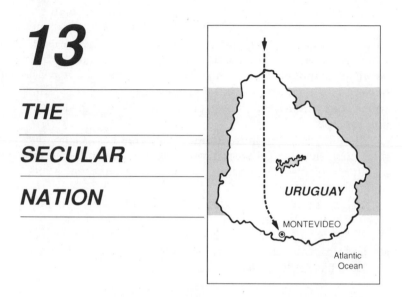

URUGUAY

MONTEVIDEO

Atlantic
Ocean

M onte vid eu!" ("I see a mountain!") a Portuguese sailor on explorer Magellan's ship is said to have shouted when he spotted the hill which now rises from Uruguay's capital, Montevideo. Although only 387 feet high, El Cerro stands out on the flat north bank of the River Plate, or Rio de la Plata, meaning "Silver River." The Spaniards who landed in 1516 hoped it might lead them to the fabled city of gold.

The Plate is really an estuary, not a river, but it led the conquistadors to the Uruguay River (Guarani for "River of

Painted Birds"), which forms the western boundary of the smallest Hispanic country in the continent: Uruguay, about the size of Washington State or of England and Wales combined. To visualize its relative size and location, I thought of South America as a bunch of grapes, with Panama its stem. About two-thirds down on the right underside I picked out a single grape. That is Uruguay. On a map, Montevideo is the same latitude as Cape Town in South Africa and Sydney in Australia.

This little nation of three million population is sandwiched between mammoth Brazil and giant Argentina, like a pearl between two clam shells. Throughout its history, the courageous nation has felt those clam shells squeeze in annexation attempts.

Uruguay was my introduction to the Southern Cone, the three countries that fill the narrowest part of the tapered continent: Uruguay, Argentina, and Chile. They represent a different South America.

"Think Europe," I said to myself as I walked through their cities. "Think Mediterranean Europe." Yet the Southern Cone decidedly is not Europe, although the three countries have strong European ties. They are very proudly South American, and each has its distinctive character.

OLD WORLD, NEW WORLD

Uruguay is a progressive little nation. Although it has the continent's highest population density, it also has its lowest birth rate and lowest infant mortality rate. Unfortunately, it reportedly has the highest abortion rate, and two out of every three marriages end in divorce. It was the first welfare state in South America, the first to abolish the death penalty, and the first to let women vote. And it never permitted slavery. Uruguay has no Indians. A monument pays respect to its last known five. Uruguay has 19 color TV stations, 75 radio stations, six newspapers, and 94 percent literacy rate.

We looked up family friends, Samuel and Ruth Lopez of WEF Ministries (originally Worldwide European Fellowship), who took Ron and me to the top of Montevideo's "mountain," El Cerro. We looked out across the Plate, which is 50 miles wide there, but three times wider at its mouth. A lighthouse dating from 1804 and an older fort reminded us of the city's Spanish history, but the big attractions for tourists are the perpetual summer climate and sparkling beaches. (My boyhood recollection of the River Plate centered around the sinking of the *Graf Spee,* the German battleship which sought refuge in the estuary during World War II.)

"There are 1.5 million people living in the city and its suburbs," said Ruth, with a wide sweep of her arm. "That's half the country's population. Eighty percent of the people live in towns and cities. What a mission field!"

I'd already read that Uruguay is the most secular nation on the continent. Christmas is called Family Day, and Easter is known as Tourism Week. One of the newspapers refuses to spell God with a capital G. Over one-third of the population claims to be atheist or agnostic, and although most of the rest would call themselves Catholic, probably only five percent of them actually practice their faith. The nation has one of the lowest percentages of evangelicals in South America.

The absence of an indigenous animistic population, combined with anticlericalism among the early ranchers, tended to prevent any superstitious form of Catholicism becoming deeply entrenched, as it has in other republics I visited. In most of Latin America, the two prominent representations of Jesus are "a helpless infant and a dead martyr," as John A. Mackay stated in *The Other Spanish Christ.*

These never appealed to the Uruguayan rationale. More recent waves of immigrants from an increasingly secularized Europe have strengthened these attitudes.

The strongly egalitarian outlook of the people helped produce tolerance and democracy. It also caused Uruguayos to react against what they saw as an intolerant, authoritarian Catholic Church. For most, the alternative was secularism, because they had never seen the liberating truth of the gospel demonstrated in Christianity. That is the tragedy of Uruguay.

HOW TO PLANT A CHURCH

"How do you start evangelizing a secular city like this?" I asked the Lopezes. "We'll take you out to dinner while you tell us. You choose the place."

Sam led us to a genuine Uruguayan pizza parlor. We sat at one of the tables surrounding a huge kiln-like oven glowing with blazing charcoal. When the chefs had put together what we ordered, they raked aside the coals and slid the raw pizzas in with a long pole. In a few minutes we had sizzling pizzas in front of us.

"Now tell us how to plant churches in Montevideo!" we said as we sank our teeth into crisp crust and hot cheese.

"Maybe we could better tell you how not to do it!" began Sam, who had been a pastor in Paraguay. "We started out with a lot of activity all over the city, but it didn't result in a local church being formed. The traditional idea was to aim for a large church to which we could invite people. That didn't work in Montevideo. First we discovered that unsaved people won't come to a Sunday morning service--that's when everyone turns out in the market to socialize. Also, people don't like to go from their own neighborhood to another for a service.

"Then I realized that companies don't have just one store for the whole city. They may have a dozen or more local shops. So we took our clue from them and started inviting people to neighborhood Bible studies. Tramping the streets was hard work, with little response. A lot of people thought we were Jehovah's Witnesses or Mormons.

"One discouraging evening we decided we'd knock on just one more door before quitting. A stooped, sad-faced woman cautiously opened the door. She showed us a Bible she'd just bought. We could see it was a Jehovah's Witness Bible, so I told her I was sorry it was not the true Bible--it had been changed. We offered to bring her the true Bible."

"In a way, we became even more discouraged!" Ruth chimed in. "When we did find someone who'd talk with us, the Jehovah's Witnesses had been there before us! The woman's name was Maria, but she turned out to be our Lydia, the woman mentioned in Acts 16, who was prepared to hear the truth and whose response opened the city to the gospel."

After Maria studied the Gospel of John for a few weeks, the change in her was amazing. She smiled and even stood up straight. Her friends stopped her on the street and asked, "Doña Maria, you've found something in life! What is it?"

Maria told them they could find out by coming to a Bible study. Before long, 30 people were meeting in Maria's house. Some asked the Lopezes to lead a study in their homes also. Soon they had studies in 10 homes.

But where could they all meet together for worship? They rented a house to meet in and prayed for something more permanent. Then one of the new believers bought a house next to his and presented the keys to the Lopezes. "This is the Lord's house," he explained.

"So that's how we got started," Sam said, cutting another wedge of pizza. He and Ruth were continuing that process in other communities. They also conducted children's clubs to reach families, and they had a discipleship and leadership training program. Members of the first Bible study group started a second one.

"There are others who are also finding response, like the Southern Baptists and Christian and Missionary Alliance," Sam continued. "But the work moves slowly in this city. If you lived here, you'd feel overwhelmed by the spiritual needs. We can use all the help we can get. If SIM would send in church planters, that would be great."

"That confirms what Luis Bush from Argentina once told me," Ron commented. "I asked him which areas of South America he felt were the neediest spiritually. He put Uruguay at the top of the list. Then Paraguay, and the south of Ecuador."

We stayed overnight at the seminary of the Southern Baptists, who first pioneered in Uruguay in 1911. The principal, James Bartley, confirmed what the Lopezes had told us. The Baptists were using the same house-group strategy to start churches.

"Are more missionaries needed?" he repeated our question. "Let me ask: When you consider that less than two percent of the population is evangelical, are you going to sit back and consign the rest to eternal judgment? In terms of eternity, missionaries are needed!"

In extensive research, Bartley found that for 30 years no church had been planted by Uruguayos. He was trying to rectify that by preparing the seminary students to be church planters. We mixed with the students and found them dedicated and friendly. One of them explained to me the mysteries of the *yerba mate* (herbal tea) he was sipping. It seemed part of Uruguayan life to walk around holding a "teacup" (usually a leather-encased gourd, but sometimes a cowhorn), with a Thermos bottle of hot water tucked under one's arm.

"You half fill the cup with a mixture of dried holly leaves or other herbs, and pour water on," the student showed us. "When the soaked herbs fill the cup, you put this silver pipe in - - see? It has a flat end full of holes. Now suck on it. When you need more hot water, add some from your Thermos. Cowboys ride around sucking their tea all day, and at night they pass it around the campfire. In fact, an idiom for 'fellowship' is 'to drink herbal tea together.' Our country has the highest cancer rate in South America, and some people wonder if it's because of drinking so much herbal tea."

"I GO TO SPIRITISTS"

The next day Ron and I took a taxi to meet the general secretary of the Bible Society of Uruguay. En route, we struck up a conversation with the taxi driver, Alcides, who had been born on a ranch.

"We're evangelical missionaries," we said, when he asked what our work was.

"Oh, Mormons! I've had lots of contact with them," Alcides responded, jamming on the brakes to avoid a truck that suddenly swung from the lane on our right across to the lane on our left.

"No, Mormons aren't evangelicals," we explained. "We believe in Jesus Christ as our personal Saviour. Do you?"

"I believe in God, but I don't go to church," Alcides replied. "I go to spiritists. And my children go to voodoo seances because there's lots of good food and they can socialize with others there. But I worry about their getting into drugs. Lots of drugs in this city--it's the Chinese who bring it in."

Ron explained the way of salvation to the taxi driver. Then as we drove past the main square in the heart of the city, Ron pointed out to me the Victoria Plaza Hotel. "The Moonies bought that hotel as their training center for Latin America," he said. "You know--Myung Moon's Unification Church. The previous military government liked their anticommunist stance and gave permission for them to put up a five-star hotel on the city block they own--but the current civilian government reversed that. The Moonies also own a bank and a newspaper."

I learned that there are more Jehovah's Witnesses in Uruguay than Baptists and Methodists together, and the Mormons have three times as many members as the largest Protestant denomination.

There was an Old World feel to the city. Wrought-iron fences and brick walls surrounded neat residences along cobblestone streets. Fresh horse droppings competed with the fragrance of purple blossoms. A workman cycled by, a long stick of bread poking out of a basket, while a matronly woman cradled her toy poodle in her arms. Fashionable blondes, brunettes, and redheads shopped at sidewalk stalls as Ron and I got out of the taxi and walked to the Bible Society office.

EDGE OF A BREAKTHROUGH

"Welcome!" the general secretary of the Bible Society, Guillermo Milovan, said with a hearty handshake. "We're glad you've come to see Uruguay for yourselves." Milovan told us that Uruguay was unique in South America for its religious liberty, with complete separation of church and state since 1918. No religion is discriminated against, he assured us.

"We noticed the Mormons and Moonies," we said. "How can they hope to be successful in a country which is so secular?"

"It's true that over one-third of the people claim to be atheists or agnostics, and 80 percent follow no regular religious practice," he replied. "But many have a great spiritual hunger."

I had read that the percentage of evangelicals in Uruguay

is only 1.9, and I asked Milovan what sector of population should be our priority as a mission.

"Students, professionals, intellectuals--the educated class!" Milovan answered, gesturing like a true Latin. "There's a tremendous need among them. They've resisted any approach until recently; now they're becoming interested in the gospel. We can reach them, but we have to approach them at their level.

"Last year the Bible Society distributed over two million pieces of Scripture--more than any other year in our 30-year history! We had planned to distribute 15,000 whole Bibles, but the demand was so great that we distributed nearly 30,000."

Before we left this enthusiastic Christian leader, I asked how he would summarize the opportunities for the gospel in his nation. Sr. Milovan leaned forward in his chair and fixed his large brown eyes on me.

"Uruguay," he stated, stabbing the air with his right hand; "Uruguay is now where other countries of Latin America were in evangelism at the first of this century. We're on the edge of a breakthrough. The doors are wide open!"

Back on the street, Ron recognized a missionary couple, Arnie and Sally Selfors. They invited us to have lunch with them while we talked.

"Before you leave Uruguay, you must have a real steak dinner," they said. "That's what Uruguay is famous for. And the cattle aren't injected with growth hormones!"

There aren't special steak houses as in North America, because most restaurants specialize in steaks. Uruguayos may eat beef at all three meals a day. They are one of the world's greatest consumers of beef, per capita, and rank second to Argentina in world beef exports.

In colonial days, the government in Madrid initially had little interest in Uruguay because it had no gold, but the young nation early discovered that its "black gold" soil produced some of the lushest grazing pasture in the world. Ever since, its economy and culture have been influenced by cowboys, beef, leather, and herbal tea--an exotic symbiosis with Montevideo's sophisticated cultures from Milan and Madrid. Government tribunals still consider requests from aggrieved Uruguayos to fight opponents in duels with pistols.

"You'll have to order a side salad if you want anything besides steak," Sally advised when we were seated in a cozy dining room off the main square. "The main course is just steak. No vegetables."

"O.K. to eat salads here?" I asked, aware of warnings in travel books.

"Oh yes!" Sally laughed. "Uruguay is one country where you can eat salads and drink water from the tap without problems. And if you did have trouble, the country has an excellent free health service!"

So we began with palm hearts, cucumber slices, and bibb lettuce. Then, on came the steak. Mine was a tender, juicy sirloin seven inches long, three inches wide, and an inch thick. And it cost only $2.75! Of course we had to keep in mind that the minimum wage was around $100 per month, but that figure has to be seen in the perspective of free services, such as education right through university.

"WHY ARE YOU HERE?"

"We're seeing a new openness to the gospel," Arnie said as we sipped coffee after our meal. "People say they have no religion, but we think that's part of the national mindset. Uruguayos have always been very independent, very democratic, reacting to any dominant authority. To be free from the pressure of priests--especially aggressive Spanish and Italian priests--people simply say they have no religion."

"That's right," Sally agreed. "So when people ask us what our religion is, we say we aren't here to spread religion. 'Then why are you here?' they ask. We reply that we're here to tell them about our personal relationship with Jesus Christ. Their next question is, 'What's that?'

"They really become interested in knowing, because the only Christ they have heard about is on a crucifix. Also, they have a great sense of disillusionment. The effect of the world economy on exports has hit the nation hard. And their ideal world of civil liberty was shattered by the Marxist terrorism of the sixties. During that guerrilla war, in nearly every family a man was imprisoned, or exiled, or killed.

"As a result of the terrorism, it became illegal to preach on the streets or for more than eight people to worship in homes. Students weren't allowed to worship on campus. But all those restrictions have been removed. Now there's a new openness. It's a great day of opportunity for the gospel."

When 15 years of military rule ended, 2500 evangelicals celebrated democracy by marching through the streets to the Plaza of Liberty, where they boldly preached the gospel. That was the culmination of an evangelical crusade by evangelist Paul Finkenbinder, known throughout Latin America simply as Hermano Pablo (Brother Paul). However, there is not the large public response to rallies which evangelists find in other South American countries.

"A lot of people who are praying with their rosaries really are searching for spiritual reality," a Uruguayan Christian leader told us. "In fact, priests are worried about the rapid growth of evangelicals. That's why the Pope is making so many trips to Latin America."

On the other hand, I learned that liberation theologians consider the Pope too conservative. During his Latin American tour that year, several Catholic theologians tried to keep him away from Uruguay, through dealing behind the scenes. The Pope heard about this and told them not to mix ideology with religion.

SEEDS OF LIBERATION THEOLOGY

Secular Uruguay provided fertile soil for the growth of liberation theology, an attempt to combine theology and sociopolitical concerns, greatly influenced by European political theology. Although most people think of Catholic theologian Gustavo Gutierrez in Peru as a main initiator, I was surprised to learn that one of the earliest proponents was a Methodist minister in Montevideo named Emilio Castro. In the late fifties he and others developed the Theology of the River Plate, an early form of liberation theology. Gutierrez and others were thinking along the same lines, but Emilio Castro was one of the key thinkers in the movement before Catholic theologians officially espoused the cause at the Second General Council of Latin American Bishops in Medellin, Colombia, in 1968.

Castro became general secretary of the World Council of Churches in 1985. We found that he was still a popular figure in Uruguay. When he visited Montevideo after the country's return to civilian rule, crowds flocked to hear him.

Castro had been a student of the European theologian Karl Barth, who is also greatly admired in Uruguay. Barth urged bringing about radical social change through restructuring society and government. One of Emilio Castro's close friends told me that Castro would not say that Christianity can be Marxist, but the WCC general secretary believes that Marxist economic analysis is a useful tool for Christians to understand society. He has been quoted as saying, "God works through Marxist revolution in order to bring all men together." Castro himself "desires to contribute to the visible unity of the church, which would include Roman and Orthodox Catholics as well as evangelicals." In a newspaper article I read, Castro described himself as a radical pacifist, saying his great goal is to include the Roman Catholic Church in the WCC family. He described a unified church, in which the Pope would not have power to appoint bishops but "may preside over world assemblies of the church."

Uruguay: secularism, Marxism, liberation theology, spiritual bankruptcy. I felt for this unique nation, asking for bread but so often receiving a stone. I also thanked God for men and women who are trying to meet the spiritual needs. Did God want SIM to play a part? The morning we left for Argentina across the estuary, my Bible reading was from Colossians 1: ". . . asking God to fill you with the knowledge of his will through all spiritual wisdom and understanding."

*Everything is meaningless. . . . The sun rises and the sun
sets, and hurries back to where it rises.*

ECCLESIASTES 1:2,5

14

MUCHO

GUSTO

AMIGO!

"FUTEBOL"

We must be in Argentina!" I exclaimed, as the stadium we
were sitting in suddenly erupted with deafening cheers. The
soccer fans stomped with their feet and punched the air with
their fists, while shredded newspaper filled the air like a blizzard.

"You're right!" Ron shouted in my ear. "Your feel for Latin
America wouldn't be complete without experiencing a soccer
game! Only here it's called 'futebol.'"

An hour before the game, the streets leading to the stadium

had been clogged with fans. Police with armored cars and a water cannon stood by to control the crowd of 60,000. Team banners streamed all the way from the top row of seats down to the playing field, which was surrounded by a water-filled moat and an eight-foot fence topped with barbed wire. Cheerleaders of the home team, Boca, had taken over the section of the stadium next to us. On huge bass drums they thumped out a rousing tempo to accompany the team song, sung to the tune of "Happy Birthday to You!"

The eruption of cheering was not brought on by a goal--the game hadn't even started. It was to welcome two of Boca's famous retired players. A helicopter landed them in the middle of the field as the crowd cheered, photographers jockeyed for shots, and someone in the stands tossed firecrackers onto the field.

From our seats near the top row, I looked out past the stadium to the roofs of derelict factories and silent derricks down at the docks. They reflected Argentina's economic woes. Those docks once competed with the stadium for noise when this giant nation, one-third the size of Europe, was a leader in beef and grain shipments to the rest of the world. That was when Argentina lived up to its name, derived from the Latin root word for silver or money: *argent.*

But this was not the time for the throbbing crowd around me to think of problems. The game had started. All around us was life with *"gusto, mucho gusto!"*

It was real Latin machismo--98 percent of the spectators were male. A brawny fan hoisted his three-year-old son on his shoulder. The lad waved a Boca pennant in rhythm with the theme song: "Give it to them, Boca! Give it to them!" A graying man wearing a Boca cap held a radio to his ear to hear the commentary. He sprang to his feet cheering whenever Boca approached the opponent's goal. Boys shinnied up the floodlight poles for a free view.

When the out-of-town team scored, the crowd fell silent. But when Boca scored, the stadium exploded with excitement. Everyone was on his feet, waving, cheering, singing, stomping in rhythm with the drums. Shirts came off perspiring bodies. I took photographs of the cheering crowd, but whenever Boca scored, it was impossible because of the snowstorm of torn-up newspaper that filled the air. Over and over, the Boca theme song swept around the stadium like an ocean wave.

I hoped that the concrete stands were well reinforced, as they shook from the thunderous applause when Boca scored the winning goal. Then the people poured out onto the streets like a human Iguaza Falls, to continue the celebration. Fortunately, the police didn't have to use their water cannon. I'd always thought of soccer as a spectator sport, but Argentine enthusiasm turned it into a participant sport. Everyone was emotionally involved.

"Mucho gusto!"

"No wonder Argentina produces world champion soccer players--like Maradona!" Ron exclaimed. "However, he plays for Italy, because they pay more."

Poster sellers tried to pick up sales by laying out posters flat along the middle of the sidewalks. The pictures were not of soccer heroes, but of the Pope, Lenin, Che Guevera, and Jesus of the Bleeding Heart.

LIFE IN B.A.

Parts of downtown Buenos Aires, affectionately called B.A., could have been in Paris, and the imposing statues were right out of Rome. Ornate old hotels rubbed shoulders with fashion boutiques. Incongruously, one was called Le Drugstore, apparently considered a modish name for a dress store. A smart-looking business woman had the improbable words "Noises off" emblazoned across her rose-colored T-shirt. Displaying incoherent English phrases on T-shirts was the current Latin American fad. I saw inexplicable slogans like "Penalty Kayak Cup," "Local Surfing Is," "Pleasure Boating Yatching Navy."

A sign in Spanish wished customers "A Happy Passover," reminding us that Easter was approaching. Big chocolate eggs and bunnies filled the windows of confectionery stores.

I felt safe in the heart of this vast city (nearly one-third of the country's 30 million population lives in the area), because the streets were filled with people of all ages enjoying the "good air" (Buenos Aires) of a warm evening.

Young lovers held hands, parents played with their children, and elderly *porteños* (the term given to the residents of this nation's largest port) strolled along the tiled pedestrian malls without fear. People on the crowded streets were dressed discreetly. I was surprised that no one wore shorts, but then I learned that some visitors have been told it is forbidden to walk around town in them! Although music cassette shops were filled with youths, the music piped over loudspeakers was classical.

Little knots of men and women were snacking in an ice cream and pizza parlor, which reminded Ron and me that we hadn't had dinner. We passed *La Estancia* ("the ranch"), a restaurant where whole sheep carcasses were being barbecued in a circle around a log fire right in the dining room. Considering that it was 10 p.m., we decided to settle for something faster and headed into a pizza parlor.

We savored our mushroom and mozzarella pizza while seated on a balcony overlooking the main floor. A smartly dressed young couple came up the stairs to find a table. The girl stopped near the top and looked up at the boy with longing eyes, as if she couldn't make the last step without a kiss. He obliged, giving her a solid buss on the lips. That wasn't enough. They enjoyed three lingering embraces before moving to their table. None of the other diners looked up. This was amorous Argentina.

Mucho gusto!

We were on our way out by 11 p.m., ready for bed, but were amazed to see customers just arriving at that hour, several with young children. Normal hours for dining are 9 p.m. to midnight. The next evening we were hard pressed to find even a hamburger place open before 9 p.m.

Of course, B.A. has the normal gamut of evils. Young people pressed into a theater to see "The Devil's Honey," garishly advertised as "Evil pleasure, forbidden lasciviousness, overflowing sadism, perverted joy." Statistics show that about half the nation's 15-year-olds smoke--a figure also true of

Uruguay and Chile. Drugs are increasingly available. Unemployment is high, and at times inflation hits 100 percent monthly. In the city, 1.7 million children live on the streets.

We walked back to our room at the aging Rochester Hotel. It boasted a uniformed doorman, and elevators out of the twenties. But it was clean and affordable. On the way to the hotel we crossed a plaza in which a giant obelisk commemorated the 400th anniversary of the founding of B.A. The night before, students had demonstrated there against the Pope's forthcoming visit. One hundred people, including the police chief, had been injured. But now the square was back to normal, with people socializing on the benches. Men chatted with men, and women huddled separately--typically Latin American. They probably had different agendas. Two young artists tried to sell us paintings. A small religious group stood in a circle singing quietly while their leader prayed at the top of his voice, punctuating his petitions with flailing arms and shouts of "Alleluia!"

I bought a copy of B.A.'s English newspaper, *The Herald*, founded in 1876. It reported on the Pope's travels in South America, under a bold headline: JOHN PAUL CONDEMNS TORTURE. (I contrasted that declaration with the fiat of a Medieval Pope, Innocent III, who legitimized torture as an instrument of the Roman Catholic Church. Latin America had felt the full impact of the Inquisition's torture chambers.) In one article, a socialist leader condemned "police brutality" at the obelisk demonstration and called for "the democratic right to express rejection of the Pontiff's visit." The nation was in the midst of human rights trials of the leaders of the previous military regime, during which 9000 Argentines simply disappeared. During the recent reign of terror the newspaper could not have been as outspoken. While a socialist leader demanded "the real separation of church and state," a Catholic leader claimed there was "a diabolical persecution of the church."

A columnist reviewed the book, *The Land That Lost Its Heroes*, written by a British journalist about the war over the Falkland Islands (*Islas Malvinas*, to the Argentines). And an editorial writer worried that negotiations with U.S.A. for a "two billion dollar rollback of the foreign debt" could be in jeopardy because Argentina supported a pro-Cuban resolution in the UN. "Not even voodoo will solve the mess in Argentina unless a lot of people start working harder or a lot of nitwits realize that Fidel passes out good cigars but the money is farther north," the writer concluded.

"DOES SOUTH AMERICA EXIST?"

I tried to imagine B.A. as it was a century before, when four evangelists from Britain visited it. The description of their trip shocked some evangelicals into action.

In 1893 British Keswick speaker George C. Grubb led the foursome, which included Harry Guinness, son of H. Gratton Guinness, who became involved in establishing Gospel Missionary Union, North Africa Mission, and Regions Beyond Missionary Union. A member of the Argentine committee of the South American Missionary Society invited the team and got them endorsed by the Anglican Bishop of South America. The Keswick Convention helped finance the trip, and Dr. Guinness's sister Lucy coedited their report under the title, *South America: The Neglected Continent* (referred to in chapter five).

The book graphically described the degenerate state of the colonists, the corruption of the Catholic clergy, and the deplorable condition of the Indian peoples. It included charts showing the great disparity between Christian workers in the United Kingdom and in South America.

The evangelists were shocked by the low level of morality: "Greed for money and abandonment to gross sensual pleasure have demoralized all classes. . . . There is no public morality to repress immorality . . . , and the priesthood is so openly immoral that its sins and follies are exposed to public view in the cartoons and the comic papers. A description of the lives of some of the priests would be soiling to the mind to narrate, and too poisonous to read. . . . Alas! too many in England and abroad entertain the idea that 'Rome is a sister church in error.' As a matter of fact, *here* it is ABSOLUTE HEATHENISM."

While recognizing the heroic work of pioneers, the book

pulled no punches, laying the blame for neglect at the door of
both denominational and interdenominational missions. "Out
of the 25 missionary societies at work in the world, only 16 are
attempting anything in the Neglected Continent," stated the
authors, charging that Asia and Africa had become the focus of
missions, to the neglect of South America.

Part of the reason for that neglect arose from the perception
of some Protestant leaders that South America was "Chris-
tianized" by Rome. This argument later became evident at the
1910 Edinburgh Missionary Conference, where South America
was kept off the agenda.

"The exclusion [from the Edinburgh agenda] of the missionary work in South America . . . has given missionaries
greater right than ever to term their field, if not the 'excluded
continent,' most certainly 'the neglected continent,'" wrote
SIM founder Rowland Bingham in his magazine, *The Missionary Witness.*

"The South American Indians are the most neglected
people of the most neglected continent." Although Bingham's
own fledgling mission was barely beginning to fly in Africa,
he was so concerned for South America that he took on responsibility of honorary secretary-treasurer of a small mission in
Bolivia. (See chapter five.)

Sixteen years before the Edinburgh Conference, *The
Neglected Continent* indicted a self-satisfied Christian public
"sitting at spiritual feasts" while abandoning the continent to a
false Christianity. The editors described a planning meeting for
a joint missions daily prayer guide. Three days were considered
too much to allot to South America; so they were reduced to
one under the heading, "Brazil, etc."

"Does South America exist at all?" the editors asked. "Has
it no place in the missionary world? What are you going to do
for it?" They quoted from a letter from a lone missionary in
Chile:

"How long shall I be left here alone?"

"We were led by the Holy Spirit to ask for blessing far and
wide," Grubb and Guinness stated. "When pleading for the
spread of the gospel in the country, our eyes were opened and

we saw with unmistakable clearness of vision the whole of the neglected continent aglow with the fire of God through the name of Jesus."

The book ended with a form for the reader to sign in commitment to pray and give and make known the support needs of missionaries. This was the travelogue that challenged the Allans in New Zealand and the Reekies in Canada, living on opposite sides of the globe from one another. They were especially touched by the poignant description of the Quechua Indians: subjugated by cruel deception, worked to death for the sake of greed, decimated through imported disease and alcohol, and spiritually enslaved by a superstitious religion.

It was to Buenos Aires that George and Mary Allan first came in pursuit of their goal to evangelize the Quechua people. There God prepared them further for the spiritual battle ahead. The rest of that story continues to live on.

As I read *The Neglected Continent* a century later, my own heart was stirred. I gave thanks that God's people did respond. If the Keswick evangelists could revisit the continent today, they'd be amazed to see the fulfillment of their vision beyond expectation. What a different Latin America I saw! New opportunities face the gospel. There are new cities, new situations, new challenges. Yet, we have to face the results of century-old problems.

CRISIS OF AUTHORITY

"I want you to meet the great-grandson of an Argentine evangelist who was active when that Keswick group arrived here," Ron Wiebe said. "He's Dr. Arnoldo Canclini, president of the Bible Society of Argentina. Both his father and grandfather preached all over the continent. He's written about 40 books and has been asked to write a paper for COMIBAM, the continent-wide missions conference coming up."

We met the energetic Argentine after hearing him preach at his Christian and Missionary Alliance church. Previously he had pastored Baptist churches.

"I'm enjoying getting to know the people of Argentina," I began. "Ron told me you'd be a good one to meet."

"I suppose I'm fairly typical!" replied the graying *porteño,* looking at me from under bushy brows. "You see, Argentines are a mixture. Both my parents were born here, but over the last three generations our family has included intermarriage with Italian, German, French, Uruguayan, and Brazilian nationals. My wife's grandfather was a Swede married to an Italian. To add to the international mix, our daughter married the son of Greek and Ukranian parents. And our son married a girl of Spanish descent."

"You say that's typical?" I inquired.

"Well, we Argentines can be divided roughly into three categories: 40 percent Italian, 40 percent Spanish, and 20 percent from other races," he replied. "But we are more proud of being Argentines than of our racial roots."

I knew the nation recently had been through several devastating experiences, and that B.A. has the world's highest ratio of psychoanalysts--something like one to every 200 people. I asked Dr. Canclini what the future holds.

"Right now the country is in a crisis of authority," he replied. "People reacted to the excessive authority of the former military regime, but now things have gone to the other extreme in democracy. Everybody wants to do his own thing.

"A lot of people don't know what to think, or which way to go. They had high hopes for democracy, but are disillusioned. They're looking for some authority figure. That's why the Pope holds attraction for many. And evangelicals face the same danger of going after personalities such as big TV evangelists instead of the Lord!"

Canclini said Argentina has not had the spiritual renewal movement seen in some Latin American countries. Attitudes differ from the rest of the continent. Catholic bishops are very conservative, and their churches are nearly empty. The more liberal ones have sided with political issues. There are special church groups, such as youth and professionals, that are attracting adherents.

"But occultism, or spirit worship, is growing fast," the pastor continued. "Just recently I baptized a man who had been delivered from spiritism. Afro-Brazilian cults are becoming popular. Pentecostals are growing fastest. One Argentine evangelist claims 20,000 conversions at a meeting, but we'll need time to see if results are solid, and to evaluate the doctrinal position. We're seeing growth in noncharismatic churches too. This is a proud country; it once was self-sufficient. But now people are disappointed in government and society. Materialism can't satisfy them. They're searching for spiritual values."

I asked about the effects of liberation theology.

"It's an important issue," Canclini conceded. "But instead of arguing over transitory theologies, evangelicals need to preach and teach the Word. Remember how the 'God is dead' debate died." He told us that SIM could fulfill a key role in Argentina by teaching the Scriptures and training leadership.

"Disciple people!" he emphasized. "The gospel is being preached and we read all kinds of conversion statistics, but new believers don't know the Word of God. Something major is going to happen in Argentina spiritually, and we must be ready to cope with it. People are spiritually hungry for the first time in history. We must preach the gospel and teach the Word!"

We left encouraged by this vigorous leader with a vision for his people. I thought of other strong evangelicals from Argentina whom God is using to challenge not only their own continent, but the world.

"MY PEOPLE ARE CONFUSED"

The driver of our airport taxi had a big nose and jaw like Mussolini's. When Ron gave him a gospel tract, he told us his father had become an evangelical. Ron asked if he had a Bible.

"No. Which Bible would I choose anyway?" he asked, sucking his teeth. "The one by Mark or the one by Luke or . . . there are so many, it's confusing!"

"Those are the Gospels of Matthew, Mark, Luke, and John," Ron explained. "They're all part of the whole Bible. Here's an address where you can buy one for yourself."

The taxi driver had a cynical opinion of the Pope's forthcoming visit. "Why should they spend millions on his visit, when he's just a man like us?" he asked.

The strains of "Eidelweis" drifted over the airport's loudspeakers. After we checked our bags we had a croissant (appropriately called a "half-moon" in B.A.) and tea labeled Big Ben, even though it was packaged in Argentina. Apart from the Falkland Islands row, the British and Argentines have been fairly good friends.

I noticed workmen rolling a scaffold away from a plaster mural on the airport terminal wall. The mural stretched two storeys high and was filled with faces and objects depicting the nation's culture. Curiously, all the faces had been cut like a loaf of sliced bread, each slice slightly out of line with the adjacent one. But the features were not grotesquely distorted like a Picasso.

"The workmen are just cleaning up the plaster droppings," I remarked to Ron. "Maybe the artist is still around--perhaps that woman over there?"

I walked over to an impressive blonde woman who seemed to be directing the workmen, and discovered that she was one of Argentina's renowned artists. I congratulated her for her sculpture and asked the meaning of the cut faces.

"Ah, my people!" she exclaimed, gesturing with both hands as if molding a clay figure. "They are . . . how would you say . . . confused? They don't know who they are or where they are going. My people are fragmented. That's what I've tried to express."

Fragmented . . . confused.

That was it. I'd been trying to understand what I was seeing, not only here but also across the continent. The artist had expressed it graphically. Twenty years before, the Argentine poet Jorge Luis Borges had in essence said the same: "All is disintegration."

As our plane rose above the sprawling city, I prayed that these lovable people would come to know the Saviour in whom "all things hold together" (Colossians 1:17).

VALIANT PIONEERS

Ron headed back north to Bolivia. My destination was westward to Santiago in Chile. En route I could see the rich grasslands of the pampas stretching west and south toward the Argentine plains of Patagonia, so named for the aborigines' "big feet." The southerly tip of the continent, shared with Chile, is only 700 icy miles off Antarctica. Before the Panama Canal was opened between the Americas, many a ship foundered in howling tempests off Cape Horn. During my research, the treacherous Magellan Straits claimed another victim: Operation Mobilization's ship *Logos,* laden with Christian literature for South American ports.

That remote area was called Tierra del Fuego ("land of fire"), perhaps so named because explorers saw Indian campfires lit to ward off the cold--or to lure travelers to their death. It was on the sea route from Europe westward to the Pacific, and Protestant missionaries soon noted the plight of its people. In the middle of the nineteenth century, British Anglican missionaries of the South American Missionary Society sought to evangelize the hostile Indians. One SAMS team, led by Allen Gardiner, died of starvation, and a later team was massacred by Indians. Other valiant Anglicans followed, and the descendants of some still live on property deeded to them by a government grateful for their selfless service to the aborigines.

When Charles Darwin first saw the Yaghan Indians of the area, he concluded they were "in a lower state of improvement than in any other part of the world," and doubted if anything could change them. Years later he was so amazed at the difference the gospel had produced in cannibals that he became a lifelong contributor to SAMS.

As I now flew westward across the continent's Southern Cone, the snow and ice I saw below were not on Tierra del Fuego. I was crossing the Andes. Aconcagua, tallest mountain in the Western Hemisphere (22,834 feet), poked above the Andean spine that forms the border with Chile. Since the beginning of my safari, I had come full circle and was back on the west coast, where the Inca once ruled. But now I was a thousand miles south of my last sighting of the Andes.

Flying over a mountain is an emotional experience for me. On the ground in a vehicle, I gradually creep up on a mountain.

At first it is a shadow on the horizon, then a scenic backdrop to the foothills. By the time I'm driving among the peaks, I'm used to them. Even then, I don't see an entire mountain all at once. As I turn the switchbacks, slopes and peaks come into my view in segments like a tourist's photos. But to fly over a mountain is disturbing. All at once, totally unprepared, I am looking down on a fallen Titan. Is it not somewhat sacrilegious for me to discover its awesome peaks, eternal glaciers, and secret valleys all in one glance? Perhaps I should be forbidden to fly over it, for it is supposed to tower mysteriously over me and lose its head in the clouds.

The ancients considered some mountains sacred. The psalmist saw them as a symbol of God's power. Even modern man attributes an aura of sanctity to mountains simply because they are inscrutable--rocky behemoths resisting man's manipulation. It therefore seems crass vulgarity for a mortal to gaze down on the bald pate of one. The mystery is exposed, the inaccessibility breached.

As I gazed down on the Andes once more, I could see no sign of life. How the Incas' messengers traversed them, I couldn't imagine. From north to south the granite ranges straddle the continent with an unchallengeable arrogance.

Yet there I was, suspended right above them. They looked unreal--the work of a geography class molding a three-dimensional map from papier mache? Or was our aircraft the papier mache?--so large and powerful in the airport, now reduced to a speck against the wall of the Andes as we crossed westward into Chile.

Jesus said, I am the light of the world. Whoever follows me will never walk in darkness, but will have the light of life.

JOHN 8:12

15

POPEMOBILE

AND WATER

CANNON

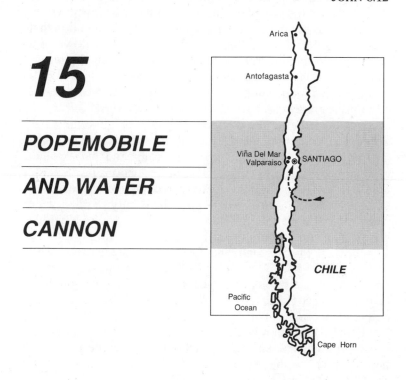

Press photographers swarmed around a scar-faced girl at the airport in Santiago, Chile's capital. She was Carmen, a student protester who became a folk heroine after she was doused with gasoline and set ablaze during a political demonstration. She went overseas for plastic surgery but came back to join in demonstrations during the Pope's visit.

Carmen's hideous face seemed incongruous as I read the immigration stamp in my passport: "The Week of the Visit of the Holy Father, Messenger of Peace." Peace, rather than violence, seemed expressed by the quilted plains surrounding the airport, flanked on the east by snowcapped mountains rising nearly four miles high. The irenic scene gave no indication of the maelstrom the city would become in the next few days.

Such was my introduction to Chile, a delightful nation that has managed to keep inflation and national debt down and standard of living up. Yet, among its 12 million population are the favored rich and the exploited poor--a point well used by a vocal political opposition still smarting from the ouster of the previous regime, which was Communist.

I could imagine the complex logistics of governing this ribbon-shaped nation, when I picked up a newspaper and saw the weather map. The country is so long and narrow that weather and road maps cut it up into three sections printed side by side, to fit it all into a handy rectangle instead of an unmanageably long strip. Although Chile is only 75 miles wide just north of Santiago, and seldom exceeds 150 miles in width, it runs 2625 miles from the northern border with Peru to the southern tip of the continent. Occupying the narrow shelf between the Pacific Ocean and the Andes watershed bordering Argentina, Chile's wildlife ranges from parrots in the jungle to penguins on ice floes. It claims land as far south as one can go on the globe, in the heart of Antarctica.

Far to the west in the Pacific, Chile has two exotic possessions. One is Robinson Crusoe Island. Yes, Defoe based his famous novel on the experiences of a Briton who lived there. Farther to the west, a tiny dot 2353 miles from Chile's coast, is mysterious Easter Island. Over a thousand huge stone figures, many weighing 20 tons and one standing 32 feet high, still protect the secret of why they were created.

"HOLY FATHER, GIVE US BREAD"

Ray Morris, SIM director for the Pacific Andes Area, met me in Santiago. The city's streets were decorated with banners in the Chilean national colors of red, white, and blue, and the Vatican colors of yellow and white, in anticipation of a papal visit. The government wanted the visit to bolster its human rights image, and Pope John Paul II wanted to project the church's image as defender of the poor.

On the day of the Pontiff's arrival, Ray and I headed for the main avenue: Avenida O'Higgins. That name seemed strange to me in a Spanish-speaking country, but I learned that O'Higgins was an Irishman who married a Chilean, led the nation's War of Independence, and became Chile's first president. The name was certainly in keeping with the European atmosphere of the city.

"The Messenger of Peace is coming!" chanted a vast crowd filling the Avenida. Church bells tolled, heralding the landing of the Pontiff's aircraft at the distant airport. The Pope's face gazed benignly from billboards emblazoned with the words, *Bienvenido, Papa!* (Welcome, Father). Newsboys sold papers headlining the visit. One paper carried a photo of the Pope embracing Carmen, the student with the scarred face.

Eager spectators filled every window and balcony. Along the sidewalk, parents hoisted children onto their shoulders. There was a festive mood as people waved memorial pennants and sang a song written to welcome "The Messenger of Peace." They cheered at anything moving--motorcycle patrol, TV film team, police helicopter overhead, or Red Cross workers dispensing water to the elderly.

Then a roar of applause arose as the Pope's airport speech boomed over loudspeakers tied to lampposts. People crossed themselves and clapped when something the Pope said especially appealed to them.

Somehow, the excited crowd kept filling in from the front until I lost my vantage point for photographs. Spotting an elderly shop owner setting up a table just behind the crowd, I asked if he'd mind my standing on a corner of it. He kindly agreed, suggesting we exchange photos afterwards. Members of his family kept pushing onto the small table, until there were 14 of us balanced precariously on it. I offered a silent prayer that it wouldn't collapse.

"This gives me good luck!" the table owner told me, taking a silver cross out of his shirt pocket. "I hope the Pope will give us a blessing as he passes, so I'll have good health."

I suddenly noticed that students behind us had unfurled a long banner and were holding it up on poles above our heads. GIVE US BREAD, WORK, JUSTICE! it demanded. Two security men on the street spotted it and tried to pull it down, but couldn't get through the crowd.

Then all heads craned forward as a motorcycle escort sped by. Sure enough, the glass-domed Popemobile was coming down the road. A tremendous ovation split the air as the ecstatic crowd glimpsed the slightly hunched, stocky figure clad in simple white. John Paul cast blessings right and left as his bulletproof dais moved quickly along. The cheering was deafening. The woman in front of me burst into tears; another kissed her crucifix. A tough-looking laborer rubbed his eyes, and the table owner laughed with joy.

It was an awesome moment for the crowd. Had they not just seen the Vicar of Christ in person? To many, this was God on earth, the one with the keys of heaven and hell--Saint Peter's successor. And he looked right at them! He gave them his personal blessing!

I felt a tug on my trousers and looked down to see a curly-haired tot trying to get my attention. "Foto!" she shouted, posing with a big grin. Why should that man in the funny little skullcap be the only one to have his photo taken!

The entourage had passed, but the protest parade was just forming. Down the road marched a crowd of determined young men and women with banners. "The people are dying! The people are dying!" they chanted as television cameras focused on them. Riot police stood by, and an armored car, mounted with a water cannon, followed at a distance. The protesters' numbers swelled as other young people joined their ranks. A shower of leaflets fell around me, stating, "Holy Father, Chile needs bread, work, justice, liberty!" It was signed "Christian Democracy."

Then, as several marchers raised their fists and shouted antigovernment slogans, the water cannon swung into action, shooting its powerful jet into the crowd. The protesters scattered and regrouped. Ray and I watched from across the boulevard. Suddenly the armored car swung around and bore down toward us. Demonstrators dropped their banners and sheltered behind a power transformer. As they were penned in by the water jet, riot police attacked them from behind with clubs.

"Let's get out of here!" Ray exclaimed as we ducked around the corner of a wall. We headed for the subway, but the entrance to the underground trains was closed because the crowd was so great. We walked a mile to the next entrance and finally squeezed our way onto a train.

Santiago has one of the best underground transit systems I have seen. The sparkling clean cars ride on rubber wheels and have horizontal stabilizers to reduce swaying. Trains run every two minutes in rush hour. We could ride anywhere in the city for the equivalent of 10 cents.

On the train, I looked at the faces of those who had watched the Pope pass. Young, old, men, women, children, affluent and poor--they had one thing in common: the need for the gift of God, eternal life through Jesus Christ. Many of them sincerely thought they had just seen God upon earth. They needed to see the Saviour, "the way, the truth, and the life."

The next day, violence erupted at a papal Mass attended by an estimated 800,000 people. Three people were wounded by gunfire and over 100 civilians and 38 police were injured in the melee.

In his address at the Mass, John Paul declared that he was "totally committed to Mary." We noted that Mariolatry seems strong among Chilean Catholics. On a hill overlooking Santiago is a large figure of the Virgin, illuminated at night. In Valparaiso, on the coast, a Madonna bears an inscription which translates: "For sure, harm will come to anyone who passes this image without respectfully praying even a Hail Mary."

While in Chile, John Paul stated that arms may be taken up as a last resort, but he was able to get leaders of the extreme political right and left to sign a commitment to search for peace and democracy. Afterward, Communists commented that the agreement did not rule out their using violence "as a legitimate tool against the government."

CHILEAN CULTURE

Ray and I stayed with Terry and Carol Thompson of the Gospel Mission of South America. Their general director, born of BIM missionaries in Bolivia, had written SIM's general director, Ian M. Hay, to offer assistance in any way needed. "There is a great deal of room for men and women called of God to labor in this country, which until now has been unusually open to the Good News of Jesus Christ," wrote Hudson Shedd.

GMSA's work began as an evangelistic outreach among military personnel, distributing Bibles provided by the Gideons. From that developed an indigenous association: the Union of Bible Centers. That name came about when the founding missionary, a layman named Bill Strong, sought to register several Bible study groups. When an official asked him the name of his organization, he said it had no name--it was just a group of Bible centers. So the official wrote: Union of Bible Centers.

Terry introduced us to the UBC General Secretary, Luis Benitez.

"This is my first visit to Chile," I told the sturdy pastor, "and I need to understand the country and the Lord's work here."

"Well, most people comment on what a long, narrow country this is," Pastor Benitez replied. "We have over 12 million population, but nearly half of them live here around the capital. Very few live in the southern part, where it's very wet, or in the northern part, where it's very dry. So that affects our strategy for reaching the nation for Christ. There's a saying that 'Chile is Santiago'--although not everyone agrees with that!"

I asked Benitez whether response to American Pentecostal televangelists has been among the unskilled or the educated.

"The biggest response is among the poorer people," the Chilean pastor replied. "But even the middle and upper classes have been impressed. We don't agree with all the evangelists' doctrinal positions, and a lot of the content is showmanship-- but the campaigns have at least got people talking about the gospel and about evangelicals.

"Chileans respect success. In Santiago there is a megachurch seating 15,000. It's really made up of many smaller ones. The church issues color-coded cards to limit worshipers to only one visit a month."

"I hear of thousands of decisions. Are they genuine?" I asked.

"Well, you have to understand Chilean culture," Benitez replied with a smile. "We're taught to be polite. So if you put on a big program, spend lots of money, have a big choir and famous speakers, the people will come out because you've gone to a lot of trouble and they don't want to let you down. They want to reward you.

"If you ask them to come forward for prayer, they'll do that too--it's the thing to do. They won't turn down a tract offered to them. They'll pray a sinner's prayer. But they may not mean it. That's Chilean culture. That's why Mormons and Jehovah's Witnesses are making such inroads--it's polite to invite them in and listen to them and agree with them."

I asked if Benitez thought that Chile is more tolerant than some other Latin American nations.

"Right!" he replied. "The protests you've heard about are instigated by small, disciplined groups. Actually, this is a very tolerant nation. I remember during the previous Communist regime, I saw a big sign: YANKEE GO HOME! Someone had added at the bottom, 'and take me with you.' Americans and other foreigners are very well accepted here. You'll hear a lot of English songs, and the fashions are European."

I'd heard that the Chilean Communist party claims to be the oldest in the world, even predating Russia's. Benitez said there are still Marxist groups at work, but Fidel Castro of Cuba has little influence. "He's looked upon as a puppet of Russia," he added.

This dynamic church leader told me that Catholics are worried about the increasing percentage of Protestants, given as anywhere between 18 and 23 percent.

"Catholic leaders hope the Pope's visit will turn people back to the church," Benitez continued. "The people themselves have great expectations that the visit will make a big difference in the country, but they are going to be disappointed. I think people will end up with even more questions, and that will give us evangelicals opportunity to tell about 'the hope that lies within us.'

"For instance, while the Pope is here, he will crown about 50 Madonnas. One of our members wants to get a photo of the Pope doing this and then print at the bottom, 'Thou shalt not worship any graven image.' Most Chileans are not going to accept the worship of images. They're going to be asking questions about that."

STRATEGY FOR THE CITIES

I commented that Chile and Uruguay are the most highly urbanized countries in Latin America--something like 83 or 84 percent of the population. I asked whether city dwellers are really being reached.

"No!" Benitez answered emphatically. "At least, not the mainstream of educated people. Most missionaries live in middle-class neighborhoods and drive away across the city to evangelize the poor. I'm glad the poor are being reached, but they're easy to reach in comparison to the educated class. And the fact that evangelicals tend to concentrate on the poor and neglect the educated, strengthens the perception that the gospel is not for the middle and upper classes. They're largely un-reached. Who's going to reach them?"

The UBC has a strategy for reaching educated urbanites. One way is to start private schools, which the government funds. Catholics make good use of that, but not evangelicals. Benitez said many parents would send their children to an evangelical school, even though some priests threaten to ex-communicate any parent who does. Evangelicals are also step-ping up television and radio programs to get the gospel into middle-class homes. Training of pastors and Bible teachers is a priority. UBC has a Bible institute but needs to provide higher level theological training. Chile has 17 universities, and in-creasing numbers of students and professional people are at-tending UBC churches.

I was surprised when Pastor Benitez said he'd be happy if

SIM sent a missionary to work in his own neighborhood. "Does that surprise you?" he asked, raising a shaggy eyebrow. "Since we are one of the few evangelical churches, people drive all across the city to get Bible teaching. We're so busy trying to meet their needs that we can't concentrate on our own city block. That's bad! If we had 800 missionaries to work among Santiago's two million middle-class population, we'd hardly scratch the surface. So if you started a church a block from my church, there'd be no competition!"

I asked about the evangelization of the aborigines.

"Only about six percent of the population is Indian, and that includes 57,000 Aymara and 80,000 Quechua immigrants," the pastor explained. "GMSA, SAMS, and Wycliffe are some of the missions doing a good job evangelizing the aborigines. Now the main unreached people are the educated Chileans.

"I can show you 20 towns of 60,000 people and more that have no evangelical witness. Some mayors would even provide property for an evangelical church or school. We have a wide-open door here--so please send SIM missionaries if you can!"

"WHY DIDN'T YOU COME SOONER?"

I heard the same thing when I looked up a longtime friend: Bill Parlane, who was visiting his son Alistair and daughter-in-law Martha in the town of Viña del Mar (Vineyard of the Sea) on the coast. Bill had been a founding council member of Regions Beyond Missionary Union, Canada, and Alistair and Martha were busy in urban church planting for RBMU. From their house we could see the sparkling bay explored by Balboa, the first European to sight the Pacific Ocean, according to a monument in nearby Valparaiso. That city became the first port of call for European ships rounding the Cape en route to North America's west coast. It also had been a favorite target of pirates, and England's Sir Francis Drake once burned it down. Now the idyllic bay was targeted by tourists' cameras.

"Why is the water reddish?" I asked. "I thought it would be blue on a sunny day like this."

"That's the Red Tide," Alistair replied. "It means the

coastal current has changed course, and toxic plankton has moved in. That's bad news for fishermen!"

I tried to imagine the panic such a phenomenon would have touched off among the Incas. Surely the sun god must be angry, to turn the water red and kill the fish! He must be appeased with sacrifice! Even a human sacrifice? The frozen body of one such sacrifice has been exhumed from the ice on top of Cerro del Torro on the border with Argentina, north of Santiago. Evidently, the victim was a strapping young brave sacrificed to mark some major event 500 years ago. He was buried facing Cuzco, "Navel of the Universe," 1100 miles to the north.

The Incas pushed their empire southward through half of what is now Chile. The ferocious Mapuches of the Araucanian tribe stopped them at the Maule River. The Spanish conquistador, Valdivia, after founding Santiago, succeeded in penetrating farther before the Indians captured him near the town that now bears his name. The story goes that the Indians said, "You want gold? Here it is!"--and killed him by pouring molten gold down his throat.

Over 400 years have passed since that day, and the spiritual conquest of a new generation in a new age challenged us now.

"Wouldn't it be great if SIM could send a couple into this area to work alongside RBMU in church planting!" Alistair and Martha said. "We're finding people ready to accept the Lord, if we can get to know them. That's not easy, because they live behind barred gates. We have to find ways of meeting and befriending them."

Martha did that with one woman, Nora, through giving her singing lessons. Nora had been depressed. As she studied the Bible with Martha, she saw her need of the Saviour. Just a month before our visit, another woman tearfully asked Martha, "Why didn't you come sooner to tell me? Why didn't my husband hear before he left me?"

While we were in the area, Ray and I visited the offices of one of the most effective Bible teaching agencies I've seen. Known as SEAN (Study by Extension for All Nations), it was begun by evangelical Anglicans serving with the South American Missionary Society. Now SEAN materials are available in about 50 languages in 46 countries and used by 64 denominations. SIM uses SEAN materials in South America, Asia, and Africa. SEAN also works with LOGOI, a U.S.A.-based publisher, to develop trained leadership through the Latin American Faculty of Theological Education (FLET).

"FLET is helping my people communicate the gospel," Roberto Henriquez told us. As director of FLET's Communication Center, he is able to apply his own experience of 20 years with government television.

Roberto told us how he had come to Christ. He had been a faithful church member, and had studied at a Catholic university.

"I even helped the priest perform Mass," Roberto said. "All I knew about the gospel was that it was for crazy people. Evangelicals were all crazy!"

Roberto's opinion changed when he got to know an evangelical family. Through them, he came to know that Jesus not only died and rose again, but that he himself could have eternal life through faith in Christ. His conversion upset his family, who wouldn't even attend his marriage to a pastor's daughter.

When Roberto and his wife decided they should take up full-time Christian work, none of his family or former friends understood. The government increased his wages and responsibilities in a vain attempt to keep him. Since then Roberto has been able to lead some of his family and government friends to Christ. The vice rector of the university, who had told him he was mad, now says Roberto did the right thing.

"Through all this, I learned what Jesus meant when He said a disciple must be willing to forsake all and take up his cross," Roberto told us. "I had to choose between following Christ or maintaining friendship with my family and employers.

"My conversion opened up a completely new world. I realized God had something to say to me, but I hadn't understood it before. Evangelicals just weren't communicating their faith. When I was a boy, I'd hear a pastor preach over the radio about being 'washed in the blood.' I thought these crazy evangelicals were telling me I had to kill a sheep and pour its blood over myself in order to be cleansed from sin. That sounded like the old pagan sacrifices."

Roberto thinks most evangelical programs are still like that--a repeat of a church service meant for believers, not designed to communicate to the unsaved person who doesn't know the Bible. FLET's Communication Center aims to train men and women to be able to make the gospel clear on TV, radio, and by other means.

As Roberto talked, he noticed my eyes following a vine that grew out of a little pot, up the wall, and completely around the four walls.

"That's my object lesson," Roberto explained. "I brought it to this office when I started here five years ago. I look after it carefully, watering it every day. When I'm away, my secretary cares for it. The vine reminds me that I, too, need daily spiritual food. Then I continue to grow."

On Roberto's walls were a Scripture verse, 14 diplomas, and a photograph of the minister of education presenting an award to Roberto for excellence in his TV program, called "All Glory to the Lord."

"THIS IS THE RIGHT TIME"

Ray Morris and I boarded a bus to return to Santiago. Like most buses, it was privately owned and operated in keen competition with others. Several times during the trip an attendant came through to ask if we were comfortable, to adjust the seats, or offer a soft drink. At one stop, a girl got on to sell photographs of the Pope. Along the road, lampposts bore the Pope's face and the words: "Holy Father, Chile thanks you for peace!"

"On the radio I've heard some of the Messianic Psalms being applied to the Pope," Ray commented. "One reference was to 'the meek Lamb.'"

Our bus passed a stopped bus which had just hit a pedestrian trying to cross the six-lane highway.

"Too bad the pedestrian got hit, but I also feel sorry for the driver," Ray commented. "In most of Latin America, the law presumes a person is guilty until he can prove his innocence.

The driver will automatically be imprisoned until the case can be heard, which could be months from now. He can be released on bail only if he has witnesses to testify to his innocence. Meanwhile, his bus will be impounded. The owner's business may be ruined before he can get the driver free and his bus back on the road. As a result of the system, there are a lot of paid false witnesses."

As we traveled, Ray told me more of his vision for SIM in Chile.

"You know, I have the same sense of God's leading about Chile as I did in 1965 when the Bolivian Indian Mission considered starting working in Peru," said Ray, who is a quiet conservative, not the flamboyant "Aussie" portrayed in some Australian movies. "It's like a strong conviction that this is the right time! We need to develop urban church planting, Theological Education by Extension, TV production in cooperation with other evangelical groups, perhaps a Christian school, and a coffee shop for youth work. In everything, evangelism and discipling are our primary objectives. That's why I'm glad Eckhard and Brigitte Nehmer are assigned here to head that up."

I had seen the Nehmers in action in Lima, Peru, and was fascinated to hear how God had brought them all the way from East Germany. When Eckhard lived there as a boy, his mother supported the family by dealing on the black market. The police got on her trail, and she fled to West Berlin with her son.

Eckhard had been raised a Marxist and was amazed at the freedom in West Berlin. But he quickly became materialistic, turning to drink and other vices. Then a friend invited him to an evangelistic service, and he decided to read the Bible.

Logically, he started in Genesis, but found it slow going until his friend advised him to start in the New Testament. There he was stunned to read Jesus' statement: "I am the way, the truth, and the life."

"I knew I hadn't found life in either Marxism or capitalism," Eckhard told me. "So I asked Jesus for His eternal life. I was amazed at the change. All at once I had no desire for alcohol or tobacco. That strengthened my faith."

Then Eckhard's mother became very ill and was admitted to a hospital ward for the terminally ill. On a Wednesday afternoon, Eckhard prayed she'd recover. When he visited the hospital the next weekend, he couldn't find her and was afraid she'd died. But the nurse explained that his mother suddenly began to improve on Wednesday afternoon, and they had moved her to a recovery ward.

After seeing this answer to prayer, Eckhard sent gospel tracts to Brigitte, whom he had met in a youth hostel. Brigitte had known him only as a carousing youth, and although unsaved herself, she accused him of ridiculing Christianity by sending her tracts. He replied that he had been saved, and she needed Christ also. Although Brigitte considered herself a good person, she started reading the Bible to please Eckhard. She couldn't understand it until she came to the verse in First Corinthians which says: "The man without the Spirit does not accept the things that come from the Spirit of God." Realizing she needed salvation, she asked Eckhard how to be saved.

Eckhard visited Mexico with a friend and became burdened for the spiritual needs of Latin America. After he and Brigitte married, they met furloughing missionaries Ingo and Christel Manhold, Germans serving with what was then the Bolivian Indian Mission. The Nehmers decided to join up too. After serving in Peru, they were assigned to start new outreach in Chile.

SINGING DUNES

"See you in Peru for Easter!" I said to Ray, who stayed in Chile a few more days. On the way to the airport, I passed demonstrators taking advantage of the Pope's presence (or really the presence of foreign journalists) in the city to make political statements. They held a banner aloft: HUNGER FOR GOD--YES; HUNGER FOR BREAD--NO. Huge effigies represented the biblical horsemen of hunger and death.

Before takeoff I bought postage stamps to mail some cards. Once again I was confronted by the Pope, this time on the stamps issued to commemorate his visit. In the stamp's background was a picture of a large cross erected beside the Straits of Magellan, signifying the Pope's travels to "the ends of the earth." I learned that the cross had to be replaced twice because violent storms destroyed the first two.

My flight passed over the Atacama Desert, the driest spot on earth. Rain never falls in some parts of the 70,000-square-mile desert. The Incas believed spirits caused the mysterious wailing and booming sounds that come from the "singing dunes," and scientists are still baffled by them.

We flew over Antofagasta, the port where George and Mary Allan landed in 1906 to board the train into Bolivia. Bolivia used to have a corridor to the sea, but Chile absorbed it as well as a chunk of desert claimed by Peru, territory rich in nitrates. The border town of Arica commemorates Chile's battle with Peru. It also boasts an iron frame cathedral built by none other than the French engineer, Eiffel, of Paris tower fame.

Once again, Peru lay before me. Not the Incas' "Navel of the Universe" this time, but modern Peru.

When I consider your heavens, the work of your fingers, the moon and the stars, . . . what is man that you are mindful of him?

PSALM 8:3,4

16

HOME

OF THE

CONDOR

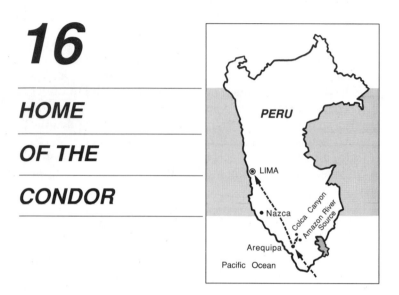

PERU

◉ LIMA

• Nazca

Colca Canyon

Amazon River Source

Arequipa

Pacific Ocean

YOU ARE AT THE HEADWATERS OF THE AMAZON, the signboard declared.

I couldn't believe it! We were only 120 air miles from the Pacific Ocean, high on the western range of the Andes in southern Peru. The mouth of the Amazon was some 4000 winding river miles away, emptying into the Atlantic on the east coast of the continent, off Brazil. It seemed incredible that the silver thread of a mountain brook, cascading from snow-covered Mount Mismi, 18,000 feet above sea level, was the very beginning of the world's mightiest river.

ON THE TEE TRAIL

I was with Wallace and Colleen Searle in southern Peru, visiting some of their students in a Theological Education by Extension (TEE) program. With the Searles was Liz Major, a professional photographer from U.S.A., born of SIM parents who served in Africa. Liz had flown to Peru at her own expense to take photographs for SIM. With her ready smile, Liz established instant rapport with the traditionally shy rural people.

We started out from Arequipa, where the Searles lived, just as the volcano Misti caught the first blush of dawn. A ring of clouds formed a royal headband befitting an Inca princess. Although Misti is over 19,000 feet, it does not retain snow very long on its cap because the slopes are warm from hot gases inside, which cause occasional tremors. Wallace Searle's Russian Jeep wound along a dirt road up and down mountain ridges. At several hairpin bends I noticed dogs sitting, as if watching for traffic coming from both directions. I'd seen the same phenomenon on other Andean roads. Dogs seem to learn that blind corners are good spots to sit, because grateful travelers, alerted to the dangerous bends by the dogs' presence, throw food to them there.

In the valleys, shepherds herded their alpacas and llamas. Some of the animals had colored tassels in their ears and bells around their gracefully stretched necks. Alpacas have softer wool than llamas, the Searles explained. Both are cameloids, but only llamas are domesticated to carry loads. Their owners never ride them and don't load them with more than 50 pounds.

"They take good care of them," added Colleen. "Sometimes they'll keep them in the house at night. That keeps the family warm too! But you have to watch out if they get angry, because they spit a very smelly saliva at you!"

"There are vicuñas!" Wallace exclaimed as we turned a hairpin corner. "They look like small llamas but have very fine, silky hair and are the rarest members of the cameloid family. They're protected."

The shy animals quickly got out of our range, kicking up clouds of volcanic dust. Clumps of sagebrush helped to hold the loose soil, but we noticed a couple men on a trail pulling up the sagebrush and throwing it on a truck.

"That's illegal, because the brush prevents erosion," Colleen explained. "Truckers like to load up with it to sell for fuel in town."

The valleys were a tapestry of greens, golds, browns, and grays, with wheat and barley ready to harvest. Contour terracing looked as if someone had drawn a giant comb across the face of the hills. These slopes have been terraced for at least 1500 years. After the Inca Empire collapsed, Quechuas under Spanish rule allowed the terracing to deteriorate, but the government is encouraging them to resume traditional methods.

Wallace explained the mindset of most farmers. Under the Incas, the community ordered their lives. Under the Spanish, the patron estate owners told them what to do. The land reform law of 1969 established cooperatives, and the managers simply took the place of the patrons in running things, in the view of the farmers. So they didn't quickly develop the private enterprise concept of growing sufficient crops to feed themselves and sell the balance in the market.

"This is changing, however," Wallace added. "The standard of living is rising, and the people are eating better, causing a shortage of local food. That means importation of beef, rice, and flour. The government is trying to restrict these imports to make Peru self-reliant."

At one place, we passed between rocky outcroppings called the Robbers' Pass, where bandits used to lie in wait for travelers on horseback. Now an enterprising gasoline vendor lay in wait for vehicles needing fuel to reach the next major town. The attendant filled a kerosene tin with gasoline from a barrel and siphoned it into our gas tank.

As ragged clouds formed overhead, Wallace got his theft-proof windshield wipers from the back of the Jeep, where he kept them to avoid theft, and clipped them in place. Two ranchers on horseback driving their sheep and alpacas hurried to reach their corral before the storm hit. We drove higher and broke into sunshine. Just when I thought we'd reached the top of the world, we came upon a wind-swept village, 14,000 feet above sea level. A Catholic church spire poked above stone houses, the roofs of which were held down by rocks. The market square was filled with women colorfully dressed in layers of petticoats and shawls. Beyond the market, we stopped outside humble adobe buildings.

"Here are the church and pastor's house," they explained. As soon as the people saw Wallace and Colleen, they hurried to embrace them. As Wallace conferred with the pastor, Colleen told us that this was one of their 13 TEE centers. Students range from 18 to 60 years of age. In the highlands, farmers are their own bosses and can take what time they want from herding their flocks. But it's not easy for farm laborers to get time off. They have to be on call 24 hours a day, seven days a week. The estate owner holds the laborers responsible for everything. If a cow dies or something else goes wrong, it's the laborer who has to pay for it. Laborers are allowed to attend Sunday morning service, so they meet for Extension classes right after.

Colleen told us about Wallace's background. His parents, William and Margaret, were the New Zealand pioneer couple who had part in the spiritual growth of Rodolfo Leigue, in Bolivia's Beni region (chapter 10). Wallace and his brother Harold grew up in Bolivia, and both became missionaries.

Wallace and Colleen have the right mindset for their itinerant life. When the villagers don't have space for them to sleep, the Searles bed down in the back of their Jeep. They enjoy the local food, but they have to be careful of alpaca meat because it can contain a harmful virus.

Wallace introduced us to a TEE group leader, Germanicio, a veterinary assistant. He and his brother had bought a farm, but his brother turned against him and built a stone wall across the property. He left only 15 hectares to Germanicio and kept the remaining 550 hectares for himself. Germanicio's area is very stony and not well watered like the rest, but his 35 alpacas produce more wool on those 15 acres than his brother's 86 alpacas produce on the larger pasture land. The villagers tell Germanicio he should take his brother to court, but he refuses to do so. When the Searles asked how he explained that his alpacas were doing better, he replied, "My alpacas belong to the Lord. He looks after them."

The Searles have their amusing moments, such as the time Wallace asked someone to bring an eraser for the blackboard he was using to teach a class. A child hurried over to a hut and brought back a llama tail, which still felt warm.

"That worked fine until a dog ran off with it," Colleen said. "The class broke up as people chased the dog to get the eraser back!"

THE ABYSS

Saying farewell to the friendly villagers, we headed on to the village of Chivay, where a sign announced we were in the vicinity of the source of the Amazon, discovered only in 1953. Our goal, however, was to reach El Cañon de Colca before nightfall. The world's deepest canyon, it was unknown to the outside world until the fifties. (Tibet has the world's deepest *valley*. The word "canyon" comes from the Spanish *cañon,* a long tube, and refers to a narrow gorge formation.)

We followed the Colca River and climbed a road carved along the face of a granite wall. The sun's last rays were mixing a witch's brew in the mists of the cauldron below us as we arrived at the lookout spot, over 15,000 feet above sea level. A white cross surmounted a stone cairn, and a plaque announced this to be the Cross of the Condor, the Incas' sacred bird.

"We want to protect the condor, the bird of greatest wing span and the heaviest of all flying birds, a bird of legend and mythology," the plaque stated. Another sign described The Canyon of the Colca: "This is the fault between the huge volcanoes of Coropuna (6425 meters high) and Ampato (6310 meters), with a depth of 3400 meters between the two mountains and 100 kilometers long." That's a rough translation from the Spanish. In nonmetric terms, the canyon is over two miles deep (more than twice as deep as the Grand Canyon in U.S.A.) and 63 miles long.

Gasping for breath, I ventured to the edge. Normally I'm not bothered by heights, but what I looked down into was frightening. My stomach seemed to drop out. An incredible magnetism pulled at my body as if to hurl me down forever through space. I shrank back from the brink and pressed against a granite crag for security. I could appreciate Psalmist David's prayer:

From the ends of the earth I call to you,
I call as my heart grows faint;
Lead me to the rock that is higher than I.

Clinging like a gnat on the wall of a high-rise apartment building, I found it impossible to comprehend the depth at my feet. The granite ridges receded down, down, down into the evening mist. The shiny thread at the bottom was really a wide, raging torrent, but so far off that I could not hear it.

From my promontory, I looked across at the solid bastion on the opposite side. I almost thought I could reach across, because there was nothing in between to give a sense of distance. Then a condor floated toward the distant mountain, and as it became a speck too small to see, I felt I was looking across a void that could never be spanned.

My companions had gone back to the car, anxious to get down the mountain before night engulfed us completely. But I couldn't leave that quickly. Sheer grandeur seemed to immobilize me. The world's deepest canyon, yet it was only a wrinkle on the surface of the earth. It still didn't reach down to the great continental plates that had thrust these lofty ramparts naked toward the sky.

I remembered reading that if the earth were shrunken to the size of a billiard ball, it would actually feel smoother than the ball. This abyss included? Yes, such is the magnitude of our terrestrial ball. Yet this earth is only a tiny bit of matter in a vast ocean of the universe, I reminded myself. The nova which had recently been discovered by a Canadian astronomer at an observatory in Chile was further evidence of that. Its light, just reaching earth, had actually started out 2500 light years ago!

Again the words of the Psalmist came to me:

When I consider your heavens, the work of your fingers ...
what is man, that you are mindful of him?

The ridiculous thought occurred to me that this abyss could engulf all the skyscrapers and concrete in all the cities of the world, all the tar on the highways of the world, and every last vestige of mankind in one Gehenna rubbish dump!

I wanted to remember this scene forever, especially when I was tempted to feel conceited about some petty accomplishment, or arrogant about man's achievements in building the highest or the deepest or the largest of anything.

Heaven and earth met as clouds enveloped the jagged peaks around me, joining with the mists rising from the canyon. I inched along the rock face to the others waiting in the Jeep. The four of us bowed our heads in prayer to thank God for the majesty of His creation and for stooping to redeem us. Then we headed into the night back to Arequipa.

"LET'S STAY HERE"

Arequipa in Quechua means "let's stay here." It has such an enjoyable climate that the Spaniards stayed to found the city in 1540 on an old Inca site, 7808 feet above sea level. Over one million people now live in the city, called The White City because local white volcanic rock is used in the buildings, giving them a sunny appearance. In fact, the sun shines 360 days of the year. Buildings are low built and without balconies because of the constant danger of earthquakes. When I was there, seismologists were predicting a major one.

Working with the Searles in Peru were Joel and Sarah Purcell, who had previously served in Ghana, West Africa. How they ended up in Peru made an interesting story. They were from a United Methodist background in U.S.A., where Joel came to the Lord through a layman's witness. After marriage, they felt they should commit their lives to evangelize unreached people, so they tried to telephone a furloughing SIM missionary from Africa whom they had met. The phone was engaged because the missionary was trying to telephone them at that precise moment! When they did talk with each other, the

Purcells concluded they should join SIM, and they were eventually assigned to Ghana.

Things went well there until the Purcells took a vacation in neighboring Togo, where Joel came down with hepatitis and malaria. They couldn't speak French (the official language of Togo), and the doctor who treated Joel couldn't speak English. Joel started on the five medicines the doctor prescribed, and became irrational. Heading back to Ghana, they found the border closed because of tension between the two countries. Sarah argued with the border police to let them across: It could be life or death for her husband. Getting nowhere, she finally burst into tears.

"I'm sick with malaria!" Joel blurted as he staggered out of the car.

"All you white people are sick with malaria when you come through here!" growled the officer. "Get going!" And he let them across.

In her concern to get back to Ghana, Sarah had forgotten the medication--which turned out to be a good thing. No one realized that the treatment was causing Joel's psychotic reactions. The Purcells had to fly back to U.S.A., where Joel was referred to a psychiatrist. He told Joel there was no underlying problem. It turned out that Joel had a reaction to the malaria treatment, combined with depression from hepatitis. He was advised to serve in a country where there is no malaria. Peru was needing church planters, so that's where the Purcells ended up.

In Peru, Joel and Sarah developed the kind of mobile gospel film ministry they had seen produce great results in Ghana. The Purcells would spend two weeks making contacts in a community where there was no evangelical church. Then a week of film evangelism would be followed by forming Bible study groups for new converts. A personable young couple themselves, the Purcells made friends in the traditional Latin American way: sitting and chatting in the public squares. Joel also found that his basketball skills helped establish rapport with city youth.

Joel got to know a Marxist university professor and asked

what he saw as the hope of Peru. "We need new people, not the present ones," the professor replied cynically. But Joel and Sarah believe that the present people can become "new creatures" in Christ. They are the nation's hope.

UNPRECEDENTED OPPORTUNITY

There was a smell of ozone, such as is given off when two electric wires cross and cause a big spark.

I had just walked into Bill Mitchell's office in his house in Arequipa. Bill, son of a Scottish coal miner, is translations consultant for the United Bible Society for Spanish-speaking South America. He was in the midst of a final check of the Cuzco dialect of the Old Testament in Quechua, translated by the Mitchells while working with EUSA.

It was all coming up on his computer monitor. Or it had been, until the moment I walked in. With the smell of hot electronic parts, a section of the first Cuzco Old Testament had just vanished from the screen. Bill Mitchell stared at the blank screen with a look of helpless despair.

This was definitely not the best moment to interview this Hebrew scholar, one of the few people I met who had a comprehensive overview of the continent. His wife, Alice, is also a scholar. The two met in Israel while pursuing their studies, hers in archaeology and his in Hebrew.

How do you greet a man when his computer has just burned up? Traditional greetings would have sounded inane, so we talked about the matter uppermost on Bill's mind: how to get repairs for a word processor in Arequipa. Not that the translation had been lost--Bill explained that it was still on floppy disks.

After Bill emerged from initial shock, he shared his joy that South America's first complete Bible in an indigenous language had just arrived. It was the Bible in Bolivian Quechua, the end result of the pioneer work started by George Allan and continued by others through the years. The Bible in the dialect used in Ayacucho (where the Shining Path guerrillas started) and a Bible for Ecuador in Quichua (local spelling), were both completed. Bill felt that these Bibles would help stabilize the language, as the Bible had done for the English and German languages centuries ago.

"With increased schooling in Spanish, why are translations in these dialects so important?" I asked.

"Even among educated people, there's a new pride in their roots," Bill replied. "Quechua is Peru's second official language, after Spanish. Not only is there new interest in the language, but also in local dialects of it. This is all part of a new recognition of indigenous rights and also of the government's emphasis on cultural authenticity. Even in the school that our children attend, the parents call for more traditional cultural teaching in such things as the arts.

"At church on Sunday, you'll notice the people singing hymns with European tunes. That is an Arequipa syndrome. Because this city has always been a Spanish cultural center, European tunes identify the people with that subculture. However, out in the villages you just came from, the people sing Quechua tunes in the pentatonic scale. It just doesn't make sense to uneducated Quechuas to sing in a seven-note scale instead of a five-note scale. European tunes sound lifeless to them."

Bill pointed out that 60 percent of Peru's population is under 25 years of age, with 40 percent under 14. Most of these will become literate and will need Scriptures in a format that appeals to youth. Even Spanish translations will need to be in the idiom of students. The Bible Societies are targeting specific classes of people or age groups and also using other forms of communication for the Scriptures.

"I note missions are reviewing their goals in South America, and many are changing their emphasis from the rural to the urban," Bill continued. "The illiterate people must not be neglected. Work among them needs to continue. But we face an unprecedented opportunity among people in towns and cities, who until recently have resisted the gospel. They are the largest unreached segment of population in the continent today, believe it or not.

"The rapid growth of urban areas brings about its own social upheaval. People suddenly find themselves in a consumer society, with secularization and erosion of traditional values. That makes them more open to hear how the gospel can meet their inner needs."

I asked about the role of the Catholic church. Bill explained that there are at least two Catholic churches. One is the traditional church, which educated youth reject because they identify it with the power structure that has supported exploitation in the past. The other is the growing Catholic charismatic movement. "It has lots of enthusiasm and emotion, but little Biblical content," Bill said. "This element presents a tremendous open door to reach people who are hungry for the Word of God but don't have anybody in the church to teach them. There is also a 'people's church' movement growing."

"Is Marxism making inroads?" I asked. "And how about liberation theology?"

"Marxist ideology is very active in such terrorist movements as the Shining Path, and of course it makes problems for Christians," Bill replied. "At the same time, Marxism in some cases creates an openness to change, away from the traditions which have held people for so long in the Catholic church.

"Liberation theology is politicized religion, and is producing its own reactions. One young man said to me, 'The priest only preaches politics, and there's nothing for us.' People applaud the priest's political activity on behalf of the poor, but they wish he would feed them with the Word of God, ministering to their deepest needs.

"If the Pope has anything to do with the appointment of a bishop, the man will be a conservative. The new archbishop of Cuzco, where Alice and I worked with EUSA for 10 years, has actually closed down the liberation theology study center there. He says he doesn't want anything to do with liberation theology in his diocese. This is all part of the tension between liberation theology and the conservative church.

"I feel we are at a very significant time in church history in South America," Bill continued as Alice brought in a tray of coffee. "Indigenous rural churches are growing rapidly, urban areas are beginning to open to the gospel, and throughout the continent there's a great mass of youth whom we must reach with the Word of God."

The aroma of coffee displaced the smell of ozone, and Bill turned back to the lifeless machine on his desk, to figure out what to do.

The next day, the Searles drove me to the IEP *(Iglesia Evangelica Peruana)* church with which SIM and several other evangelical groups work. We passed Catholics coming out of early Mass with little crosses made from woven palm fronds. It was Palm Sunday. The ornate facade on the Catholic church gave its date as 1710. After midnight on Easter Sunday, the Catholic faithful would take part in an interesting ceremony. They would burn an effigy of Judas and read his "will," which in reality would be a list of current criticisms of city authorities.

IEP's Mount Sinai church was in a poorer suburb. A Christian neighbor had donated a section of his property for the church to put up a building. There was a great heap of sandy earth in front of the church from a trench the members had dug for the installation of water and plumbing. Residents have to pay for installing their own plumbing, water, and electricity, and also, if they can afford it, paving their street.

The church had no pastor, but the elders carried on an effective ministry. As we arrived, Sunday school was still in progress, and a group of children were singing: "It doesn't matter what your color or race is, God loves us and we need to love each other." A motto at the front of the small auditorium said in Spanish: GOD IS LOVE.

MYSTERY LINES

It was time to leave The White City and head north to the capital, Lima. At the airport I bought a bottle of mineral water (visitors to Peru are advised not to drink tap water), bottled by the Society of Public Benefit of Arequipa. Under the brand name "Jesus," the label bore a drawing of volcanic Misti and a declaration that the water was free from bacteria.

On the flight northward to Lima, I looked out on the mountains rising majestically on our right. Somewhere over there, Cuzco was nestled among them. It seemed like years since we were there. To the left was the ocean blue, across which the sun god sailed off into darkness every evening. Down below us, the coastal plains were bleak and dry, with only ribbons of green along the rivers that vainly seek to reach the sea before evaporating in the desert. Peru has South America's second largest desert (10,000 square miles), as big as England or the State of New York.

This area includes the mysterious Nazca Lines--geometrical figures and shapes of creatures cut into the stony desert by a highly developed civilization that reached its peak 800 years after Christ. Tourists, anthropologists, and occultists are still arguing over the meaning of these enormous figures, which can be seen in entirety only from the air. A German woman has studied the lines over the past 30 years, mostly from the top of a stepladder.

Theories abound as to their meaning: an astronomical calendar; a map illustrating the Tiahuanaco Empire; tracks for running contests; a site for Nazca hot air balloon launchings; and, of course, messages left by aliens from outer space! The proponents of each theory have their documented support, some published in books. To me, the most plausible explanation is that these were religious symbols laid out for deities in the sky to view.

Scientists are also arguing about whether civilization in Peru sprang from a fishing economy on the coast or from a mixed agricultural-maritime economy. They all agree there is evidence of structured society as far back as 2100 B.C., which is 3500 years before the Incas. The dryness of the coastal plain has preserved ancient artifacts, including some of the greatest examples of weaving and tapestry found anywhere in the world, dating 2000 years before Christ. Peruvians are understandably proud of the heritage of these civilizations, advanced and sophisticated for their day.

Peru is almost twice the size of Texas. The coastal region, 11 percent of the country, holds 45 percent of the 21 million population. The central mountainous area covers 26 percent of the country, holding 50 percent of the people. These live at the barest subsistence level, outside the money economy, and they have the lowest literacy rate of any comparable group in the continent. The eastern flank of Peru, from forest slopes to lowland jungle, covers about 63 percent of the country but holds only about five percent of the population. These live along the cultivable riverbanks and on the high plateau surrounding Peru's side of Lake Titicaca.

In 1535 the Spanish conquistador Pizarro established Lima as his communications capital with Spain. It was there that he, in a kind of just retribution for his own cruelty, was assassinated.

At one time the vice royalty of Peru also embraced Argentina, Bolivia, Chile, Colombia, and Ecuador. From its founding until the independence of South America's republics, Lima was the chief Spanish city on the continent. At the beginning of the 18th century, few European cities could rival its opulence. Spanish rule was finally overthrown by Simon Bolivar and his colleague General Sucre, when the last Spanish troops capitulated at Callao on January 22, 1826. This was followed by a temporary confederation between Peru and Bolivia in the 1830s.

"GOD PLANNED OUR SEATING"

On the flight to Lima, my fellow passenger was a handsome young man of 25 returning from a four-month overland journey to Brazil. Employed by a travel agency, Raul was interested in seeing other countries for himself. He spoke Spanish, Portuguese, French, and English.

Raul had heard a radio report about the violent demonstrations in Chile during the Pope's visit. That and the guerrilla activity in Peru shocked him. He didn't see how the country could settle its own problems: Help would have to come from some major power like Russia or U.S.A. He'd heard of the train bombing incident in Cuzco and was distressed that terrorists would try to harm innocent tourists.

"It's good we can find God's peace in these turbulent times," I commented. "Do you read the Bible?"

"Yes, of course," Raul replied. "I'm a good Catholic. Two

years ago I was baptized by the Spirit in a charismatic group led by my priest."

"Do you have a personal relationship with Christ as your Saviour?" I asked.

"I know I sometimes sin," Raul said, looking out the aircraft window and then back at me. "When that happens, I go to see my priest to confess my sins to him."

"I'm an evangelical missionary, and I like to help people get to know God," I explained. "The most important thing I can do is show you that Christ is your High Priest and has provided His life as an eternal sacrifice. By accepting Him as Saviour, you can have your sins forgiven and receive eternal life."

Raul listened intently and accepted a booklet explaining the way of salvation. Before we landed, I prayed with him and told him about the evangelical churches in Lima.

"I think God planned for us to be seated together!" the young travel agent said with a smile as we parted.

I wondered how many other people like Raul are waiting for someone to go to their "chariot" (Acts 8:29) to explain the gospel.

You shine like stars in the universe as you hold out the word of life.

PHILLIPIANS 2:15,16

17

REACHING

PERU'S

JERUSALEM

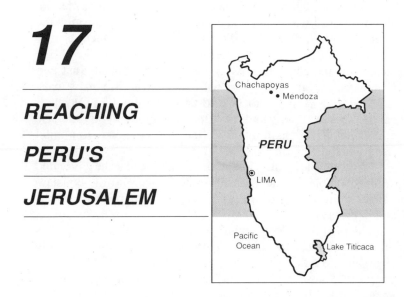

$\mathbf{A}$s our jet banked into its final approach to Lima airport, I looked down on a harbor filled with ocean freighters and fishing vessels. At one time, Peru caught more fish than any country in the world, but recently El Niño had been playing games with the fish-packed ocean currents.

Lima sprawls along the coastal plain with eight million people, one-third of the nation's total population. By the end of the century it will be larger than New York City. In the last five years, 12 percent of the people have poured in, and 1000 more arrive daily. Squatters in shantytowns around its perimeter number more than the total population of some Central American nations.

"YOU HAVE TO BE ALERT"

Ray Morris, having returned to Lima from Chile, met me at the airport. I was glad that he, not I, was driving through the unpredictable traffic. Cars didn't keep to their lanes. Sometimes two would attempt to drive in one lane. Added to the chaos was the constant possibility of being robbed. Just two months before, armed robbers followed a Wycliffe missionary from the airport to his house and tried to force him into their car. He shouted loudly and they fled after grabbing his suitcase and wallet. Thugs held up an airline bus on its way to a hotel and robbed the entire aircrew.

"You have to be alert all the time," Ray said as he navigated around potholes. "The Lord gives us peace, but the constant danger from robbers or terrorists makes many people nervous and depressed."

I slept at the SIM guesthouse. The next morning the sun's orb didn't visibly rise. Instead, the darkness of night slowly changed into a dull gray. From my open window I looked out on ghostly shadows of buildings looming through Lima's *garua* mist. My arms and face tingled from the city's acid pollution. However, doves and finches flitted outside my window among the orange blossoms of a tulip tree, relieving the gloom. By noon the sun had burned off most of the smog, but it would be back the next morning--and in a few weeks' time the people would not see the sun all day. Between June and October, a cloud blanket covers the coastal shelf, but no rain falls. The *garua's* gloom contributes to mental depression in the city.

I saw two sides of life in Lima. One was a suburb of upper income people with luxurious homes and manicured gardens worthy of Palm Springs, California. Spreading shade trees and red-blossomed bougainvillaea shrubs lined the avenue where embassies were located. A supermarket was stocked with every type of produce I would expect to find back home.

The "other Lima" held more people: squalid shanty sub-urbs of peasants who pour down from the hills to find a living in the big city. The highway median and sides were covered with piles of garbage. Two boys walked through the rubble, listening to a transistor radio one carried on his shoulder. He was wearing a second hand T-shirt that announced: "I Love New York." Ranging up the hillsides were dusty shanties, some with TV aerials. Ragged children were trying to sell items, to make a few intis.

HOPE IN THE SHANTYTOWN

I wandered through one of the shantytowns. Some of the shacks were made of cardboard and woven matting, but others were built of rough mud blocks. I was surprised at the cleanli-ness of the lanes between the shacks. Inside, the ground was swept clean, and some owners had planted cactus plants and the odd flower, which were covered with dust and barely hanging on to life. Children kicked a ball with their bare feet. One girl was especially proud of the piece of red plastic she had found in a dump and had tied in her hair, and a little boy was delighted with a bent tricycle wheel he found. Obviously, these people had self-respect and were simply seeking to sur-vive. It was hard to realize they felt better off living in these conditions than back in their isolated villages, without oppor-tunity to advance themselves. The main question was whether they went to bed hungry.

I met an American medical couple who had worked for 10 days in a Lima shantytown. It had been hit by a mud slide after an unprecedented rain. The Americans were surprised to find that although the people were poor, they had a sense of pride in their surroundings and were very friendly. They had strong family ties. Children took it upon themselves to protect the medical team from pickpockets and mugging and Shining Path agitators. The couple, who were with a relief group from a church in Ohio, did find a lot of tuberculosis, parasites, and malnourishment, although they were surprised at how the people seemed to find basic food.

The hope of these people is to subsist long enough to find

some kind of employment and improve their lot. They were living much as they had been living back in the hills, and that was a miserable life. However, here they always hope for improvement.

Isaias and Maria were a couple making that transition. To a visitor like me, from a suburb of tidy streets and homes and gardens, the half-built houses on their dusty lane looked like a depressed ghetto. Actually, it was upward mobility, to use a sociologist's term.

Sixteen years ago, Isaias and his family had left an isolated village over the hump of the Andes east of Lima, at the headwaters of the Amazon. Looking for work in Lima, they subsisted in a cardboard shack at first, until they were able to buy a tiny plot and start building. The ground floor was completed; that is, the walls were up, even if only raw cement and brick lined the rooms. Sunlight stabbed between pieces of used corrugated metal which formed a temporary roof. Steel rods poked up along the top of the walls, so that as Isaias earned more money he could begin adding a second floor.

It had taken 10 years to put up their small house, but the family members were thankful they had a roof over their heads, even if nothing seemed finished and there were piles of rubble outside. That was Lima's way of life, and it didn't seem to bother anybody.

Isaias and Maria are evangelicals. They make a living by selling fruit and by welding frames for doors and windows. Their son was studying to be a teacher; one daughter was studying dressmaking; another daughter was a seminary student, aiming to be a missionary to the people of the mountain where she had been born.

"I'm glad you've come," Isaias told me. "I've wanted to write believers in other countries to tell them what things are really like so they can pray for us. I've wanted to tell the missionaries who used to work here, to encourage them. But I don't know how to reach them. I'm glad you're writing a book.

"We've had hard times," continued Isaias, who is an elder in his church, "but the Lord said to be faithful until He returns."

I asked him whether the Shining Path terrorists bother the

Christians. He started to reply, when his children motioned him to lower his voice.

"They're all around us," Isaias whispered, "and they make it difficult for believers. They infiltrate the churches to find out how strong they are and what they're doing. We need wisdom to know how to handle this."

As Isaias talked, one of his daughters stepped outside to the front of the house to make sure no one was listening.

"Three of the young people active in our church, including our daughter who is at seminary, have been targeted by the terrorists to silence their witness," Isaias added in a low voice, glancing at his children.

The laughter and banter we had been enjoying stopped, and the shadows in the house seemed to deepen as the family told about the serious situation around them. Isaias asked about believers in other countries. His face brightened when I told him about Christians I had seen living for Christ in Communist countries.

"Jesus said He will build His church, and even the gates of hell will not prevail against it," I reminded the family. "What shall I ask the believers in other countries to pray for?" Isaias listed three things:

• That those who come to the Lord will be faithful to Him, even in persecution.

• That Christians will be more on fire for the Lord, witnessing to their neighbors.

• That the children of Christians will be well grounded in the faith, even if their parents are separated from them or die.

Maria chased out a chicken that had wandered into the room as she set a tray of Inca Kola on a table.

I noticed musical instruments in the room: a guitar, drum, bamboo flute, and castanets. I asked if the family would sing a hymn. The words they sang were from Isaiah 25:1,4:

"O Lord, you are my God; I will exalt you and praise your name.... You have been a refuge for the poor, a refuge for the needy in his distress, a shelter from the storm and a shade from the heat...."

Before I left, Isaias prayed. I felt I was in the presence of New Testament Christians living at the end of the 20th century.

Isaias and his little church in the shantytown are part of a network of 50 IEP churches SIM has worked with in Lima. They belong to the Evangelical Church of Peru *(Iglesia Evangelica Peruana,* or IEP). The members range from laborers to people in the professional bracket. About a thousand people attend Sunday morning service at their largest church, Maranatha.

"We're challenged by the real mission of the church!" Pastor Ernesto Palermo told me when Ray Morris introduced us. "We know we're to be the light and salt of the earth, and for us that means not only Lima but outreach into the mountains and the jungle."

Ernesto showed me a map of their "Jerusalem," the city of Lima, with little pennants locating their church and eight locations they have targeted to plant new churches. They were holding open air services to get these started. In the coming year, they had plans to train 100 of their members in church planting, establish 50 new prayer groups, and plant five of the eight new churches.

Maranatha also supports missionaries to reach their "Judaea and Samaria." One Peruvian missionary started 20 churches in three years. The mother church brings leaders from these churches into Lima for two months for discipling in leadership. These go back to their villages, returning in six months for another two months of training.

Talk about commitment! No wonder the IEP churches were growing at the phenomenal rate of 10 percent per annum. Ray took me to visit the president of this interesting group. A balding man with mahogany skin and gray lamb chops, Pablo Pecho told me that IEP was founded as a local church in 1895, registered with the government in 1907, and established as a denomination in 1922. A prime mover was John Ritchie, a remarkable Scotsman who served with Regions Beyond Missionary Union and Evangelical Union of South America and who contributed much to both church and nation. Now throughout Peru there are over 1400 IEP churches in 50

Above Right: The wealthy can buy almost anything ("todos") in this supermarket, but most Latin Americans are limited to subsistence-level foods purchased in local markets **(below).**

Men and women anxiously scan a list of jobs posted by an employment office. Most will not have the skills required.

THE ECONOMY

Photos by W. Harold Fuller

For centuries cowboys have herded their cattle in the lowlands. **(inset)** Now the lush plains attract poverty-stricken highland farmers, and many grow drug crops for quick cash. In some parts, terrorists extort payment to protect drug producers.

Increasingly, rural children like this llama herder are swept along in the flow of people to the cities, where promises of prosperity often turn into misery and horror. **Right:** This street child watched his drug-crazed brother kill his baby brother.

In Lima, children play in the rubble around houses being built by their parents—a process which may take twenty years or more. One third of Peru's population lives in the sprawling capital city of Lima.

While container ships unload in busy ports **(above),** urban squalor increases **(below).** Latin America's economic problems are complicated by philosophical views and have no simple solution.

SIMer Paul Bentley **(inset)** helps train church leadership, discipling believers so they can reach other communities with the gospel.

PEOPLE REACHING PEOPLE

Returning to Bolivia after several months' absence, SIM missionary Dianne Guta **(L)** is welcomed with a traditional embrace by a Quechua woman. **Below:** One-on-one relationships are important in evangelizing educated people in cities like La Paz.

Above: Children learn crafts and Bible truths at a Christian camp.

As women prepare a meal for the visitors, evangelist Julian Coronel instructs rural believers in witnessing to surrounding villages.

Braulio and Anna Maria organized the building of this church in the village where their lives were once threatened because they were evangelicals. Braulio has since served as village mayor.

Above: Trying to cope with their own problems, pedestrians hurry past an amputee beggar on a Sao Paulo sidewalk. **Below:** Argentine soccer fans forget their national and personal problems as their team scores a goal. Disillusioned, reaching out for meaning in life, city people represent the greatest need for the gospel in Latin America today.

presbyteries, five missionary outreach centers, 55 TEE centers, plus a residential Bible school and night school. SIM is one of six mission agencies which have worked with IEP, the others being EUSA (U.K.), the German Mission, RBMU, South America Mission, and the Swiss Indian Mission.

Our conversation was interrupted when the general secretary popped in to inform the president that there was an important telephone call for him in the office of a company down the hall. As we left, Ray explained the problems of getting a telephone in Lima.

"The only way is to pay for shares in the telephone company!" Ray joked. "It cost us several thousand dollars to get a line into the SIM office, and even more to get a line into our house. That's just the installation charge; the monthly fee is additional. IEP avoided the huge initial investment by renting someone else's line, but recently the owner took it back for his own use, so now they don't have one in the office!"

As we drove through the city to an appointment at the Lima Evangelical Seminary, Ray explained more about the training need in Peru.

"The need seems limitless," he said. "In Lima alone, to have one evangelical church for every 10,000 population, we'd need 700 pastors. If we had 10 missionaries in Lima, and they each planted one church every year, they still couldn't keep pace with the population growth rate of 3.8 percent. While we still need missionaries as church planters, we must emphasize training leadership so the churches will have more evangelists and church planters to expand their missionary outreach.

"SIM is training leadership through Theological Education by Extension classes. TEE is a great discipling tool. But it's also our most effective evangelism tool, because students go out and witness as they learn more of the Scriptures. Wherever we conduct TEE classes, we see new church growth.

"Another project we're developing is a Christian Communications Center for Lima, in partnership with Radio HCJB. This will prepare church leadership with skills in using communications media. We also have a mobile film ministry. Cinevan of Hope, it's called. It really draws the crowds."

"WE'RE IN A SPIRITUAL WAR"

Ray pointed out that TEE groups help combat the inroads of cults and sects. Mormons are very aggressive, with young missionaries from U.S.A. helping establish impressive temples which attract the middle class. We drove past a block-long complex built by Jehovah's Witnesses. Another sect, The Children of God, was investigated after several parents claimed their children had been kidnapped and forced into immorality.

A new indigenous cult is called The Israelites of the New Pact. They sacrifice bulls and sheep and deny the eternal sacrifice of Christ. Their clothing, worship, and lifestyle (including concubinage and polygamy) are right out of the Old Testament. When police raided one of their temples, they found preteen girls tied up in sexual bondage. On one occasion, the cult leader, like a modern-day Moses, took a group into the jungle to find "The Promised Land." He requires all adherents to sell their goods and relocate in the jungle. At least one IEP congregation has been deceived and destroyed by this cult.

"Unfortunately, anyone who's not a Catholic is classified as evangelical," explained Ray. "That includes cults. When we go to a village and ask if there are any evangelicals, the people sometimes ask, 'Do you want the beer kind or the nonbeer kind?' At least the people can see that much distinction."

When we arrived at the seminary, we found the high iron gates heavily locked--not unusual for any institution in Lima, because of bomb threats. When we got inside, we met the principal, Dr. Hector Piña. One of three evangelical schools in the city (the Assemblies of God and the Christian and Missionary Alliance operate the others), the Lima Evangelical Seminary is interdenominational. It was started in 1933 as a Bible institute by C&MA, the Free Church of Scotland, and EUSA (U.K.). In 1985 it became the first evangelical seminary in Latin America to receive government accreditation. SIM and The Evangelical Alliance Mission (TEAM) now serve on the board as well.

"You can see the kind of city that surrounds us," the principal told me, when I asked about the emphasis of the seminary. "We need to bring the whole Word of God to speak to all of man's needs, not just little bits of it. Some evangelicals are good in their theory, but not in applying it to real needs."

"How do you prepare students to face liberation theology?" I asked.

"Of course we don't teach it, but we help our students understand what it's saying," Dr. Piña replied. "Liberation theology has actually prodded evangelicals to think more deeply about the concerns of the whole man. When our students leave here they have a great advantage, because they understand the relevance of Scripture to life in Latin America, and at the same time they understand what is so wrong with liberation theology. "

At the seminary two German couples had been teaching on behalf of SIM, seconded by their German mission boards. Jurgen and Monica Ehrich were there, and Eckhard and Brigitte Nehmer had moved on to Chile after a number of years at the seminary. Apart from lecturing at the seminary, both had been active in evangelism and church planting among the squatters on the outskirts of Lima.

Lima was the site where the World Council of Churches signed their *Lima Agreement* on Baptism, Eucharist, and Ministry in 1982. Leaning decidedly toward Catholic and Eastern Orthodox teaching on the subjects, the Agreement is based on tradition more than Scripture. The city has also produced a lot of thinking about liberation theology. I tried to meet its best known exponent, Professor Gustavo Gutierrez, at the Catholic University of Lima. Another professor, Father Crespo, told me that Gutierrez rarely came to the university now, for he spends most of his time in writing and travel. Professor Crespo said that many of Gutierrez's students misunderstood his teachings, and that he was not really advocating dialectic Marxism. I asked the priest what he would teach students about sin. He replied that sin is societal, and salvation needs to be societal.

As I walked among the thousands of keen young students on campus, my heart ached for them to know the liberating gospel rather than the false gospel of liberation theology. I had studied enough of it to know that men like Catholic Gustavo Gutierrez and Protestant Emilio Castro had fused Barthian concepts with Marxist ideology to produce a religio-political system. Although Gutierrez has publicly decried violence, many liberation theologians press for violent revolution. God is in favor of this, they argue, because He put His Son to a violent death on the cross. Ray Morris showed me a cartoon circulated by liberation theologians, distorting the story of the Passover to make it say that God told the *Israelites* to rise up and slay the firstborn in every Egyptian household in order to be free from political oppression!

"We need to help IEP pastors understand what liberation theology is really saying and how to answer it scripturally," Ray said. "At the same time, we need to understand the Latin American background to all this. It's difficult for us as foreigners to realize the deeply emotional concerns of Latin American evangelicals. Over the past five hundred years, their countries have suffered political and economic abuse--unfortunately, much of it in the name of a state church. As Scripture says, we need to bear one another's burdens. This is particularly true of us as missionaries in helping to share the heavy burdens of societal concern that press upon our evangelical brothers and sisters."

I thought of the Peruvian evangelical theologian Samuel Escobar, who states: "The theologies of liberation are a challenging debater, but for us they are not a theologically acceptable alternative." However, he stresses the need for evangelicals "to evaluate their role as God's people in the turbulent socio-political environments in which He has placed them."

SIM was doing just that, I was glad to note at the staff prayer meeting that night. The missionaries discussed helping IEP with a family orientation center which assists 130 families in one of the slums not served by a government program or other agencies. They prayed for SIM's rural agricultural and health projects, as well as the theological and church planting ministries being carried on under stressful and sometimes dangerous conditions.

Appropriately, the Scripture reading was taken from Ephesians:

Put on the full armor of God. . . . For our struggle is not against flesh and blood, but . . . against the spiritual forces of evil in the heavenly realms.

"I'm very conscious we're in a spiritual war," Ray told us. "Nowhere else have I felt the oppression which I feel here in Peru. We can be sure that everything we do for the sake of the gospel will be opposed by Satan. We need much prayer!"

Myrtle Morris served refreshing passion fruit juice that evening in their home, as we chatted further. I discovered that Myrtle started out as a school teacher in rural U.S.A. Ray was from an Australian city, Sydney, and as a young man was part of a rescue team on a surfing beach.

"My spiritual battle was over the control of my life," Ray said. "I knew that if I became a Christian, I would have to let God control my life, and I wanted to do it myself. Then an SIM missionary, Bob Jarman, showed me John 1:12: 'to all who believed in his name, he gave the right to become children of God.'"

Ray and Myrtle met and married in Bolivia. Together they have produced seven TEE program books, between treks with Quechua believers up and down the Andean hills. They learned a lot of the local culture, including appropriate mountain greetings. After the normal greetings, the next one is, "Are you going up the hill?" The appropriate reply is, "Yes, I'm going up the hill." On the way down, the greeting will be, "I see you're going down the hill."

"It's just a formality, like our asking, 'How are you?'" Ray explained.

KILLERS IN EDEN

"At the prayer meeting tonight you mentioned about visiting the northern highlands. Tell me more about that," I prodded Ray. "I guess I won't be able to get up there on this visit."

"You'd need at least a week, and perhaps two," Ray replied. "By road, the trip would take several days, and during the rains the roads are impassable. You could get there by air in a little more than an hour, over the Andes. The problem is that there's only one flight in and out a week, and it's booked way ahead of time. Even if you have a confirmed booking, you may not find a seat available. People tell me that drug traffickers take the seats."

On a map, Ray pointed out where he had been in the Amazonas district of Peru, bordering Ecuador, Colombia, and Brazil. SIM assists IEP with projects in two centers: Chachapoyas in the highlands and Mendoza down on the jungle slopes at 6000 feet. The highest mountain in Peru, Huascaran (22,204 feet), keeps watch over the whole area. It was in these highlands that at least 20,000 people died when a major earthquake struck in 1970, causing the greatest ice avalanche disaster ever recorded.

This is also the region in which the ruins of Kuelap, an ancient city twice the size of Machu Picchu, had just been discovered from the air. Some of these sites in northern Peru predate the Incas by a thousand years. A recently discovered tomb has revealed "the most elegant jewelry ever found in the Americas," according to the National Geographic Society.

Kuelap may have been discovered only recently, but the Indians living across the valley had already discovered something more precious than ancient jewelry. They found the gospel, and now there is an IEP church there, witnessing about the living God, the eternal Creator. RBMU missionaries from Britain pioneered the area. IEP asked SIM, as a sister mission of RBMU, to help extend the work.

In this area on the western rim of the Amazon basin, botanists have discovered the world's richest known diversity of tree species. They had thought that southeastern Asian forests held that record, but no more than 200 tree species per hectare have been found there, and only 120 species per hectare in central Africa. The Amazonas region of Peru contains up to 300 species per hectare. There are also killers in that jungle--not only killer piranhas in the rivers, killer jaguars in the forest, killer bees (an African import), and killer spiders, but a killer plant as well. The *matador* is a vine that winds around trees until it suffocates them.

The region is a South American Garden of Eden, with a

record number of species of butterflies, amphibians, reptiles, birds, mammals, and trees. Unfortunately, the people have suffered from isolation. Their diet has been limited chiefly to starchy roots, whereas the fertile soil could produce a widely nutritious diet for them. A Peruvian agriculturalist working with SIM-IEP, Walter Aliaga Lino, has introduced experimental gardens which have aroused a lot of interest among the local people. His gardens can average three to six crops annually, depending on the particular vegetables. Families are beginning to catch on to this and are growing carrots, tomatoes, lettuce, and cabbage. SIM introduced rabbit and guinea pig breeding to provide protein in the diet.

When the conservative villagers resisted the new foods, the local IEP church put on cooking demonstrations and distributed samples at a community fair. The Canadian and Australian governments have helped with funding because of the impact the project is having on the entire community.

As Ray described the agricultural projects, I could readily understand how significant these are, not only in helping the people physically, but also in strengthening the churches' credibility in the community, especially in a country beset by drug trade and guerrilla activity.

AIRPLANE EGGS

New Zealander Heather Simpson had gone into the area with a Peruvian co-worker, Damaris Rivas, to organize TEE studies to strengthen the believers, protect them from the inroads of cults, and motivate them to reach out to others. I was fascinated by Heather's description of the quaint people. They are called Huayachos and may be descended from Scandinavian or German immigrants of the last century. For months at a time, rains isolate them in their mountain redoubts.

Blond-haired and fair-skinned, with blue or green eyes, they have an above-average percentage of dwarfism, deformity, and insanity as a result of intermarrying. The term "Huayachos" has become synonymous with naive, folksy people. "They have a great sense of humor and enjoy telling interesting stories on themselves," Heather said. She told me one of their favorites:

Ortiz was intrigued by airplanes he saw flying overhead. When an airstrip was built nearby, he carefully observed the aircraft that landed. He decided that if he built one to look just the same, he would be able to fly. So he made it out of wood covered with leather and put it on the roof of his hut. When his musical group traveled to another village one day, he told them he would catch up to them in his plane.

"I'll get there before you do!" he boasted. After they left, he got up on the roof, sat in the leather "aircraft," and told his wife to push him off. She refused at first, but he finally persuaded her with threats. He fell to the ground, suffered concussion, and soon died.

The villagers thought Ortiz had a good idea basically and discussed what went wrong. Obviously, a plane made out of leather was not the right way to go about things. By logical deduction, they figured that since airplanes fly like birds, they must also lay eggs, and if the villagers could find one, they would be able to hatch an airplane for themselves.

Off they went to the airport to ask where they could find an airplane's egg. The airline agent helpfully suggested they could unload the next air freight flight that came in, and keep any eggs they found. The Huayachos gladly did this, and the agent enjoyed a rest while they did his work!

Getting back to more serious matters, Heather told me how she and her colleagues helped the women set up a knitting cooperative to help their economy. Speaking of the economy, I learned that Heather had saved enough money to buy a small motorbike, but before she could purchase one, the price doubled.

BLOOD AND GOLD

Although I'd been intrigued by these stories about the northern highlands, everything around me told me that I was still in Lima. This City of Kings had many reminders of its Spanish past, including the oldest bullfight stadium in South America (the best seats sell for $180 per fight). Religious art in the churches was some of the most gory I saw in South America: victims being disemboweled, blood gushing from their eyes, noses, mouths, and ears. The most horrifying exhibits are in the Museum of the Inquisition. The Court of Inquisition tried heretics from 1570 to 1820. The cruel torture of victims, many of them evangelicals refusing to deny their faith, are realistically recreated in wax figures and instruments of torture.

The Gold Museum showed me what lured the Spaniards on to Peru in their quest for El Dorado. The Spaniards came from a society where gold represented purchasing power and wealth. To the Incas and their predecessors, it had no monetary significance but was valued for its religious and esthetic use. The Indians called it "sweat of the sun" and could not understand the Spaniards' greed for their beautiful metal.

I was amazed at what Indian artisans did with it. There were garments, ornaments, vessels for food and drink, ceremonial spears, long gold gloves with movable finger joints, and a death mask--all made of solid gold. Fabric vestments, preserved in the desert dryness, were covered with small gold disks sewn on, along with mother-of-pearl, gemstones, and coral. The privately owned museum contains the world's largest collection of pre-Columbian metals found in South America, and its items have been exhibited in the world's leading museums.

At the Museum of Anthropology and Archaeology, I saw a wider range of Peru's ancient cultures. An obelisk dating from the Chavin Period, around 1000 B.C., depicts a divinity connecting earth, water, and all the living elements of nature. I gazed in awe at beautifully molded ceramics dating a thousand years before Christ. These depicted vegetables, fruits, animals, means of transport, social activities, arts and crafts, various infirmities, instruments, warfare, and religion.

Amazingly, these cultures did not have any form of writing, but their ceramics did leave graphic descriptions of their society. Human fertility must have been much on their minds, from the number of genitals and sex acts graphically displayed. Perhaps most amazing was the evidence of brain surgery performed. I saw skulls that had been operated on, probably to remove tumors. The patients must have survived, modern surgeons believe, because there is evidence of further bone growth after surgery.

"MEET ME AT THE SENATE"

"The senator says he can see you at 9 a.m.," Ray Morris told me. "I'll pick you up at 8:30."

I had asked for an interview with an evangelical senator, Dr. Jose Ferreira Garcia. He welcomed us at the front door of his very ordinary bungalow sandwiched between other ordinary houses in a middle-class neighborhood. Dr. Ferreira was a short, unpretentious man with balding head, graying sideburns, and a handsome moustache that set off his olive-colored skin.

We sat around an antique coffee table covered in hand-tooled black leather. Above us was a crystal chandelier, and on the walls were family photographs. A large photo showed the chancellor of the university awarding the senator an honorary degree.

"I understand you're an authority on Chinese food!" I began, knowing that Dr. Ferreira's grandmother was Chinese and his nickname was El Chino.

The senator threw back his head and laughed. "Next time you come, I'll prepare a Chinese meal for you!" he replied.

Born of a Brazilian father and a Peruvian mother, as a child he lived with his parents, growing rubber in the jungles of Amazonas. When the rubber trade collapsed, the family moved to Iquitos, the farthest inland navigable point for shipping on the Amazon River, and Peru's main trade outlet to the east.

The boy Jose was obviously a self-starter. When he couldn't continue formal education for lack of family finance, he studied by correspondence while working. Moving to Lima at the age of 18, he earned his high school certificate at night and then went on to university to study economics and accounting. He ended up as an accountant for a mining company in the world's highest city, Cerro de Pasco (14,107 feet), where he helped develop the work of IEP. The city eventually elected him mayor, and then, to his surprise, he was elected senator for the region--a post he has held for over 30 years.

"I don't remember the date of my conversion," Senator Jose told us, "but I do know that Jesus Christ is my personal Saviour. I also believe that any position I have held is because God wants me to serve Him to help my country and encourage evangelicals."

The senator was indeed doing that. Bustling around his house were two men he employs full-time just to handle his Christian ministries. He had been busy since 8 o'clock that morning telephoning city officials to get approval for the Christian and Missionary Alliance to conduct a series of evangelistic meetings in Lima's main square. So far he had obtained everyone's agreement but still needed to contact Lima's mayor. Robert Anderson, general director of the South American Mission, had told me how helpful the senator is. Bob had known the senator and his family personally for many years, and it was he who earlier had introduced me to Dr. Ferreira by correspondence.

"Peru is a great country," I said. "Tell me what makes it run."

The senator looked at me with pain in his eyes as he told me about Peru's economic problems. As chairman of the Mining Commission of the Senate, he was especially concerned by the current low prices overseas, since mining accounts for 50 percent of Peru's GNP.

"But our biggest problem is the drug trade," he added. "Drug money comes into the country in U.S. dollars but entirely bypasses the economic system, going into the pockets of profiteers instead of enabling the government to develop the country."

"What's the solution?" I asked, knowing that Peru, Bolivia, and Colombia provide 99 percent of the world's cocaine.

"If there were no market for drugs overseas, we wouldn't have the problem to face here!" he said, slapping his knee.

Before we left the senator's home, he committed us to the Lord in prayer, thanking God for the ministry of Ray Morris and other missionaries.

"Can you meet me at the Senate this evening?" the senator asked as we were parting. "Then you can see how the country runs!" When I later arrived outside the Senate, an aide of Senator Ferreira was waiting for me with a signed security form which got me past several armed checkpoints, all on the alert for terrorists. Once safely inside, I had toast and coffee with the senator in a carpeted lounge with oil portraits of dignified senators gazing down at us. Secretaries and aides flitted busily back and forth, carrying dossiers.

When the Assembly call bells started to ring, the senator and his secretary escorted me to the diplomatic gallery. As we passed along the corridors, people bowed or curtsied to Dr. Ferreira, who seemed embarrassed by the attention. "Senator Ferriera is very important to us," his secretary explained. "He is so human; he considers us and helps us!"

The Senate chamber, dating from 1860, was four storeys high, with colored glass in the vaulted atrium and ornate friezes covering ivory-colored walls. As I entered, the senator responsible for the interior had just wound up a long speech. Two other senators jumped up and started to shout and rave, pounding their desks. The president of the Senate tried to shut them up, while TV cameramen roamed at will to film the action. Senator Ferreria's secretary whispered that they were Communist members of the Senate.

Voting was carried out in the traditional manner of slamming one's open hand on the desk top. Both yea and nay votes were indicated in the same way, and if there was any question as to which had "the upper hand," each person stood up to register his or her vote.

I learned that the government annually deals with 12,000 legal documents and passes 120 new laws each year, while annulling others. Peru seems obsessed with legal jurisdiction rather than personal moral conscience. Legalism tends to affect churches as well, and legalistic religions such as Seventh Day Adventists have wide followings.

I left the Senate thankful for the unusual opportunity Dr. Ferreira had given me to see something of the nation's highest level of government. And I thanked God that the power of the gospel was being demonstrated in the life of a humble believer at that level.

NETWORKING IN THE CITY

In Lima I was glad to see much networking between evangelical missions and churches. SAM and RBMU both provided SIM with visas from their own quotas when SIM had no available visas for additional missionaries arriving. While I was in Lima, RBMU missionaries met with Ray Morris and me to discuss TEE ministries.

Christian and Missionary Alliance has an unusual church planting project in Lima. To make an impact on educated and professional classes, the Alliance invests in a property on a main street, erecting a building which will attract the attention of residents. Two weeks of evangelistic meetings are followed by two weeks of discipleship, and so through the year the church is built up. The newly formed church pays back 20 percent of the cost of the building into a national church building fund, plus giving to missions. The main C&MA church in Lima has a membership of over one thousand and gives nearly 50 percent of its income to support other work.

Although such policies are not followed everywhere by C&MA, and certainly are foreign to many other evangelical groups, the particular circumstances of Lima made this an effective strategy for urban evangelization. It was made possible through the generosity of American businessman R. G. LeTourneau. When he couldn't get his business profits out of Peru, he plowed them back into missionary work under a trust fund.

"People used to think that missionary work was riding a donkey in the mountains, and that the big cities were unreachable," Eugene Kelley, coordinator for C&MA's urban church planting, told me. "Now they see we can fill a tremendous spiritual vacuum in the cities, and that braving the traffic of downtown Lima is just as valid a missionary environment as the jungles!"

I visited another effective gospel ministry in Lima: Radio del Pacifico, started by TEAM but now an independent ministry supported through local contributions and income from paid advertisements.

"We recognize that missionaries gave us the Word of God," Petronio Allauca, counselor for the station, told me. "But they didn't teach us to give. They didn't think in terms of turning things over to us. This may be a problem not only in Peru but throughout Latin America. In the meantime, the national church has grown, the country has changed, and we have to learn to take responsibility. Sometimes our learning causes reaction among missionaries from overseas because they don't understand we have to grow on our own."

Petronio told me that his staff members have personally felt the effect of the Shining Path. One day a band of terrorists burst through the door, herded all the staff into a tiny washroom, and locked them in, along with a bomb. While some of the terrorists shouted threats to the staff, others broadcast revolutionary announcements over the air. After the terrorists left, a staff member was able to crawl out the washroom window and call the police, who came and defused the bomb.

As I left the radio station, Easter hymns were playing over the studio loudspeakers, reminding me that this was Peru's Holy Week. People told me that in the next few days I'd see Easter celebrated in a way I'd never forget.

The sun of righteousness will rise with healing in its wings.
MALACHAI 4:2

18

DEATH

AND

RESURRECTION

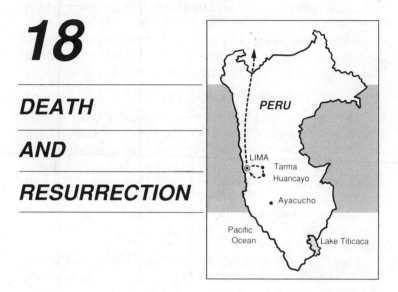

PERU

LIMA
Tarma
Huancayo

• Ayacucho

Pacific
Ocean

Lake Titicaca

Terrorists have blown up the main bridge on the road to Tarma," Ray announced, "but we've talked with a traveler who got through over a mountain mining trail. Are you game to try it?"

Ray had told me about the Easter Festival at Tarma, a little mining town at 10,000 feet, founded just 13 years after Pizarro first stepped on Peruvian soil. Tarma's distinction is a quaint Holy Week Festival in which villagers create carpets of colorful flower petals in the main plaza. SIMers Phil and Sue Manley, in Lima for vehicle repairs, offered to take me via Tarma on their way back to their home in Huancayo.

"I'm game!" I replied. Early the next morning I set off with the Manleys in their Toyota Landcruiser. Outside Lima we passed fields of lima beans and bright orange marigolds, which are grown as chicken feed additive. People were washing their clothes and themselves in an irrigation ditch that also supplies the drinking water for a satellite town of 100,000 people. Many of them worked in a nearby Volvo bus assembly plant.

"GOD IS SO BEAUTIFUL"

The trip gave me a chance to get to know the Manleys, a Kiwi couple, as New Zealanders call themselves. Phil and Sue were opposites in many ways--he from a protected Christian background, and she from a broken home. Their very different natures complemented each other, and they obviously loved each other and God. Traveling with them was a refreshing experience because they were not traditional in their outlook, but very frank, direct, and simple. Perhaps "uncomplicated" is the word.

Phil, from Auckland in New Zealand's North Island, took his Christian faith for granted as he grew up. Then he met Sue, who hailed from the birthplace of Bolivian Indian Mission's founder, George Allan, in the South Island. When Sue was converted, the radical change in her life convinced Phil that Christ would have died for him personally even if he'd been the only person in the world.

Sue can now talk about her childhood: the terror of rejection and physical abuse. But one of her sisters still can hardly speak because of her childhood trauma. Sue's mother died when she was three. Her stepmother was schizophrenic, and when that marriage ended in divorce, the family broke up. Sue was 14 when her father married the third time. By then she was numb with mistrust of all adults.

"At the age of 17 I emerged into the world, feeling as though I had lived a hundred years," Sue said, gazing out the car window. "When I finally came to know God, I was amazed that He desired me in every sense of the word. I still am amazed at the gentleness of His touch as He remolds my mind. He is so utterly beautiful!"

"You're an unlikely type to become a missionary!" I commented. "How did that happen?"

"About a month after my conversion," Sue recounted, "I stood gazing at the dusty, yellowed photographs of a bunch of missionaries and seemed to hear God say, 'You're going to be one of those things.'"

"Are you kidding?" Sue remembers asking God.

"Nope," Sue says God answered.

"But what are they?"

"You'll find out."

"It reminds me of the way Hudson Taylor put it," Sue added. "He said, 'God has His own universities and way of training men and women. There is a school of sorrow, a school of trial and persecution, and men who have not graduated in that school do not prove very good helpers for the churches.'

"After studying at God's universities, I am now one of those 'things'--probably getting dusty and yellowed and out of date!

"I really have to laugh when I hear people say they can't do something because it's too difficult," Sue continued, her green eyes dancing in her freckled face. "I say to them, 'Of course you can. Do it by God's grace!' When folk tell me they don't know how to be Christian parents because their parents weren't believers, I tell them, 'Mine weren't either. God can help you to be the parents you should be.'"

The Manleys told me their marriage had early tensions, because Phil had pat answers from the Bible, and Sue had pat answers from experience. They had to struggle in prayer and Bible study before they understood each other and understood God's working.

"The experiences we had before coming here were God's preparation for missionary service," Phil and Sue said as the Landcruiser left the coastal plain and started climbing into the hills. "For instance, we saw God turn around the life of our teenaged adopted son, who was into crime and drugs. Today he and his wife are helping troubled teenagers find the Lord."

We climbed a corkscrew road up the mountains for an hour, until we finally reached a pass at 15,889 feet. A postcard panorama lay before us, with a glacier saddled between snow-capped peaks.

At a mining town, a truck driver told us that nothing was coming through from Tarma. We squeezed past a bulldozer the government had sent to improve a mining trail that struck out across the mountain ridges, bypassing the bombed bridge. Other vehicles were attempting this route. Heavy trucks lumbering over the trail in both directions had difficulty negotiating the hairpin turns. In some places, they found themselves nose-to-nose, and at times one had to reverse to let the other pass. Enterprising boys pretended to fill in boggy spots, where mountain springs crossed the trail. They demanded payment for enabling vehicles to pass. Most drivers shouted at them to get lost.

"Oh, no! We're in trouble!" Phil exclaimed as we rounded a hairpin turn at the crest of a hill. On the trail below us, 30 vehicles were lined up behind a long truck wedged in the cliffside at a sharp switchback. The trail was completely blocked. The line of vehicles grew on both sides while men worked to clear the blockage. It was cold at 16,500 feet, so I slipped my wool sweater on.

UNHOLY WEEK

"In Peru, this week is called Holy Week, not Easter," Phil explained as we waited. "Some Catholics believe that if they eat red meat during this week they'll be guilty of partaking of the body of Christ. Tomorrow's Good Friday, and many will go into the hills and pick herbs. They'll take them down to the river and bathe with them for purification. There is a Mass held every morning during the week, as people prepare for the fiesta at the end of the week. Sunday night they will drink seven types of soup to purify themselves internally.

"Last Sunday people took home palms blessed at church and placed them in their houses to bring good fortune. During the week they'll carry images of Jesus and Mary through the streets. Mary will wear a black veil. Most Catholics here believe that Jesus is literally dead on Good Friday, so they feel they have license to rob and drink and be immoral. Then when Jesus arises on Sunday, they can celebrate with more drinking and immorality. They believe that the priest can forgive all this when they go to confession."

At last the lineup of vehicles started to crawl ahead again, and we entered Tarma after dark. A banner across the main street announced: "Welcome to Tarma. Coca Cola and Sprite are here during Holy Week."

A kindly man came up and warned us to be extremely careful of pickpockets, indicating how we should hold our camera bags under our arms. A novel trick used by pickpockets is to "accidentally" smear mustard or manure on a tourist's clothes when passing in a crowd. While the tourist tries to wipe it off, the pickpocket helps himself to wallet, purse, or camera.

A Good Friday Eve Mass was in progress in the cathedral in the town square. Armed soldiers stood on the alert outside the doors and searched our bags before allowing us to enter the cathedral. Worshipers purchased incense candles, placing them to burn before paintings, Madonnas, crucifixes, or images of saints. A youth choir sang a modern chorus: "A new commandment have we been given, that we love one another." People went forward in groups, to kneel at the altar as the priest placed wafers in their mouths and held the communion cup to their lips.

"They believe the priest has miraculously changed the wafer and wine," Phil whispered, "so they think they're actually eating part of Christ's body and drinking some of His blood."

After the Mass, the people poured out of the church to form a procession behind a figure of Jesus, dead on a cross. The men carrying the image chanted and swayed slowly back and forth as they proceeded around the square. Lilies and lighted candles surrounded the crucifix. The procession was led by the priest and altar boys, while a brass band played mournfully. Bringing up the rear was another group carrying a queenly statue of Mary, also surrounded by candles.

The people lined the square very reverently as the procession made seven stops, in keeping with the seven Stations of the Cross. The priest made a brief oration at each stop. Behind the worshipers lining the square, others who had come to Tarma for the fiesta were milling around buying food and articles stacked along the sidewalks. On a hill behind the town, a line of lanterns twinkled in the night as pilgrims ascended to worship at a shrine.

We wanted to reach the Manleys' house in Huancayo that night. Fortunately, we now were back on the main highway. As we sped through the darkness, Phil and Sue told me about their work. They and an Australian couple, Phill and Diane Marshall, were SIM's missionaries at Huancayo, which is a center for about twenty TEE groups in the surrounding countryside. The Searles, with whom I had traveled the previous week, had started that program before moving to Arequipa.

"We have an excellent Peruvian staff," Sue said. "Gloria Chavez started studying TEE in 1978, and now she looks after the office in the mornings and studies at a university in the afternoon. Then two other staff members, Moises and Eloy, itinerate among the TEE groups. They help train lay leaders who mobilize the believers to witness. It's exciting to see the results! In just seven years, the number of churches in one district multiplied from ten to over one hundred.

"The last time I was up here I drove through a blizzard!" I said. "But the scene that really sticks in my memory is a visit Ray Morris and I had with a pastor and his family who had just come in from the lowlands. They really looked dejected. They had been forced to flee their church in the jungle because of hostility from the coca growers. I remember Ray having prayer with them to encourage them. How about the drug trade now?"

"It's worse!" Sue replied. "Peru and Bolivia are at the top of the list of coca producers. Planes pick it up from hidden airstrips in the jungle and take it to Colombia. Traffickers try to pressure even Christians into growing the stuff; some who refuse have had to move out of the area. People in town disappear and nobody dares say anything. In one week we had two hotels and a theater blown up, a couple of houses damaged, and, of course, the usual dynamiting of power line pylons and transformers, leaving us in the dark. Sometimes at night we hear gunfire. But God gives us peace. We know He is in control of our lives."

I remembered Heather Simpson, who had moved to Peru's north, earlier telling me how God had protected her when she worked in Huancayo. She was fairly naive when she first arrived, and was upset to find that no one trusted anyone else, whether Christian or not. As a missionary, Heather wanted to trust people and develop friendships, but she had to learn to be on her guard while showing the people Christ's love. Her close Peruvian friends explained that her visitors might easily be sizing up what was in her house, and how the doors and windows were locked. They told her not to wear glasses, costume jewelry, or wristwatch when she went out on the streets.

Once Heather took a visiting friend, Joan, to a TEE seminar in a quiet village where guerrilla activity had been unknown. At night Heather and Joan crawled into their sleeping bags in a shepherd's hut, with the doors carefully barred. Suddenly they were startled awake to find four men attacking them. One had a knife. Heather prayed aloud in Spanish, and the four men ran off into the darkness, scooping up the girls' clothes as they fled. Heather and Joan didn't know what caused the men to leave in such a hurry, but they spent the rest of the night praising the Lord for protecting them.

At sunrise they ventured out and told the believers, who were shocked at what had happened in their "safe" village. Joan was worried about her passport, which she had left in her jacket. After three days of ministering, the two women walked out to the main highway with other believers, to take a bus back to Huancayo. A truck loaded with people passed them. Someone tossed an object out of the truck into the grass--it turned out to be Joan's passport! That was another answer to prayer and cause for thanksgiving.

"Did that experience make you nervous about staying in the villages?" I asked.

"No, I'm thankful to say," Heather replied. "The same kind of thing can happen back home in my own country, whether to singles or couples, men or women. But the incident did make me and the believers more careful. Now Christian women always sleep in the same building with us."

Heather told me she had to unlearn the suspicious, aggressive Huancayo attitudes when she later moved to work among the gentle and naive Huayachos of Mendoza (chapter 17).

SHINING PATH TERROR

We arrived at the Manleys' house in Huancayo well after midnight. It took us about five minutes to open all the bolts and bars on the wooden garage doors and roll up the metal security door inside it.

"As you can see, we don't take any chances!" Phil explained. "Recently a neighbor lost everything, including his car, when robbers simply put a chain around the handle of his garage door, hooked up the other end to their pickup truck, and backed off, taking the entire door with them."

We all had to get some sleep, but in the morning I asked Phil to tell me how the churches were coping with the terrorist problem. I knew that the Shining Path movement *(Sendero Luminoso)* had been started by university students from Ayacucho, further down the main road. The name came from a prophecy of the Peruvian Communist, Mariategui: "Marxism-Leninism will open the shining path to revolution." My travel guidebook warned: "The activities of the Maoist guerrilla movement, *Sendero Luminoso,* are spreading. Avoid visiting places where they are reported as particularly active. They have no love for foreign tourists. Since it has been linked (supposedly) with the drug trade, police and army searches have increased."

That increased security caused the authorities in two provinces to ban ponchos and overcoats in spite of the cold, in case they concealed bombs.

"Churches are pressured from both sides," Phil explained. "Local government officials told pastors of one denomination that they mustn't preach from a certain passage of Scripture, and the guerrillas told them they must not take up a church offering, which the terrorists look upon as a capitalist idea. The leaders were courageous and told the government officials they would continue preaching from all the Scriptures, and they told the guerrillas that the people willingly give their offerings to help others.

In some of the more active areas, I learned, armed terrorists enter churches to threaten worshipers. They tell pastors they'll be back in a month to check up on what they are preaching. They threaten Christian schoolteachers who don't teach Communist doctrine. In the Ayacucho area nearby, terrorists murdered six Pentecostal Christians. In one village, soldiers ordered Presbyterian worshipers to sing hymns loudly, while they took six men outside and shot them.

Peru's National Council of Evangelicals (CONEP) has a relief program for members affected by terrorism, and has issued a call for prayer worldwide. CONEP's human rights office listed 12 pastors and 74 laypeople assassinated in a three-year period, from a cross section of member churches, including IEP.

Although the Shining Path movement developed momentum in 1980, it actually dates back to the 1960s, when Abimael Guzman, a philosophy professor, founded a Maoist party in Peru. His small band of disciples at the university in Ayacucho praised Guzman for going further than Marx, Lenin, and Mao, who, they believed, had compromised revolutionary ideals. When the highland Indians did not readily accept the revolutionary teaching of the intellectuals, the Shining Path turned on them, killing those who would not cooperate. An estimated 10,000 people died in the first seven years of the movement's existence.

Facing increased security forces in the mountains, the Shining Path took to bombing cities in order to disrupt the profitable tourist trade and intimidate the people. Lima experienced 40 bomb blasts in one 10-day period. Typical of terrorist ruthlessness was the action of three gunmen who entered a hospital in Lima, disguised as doctors. They killed three police guarding captured terrorists who were receiving treatment.

Ayacucho was proving true to its name: "Corner of the Dead." A number of families had each lost at least one member to terrorists, and had moved into Huancayo. One Catholic family moved after their cattle's throats were slit and their son's house bombed. Missionaries in Huancayo were careful not to further endanger the lives of believers in Ayacucho, since a pastor and his family were shot after a missionary (not from SIM or IEP) had gone to encourage them.

The Shining Path, known as "the most vicious terrorist group in the world," follows the Maoist formula of creating anarchy. This has produced paranoia in many communities. A Christian student in Huancayo told us she had seen pinned on the university bulletin board a list of the next people to be eliminated. In Huancayo, when the terrorists blow up a power transformer at night and the lights go off, a hammer and sickle usually appear on the dark hillside, formed by lanterns of Shining Path members.

The movement uses a subtle maneuver to infiltrate the churches. They offer scholarships to men and women to study at seminaries, mainly outside the country, where liberation theology is taught. The Manleys know a Presbyterian minister's wife who left Shining Path when she was converted, but unsuspectingly accepted one of the scholarships. When she returned to Peru, she rejoined the terrorist movement.

(SIM eventually had to withdraw its missionaries from Huancayo temporarily, not only for their own safety but also to avoid endangering Peruvian believers by being seen with them.)

HIGHEST STANDARD-GAUGE RAIL

"You're going back to Lima by train with Dr. Phill Marshall," the Manleys said. We climbed on board the passenger train that travels the highest standard-gauge tracks in the world. When we started out, the stream beside the tracks was flowing eastward toward the Amazon, in the opposite direction to our travel, for we had not yet reached the top of the pass. When we did, at 15,681 feet, water started flowing westward, down to the Pacific. There are 65 tunnels on the twisting line between Huancayo and Lima, keeping the train driver blasting on his diesel horn most of the way, to warn people and animals to get off the tracks.

"My wife is amazed that God should send us to such a beautiful place!" Phill exclaimed as the train traversed a fertile valley. Phill Marshall studied medicine in Sydney, Australia, and Bible in New Zealand, before contacting SIM about possibilities for missionary service. His wife, Diane, is a nurse. The couple ended up in Huancayo, where they developed a ministry coordinating health projects with Theological Education by Extension methods.

"We can't impose new ideas on the people, even if they're for the betterment of their health," Phill commented. "We have to bring about a change within the people, so they'll be motivated to take care of their health. I see the spiritual results of TEE Bible studies being very central to changes in attitude."

Phill's voice was drowned out as we rattled over a new bridge which replaced one blown up by guerrillas a few months before. The twisted girders of the old bridge were still lying beside the tracks. In the last couple of days, terrorists had twice attempted to blow up another newly replaced bridge just outside Huancayo. On our train, armed guards kept constant watch, especially at stations where we stopped.

"It's a pity to see that the concept of the Good Samaritan is foreign to many people in Peru," Dr. Phill told us as the train rumbled on. "I think that's because people have to be so suspicious of strangers. I remember a group of Christian New Zealanders who came to Lima to demonstrate their faith. They tried to help elderly people cross busy streets, or shop for them, or clean up their shanties. They had to quit because everyone suspected they were really trying to molest and rob the elderly.

"The same thing applies to helping someone who is injured. People don't stop to take them to the police, because the police would charge them with having caused the injury. I remember the last time Phil Manley drove to Lima. He came upon a taxi driver whose car was totaled by two trucks coming around a curve. The taxi driver was amazed that Phil stopped and took his six injured passengers to the hospital. No one else stopped to help."

The train lurched to a stop at 5000 feet altitude, where there was no space for a hairpin curve to be built. Instead, the trainmen disconnected the engine, which moved on to a large turntable. Four men pushed the turntable so that the engine rotated; it bypassed our passenger cars on a siding, hooked up to the rear of the train, and pulled us backwards the rest of the way down the mountainside into Lima.

GOOD FRIDAY ON THE PLAZA

It was the afternoon of Good Friday, so as soon as our train pulled into Lima, we hastened to the main square to catch a glimpse of one of the major events of the year: parading an image of the body of Jesus on an open coffin through the streets. The Plaza de Armas is considered one of the finest public squares on the continent, ringed by the impressive Cathedral of Lima, the Archbishop's Palace with its ornately-carved mahogany balconies, the City Hall, and the glistening white Government Palace.

It was in this square that many Protestants were put to death for their faith during the Inquisition. Now the plaza swarmed with the citizens of Lima plus thousands of visitors. A Good Friday Mass was in progress in the cathedral, which bears the coats of arms of Lima and of Pizarro, whose mummy lies in a crypt.

We noticed a movement of people outside and hurried over in time to see pallbearers leaving the side door of the cathedral with an effigy of Christ on a bier. The figure was life-size, with a wig of human hair and only a loincloth. Red paint graphically marked the spike holes in the hands, the spear wound in the side, and the bleeding scars from whip lacerations.

People gazed down from their balconies as the pallbearers moved slowly along a side street. Some threw rose petals on the body. A little boy ran out to pick up some of the fallen petals, which to him and his family would be holy. An elderly woman, tears streaming down her cheeks, lovingly traced over the limbs of the body with a palm leaf cross, then hugged the palm cross to her heart and wept some more. Tears came to my own eyes as I saw her devotion and realized her spiritual emptiness.

Floodlights switched on around the square as darkness fell. Cameras around our necks, we hastened back to the plaza to photograph the final ceremony. The crowd was thickest in front of the Government Palace, and we despaired of getting close enough. However, the people were obviously accustomed to having foreign photographers attend these processions, for they opened a path and pushed us through to the very front. We found ourselves standing with reporters in a cleared spot almost under the balcony of the Government Palace. Armed soldiers and police with vicious-looking guard dogs held back the surging crowds. I was surprised that they did not check our camera bags or frisk us, when we were standing so close to the center of action.

The broad sidewalk in front of the palace was covered with flower petals in the form of a cross. City and national dignitaries took up their places in the middle of the road to welcome the parade, which we heard approaching down a side street. First came the bishop's ecclesiastical guardsmen, feathery plumes on their medieval helmets. Then the doors on the floodlit palace balcony swung open, and President Garcia, his wife, and the bishop came out and stood at attention.

A hush fell over the crowd as a woman bearing a brazier of burning incense appeared, followed by the pallbearers carrying the effigy of the dead Jesus. It was the same figure I had seen before, but now reclining in a glass-sided casket. On each corner of the casket a golden angel folded its wings. Two dozen black-robed pallbearers swayed mournfully back and forth. When they arrived in front of the palace, they lowered the coffin onto a gold-painted stand on the carpet of flower petals.

The president, a handsome, dark-haired man, and his petite blonde wife knelt in prayer on the balcony, facing the coffin. I remembered Samuel Escobar telling me that he and the president's mother had attended the same evangelical high school. Whatever the president's personal beliefs, he was fulfilling his expected role in this ceremony of national importance. The band took its place behind the casket, and a trumpeter played the "Last Post" while the group on the balcony stood to their feet.

Suddenly, an electrifying wave seemed to go through the crowd as a life-sized figure of the Virgin Mary arrived in the procession. In contrast to the pathetic figure in the casket, the radiant Madonna fulfilled the Catholic concept of The Queen of Heaven. Her image seemed alive and triumphant as it was placed on another gold-covered stand on the carpet of petals. Two sergeants, one black and one white, stepped forward to place bouquets before her image, and once again the president, his wife, and the bishop knelt on the balcony, bowing to the Madonna. The image bent forward twice, as if acknowledging their homage.

There must have been a million people in the plaza and its side streets. I turned around and looked at the sea of faces behind me--intent, solemn, seeking salvation through a distorted gospel. As I compared the lifeless form of Jesus with the vibrant figure of Mary, I suddenly saw the procession in an Indian context: The son of the sun, the Inca, was dead. But the earth mother was triumphantly alive! Holy Week was a contemporary way of "tying down the sun"--of controlling mysterious forces.

"I BEHELD HIS GLORY"--IN A SLUM

Far away from the pomp, the ceremony, the tragic delusion in the plaza, I dropped in on a humble family the next day. Arnoldo Merga had come down from the hills about twenty years before, to live in a bamboo shanty on the outskirts of Lima. Before he was saved through the witness of an aunt, he drank a lot and chewed coca leaves. The living Christ changed him and then changed his parents as they, too, became believers.

Arnoldo is now a secondary schoolteacher, but his wages are only half enough to support his wife and three children. So he sells books on the street, and his wife does sewing for other people. They both embraced me and thanked me for coming from so far away to see them. They invited me to attend a service in their church that night. Because of the gross misconception of Easter in the minds of most people, IEP churches do not make a big thing of it. Instead, they preach on the last statements of Christ, one for each evening of the week, as an evangelistic series to take the place of the traditional Catholic Stations of the Cross.

"The Bible doesn't tell us to celebrate Easter," Arnoldo explained. "But we are commanded to remember Jesus' death and resurrection. So that's what we do."

When we arrived at the church in a dusty lane, I found it was a simple room about 40 x 30 feet in size, with a rough cement floor and whitewashed walls. On a side wall was printed Philippians 4:19: "My God will meet all your needs according to his glorious riches in Christ Jesus." On the bulletin board was a copy of the Spanish edition of the poster, "Reaching the World for Christ."

I sat on one of the low benches, a dead oversized cockroach lying between my feet. A woman led the 40 worshipers in singing, accompanied by Arnoldo on his piano accordian. Then we watched a Spanish edition of the film, *I Beheld His Glory,* projected on a sheet suspended at the front of the room. Women wiped tears from their eyes as they watched Mary at the tomb. The armor on the Roman soldiers reminded me of medieval Spanish armor I'd seen in one of Lima's museums. The clothing seemed in keeping with Quechua ponchos. The round loaf that Jesus broke and passed to the disciples could have come from a local bakery.

The Jesus we saw portrayed was so different from the hopeless scene of Friday night! After the film, Arnoldo again explained that Jesus is the living Saviour.

When the people heard I'd be leaving the next day, they embraced me and kissed me on the cheek. "Greet all the believers in your country!" they said, making me feel like a visiting apostle.

There were no gold-plated crosses; there was no incense burning, no band playing, no procession chanting. Instead, the Spirit of the risen Christ was alive in the hearts of these humble believers. I beheld His glory, not in the cathedral, but in a dusty slum.

Outside, the air hung heavy like a pall. Skinny dogs barked a chorus. Young people hung around the rubble-strewn streets.

In the darkness, Lima was still there. Lima needed to know that Jesus Christ, the Saviour, lives. Such a vast task lay before the disciples of the risen Saviour! But it was not an impossible task. The Scripture echoed in my mind:

Jesus came to them and said, 'All authority in heaven and on earth has been given to me. Therefore go and make disciples of all nations...and I will be with you always, to the very end of the age'

Even in seething Lima.

In my travels through South America, I kept running into Marxist and Maoist concepts. I wondered how much Latin America's first Communist state, Cuba, had influenced other countries. What lessons could the churches in Cuba teach my own country? I would soon find out.

Why do the nations rage and the peoples plot in vain? . . .
Kiss the Son, lest he be angry.

PSALM 2:1,12

19

THE

CARIBBEAN

CAULDRON

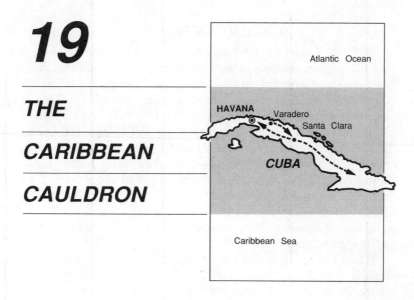

Atlantic Ocean

HAVANA

Varadero

Santa Clara

CUBA

Caribbean Sea

From 30,000 feet, the basin of liquid turquoise looked deceptively peaceful. I was flying over the Caribbean Sea on my way to Cuba. Tucked in with my passport was a cable: WE INVITE YOU TO BE WITH US IN OUR NATIONAL CONVENTION AND PASTORAL SEMINAR. With it was a backup letter from the New Pines Evangelical Convention of Cuba, which had invited me.

I prayed that in God's goodness those two documents would help me get a visitor's visa upon landing, for months of hassle with Cuban consuls had failed to produce a visa that would permit me to preach at the convention. Finally a consular secretary said I could go in as a tourist and pick up a visitor's visa upon arrival. That still wouldn't let me preach. So I had to leave for Cuba in faith that God would provide the permit to minister.

ANCIENT EMPIRES

Now the Caribbean stretched below me, changing tones of blue like a jewel rotating in the sun, from azure to aquamarine, from cobalt to sapphire to turquoise. The jewel was set with bits of coral reef, golden sandbars, and green islands.

I wondered what went through the mind of Christopher Columbus in 1492 when he entered the Caribbean. He first encountered the peaceful Arawak people, who eventually were wiped out. It was the ferocious Carib tribe after whom the Caribbean area was named. The Spanish called them *caribal,* from which our English word "cannibal" evolved. The continental name, America, was derived from the first name of an Italian sailor, Amerigo Vespucci, whose account of the exploration was published in Europe.

Thinking he'd reached Asia, Columbus called the swarthy-skinned people "Indians." He'd really happened on people whose ancestors had found their way from Asia across the Bering Strait in the Arctic, and perhaps from Polynesia in the Pacific. Certainly the monolithic figures guarding their stone temples identified them with cultural roots found all around the Pacific rim, from Japan to New Zealand, from Hawaii to Peru.

Long before European explorers discovered this New World, sophisticated empires rose and fell. The Maya of Central America flourished for over three millennia, collapsing nine hundred years after Christ's birth. They used the zero long before Europeans borrowed it from Asia. They accurately predicted each equinox and solstice and eclipse of the sun. Their astronomers calculated the solar year at 365.2420 days. (Today's reckoning, using the latest space technology, is 365.2422 days!) Their cities rivaled any found in Europe. Yet they did not use the concept of the wheel.

They played tournaments with hard rubber balls and often sacrificed the losers to the gods at the top of their pyramid temples of the sun. Why the Mayan and subsequent empires collapsed is still a puzzle. Did barbarians sack their cities, as the Vandals sacked Rome? Did the miserable masses overthrow their oppressive oligarchy? Amazingly, many of their well-planned cities and fortifications were suddenly abandoned and forgotten, it seems. Whatever the reason, when the Spanish conquistadors arrived in the early 1500s, they quickly overcame the remnants of once proud empires. Slaughter in the name of religion, however, was not an unfamiliar pattern to the aborigines of the Caribbean and Central America. At the dedication of an Aztec temple just five years before Columbus arrived in the area, 80,000 captives were sacrificed by Indian priests. Apart from the Spaniards' carnage of conquest, they brought death to many more through imported European diseases: smallpox, measles, whooping cough, and syphilis.

The Spanish invasion turned Central America's face away from the Pacific to the Atlantic, introducing the Spanish language, culture, and Catholic religion. African slaves, brought over to work on plantations, added to the Caribbean melting pot. Shem, Ham, and Japheth joined together in a new racial mix, and their gods formed a religious brew of Asian-rooted shamanism, European monotheism, and African fetishism.

At one time Spain controlled not only the Caribbean and Central and South America, but also Florida and most of the west coast of North America. The Caribbean was Spain's hub for the Americas, a staging point for officials passing to other countries. For political and monetary reasons, Madrid insisted that all cargo pass through the Caribbean. For instance, shipments from Europe to Buenos Aires, Argentina's Atlantic port, first had to pass through Panama on muleback, then by ship to Peru or Chile on the Pacific coast, and finally by mule over the Andes eastward to Buenos Aires.

Rumors of spectacular wealth also brought to the Caribbean British, Dutch, and French buccaneers, so called because of the smoke-dried boar's meat *(bucan)* they lived on.

Now my own voyage of discovery was taking me into the

middle of a melting pot of twenty or so nations, ranging in population from St. Kitts' 40,000 to Mexico's 83.5 million. To the north was U.S.A. To the south were Colombia, French Guiana, Guyana, Suriname, and Venezuela. In the west was the Mesoamerican isthmus, and forming the eastern edge was a 2000-mile-long string of islands. The Caribbean's 25 island groupings include 33 million people: 20 million Spanish, seven million French, six million English and Dutch.

Many Caribbean and Central American nations are crippled by national debt, suffocated by poverty, fractured by politics, terrorized by guerrillas, dominated by drug lords, and on top of all that, pressured by West-East rivalries. In one Venezuelan official's opinion, "The Caribbean states are not the Third World. They are the Fourth World."

I was heading right into the center of that seething cauldron--or was Cuba the eye of the storm? I had been in a number of Communist countries in other parts of the world, but I found myself a little apprehensive about landing in Cuba.

THE REVOLUTION

I'd read about the takeover of Cuba by Marxist Fidel Castro and his small band of guerrillas--at one time reduced to only 12--on January 1, 1959. They found popular support throughout the island because of the corruption and brutality of the previous dictator, Fulgencio Batista. At the time, even evangelical pastors thought Castro was God's answer to the discrimination against them by a pro-Catholic government. Evangelicals were chiefly from the poor class, and they agreed with Castro's statements on behalf of the poor. Besides, Castro's group did not initially reveal the atheistic, anti-Christian side of Marxism. Cubans in general were never deeply religious, anyway.

But after Batista fled and Castro triumphantly entered the capital, Havana, things changed radically. Marxist ideologues confiscated landowners' property--including that of Castro's father--forced farmers into collective farms, and nationalized all private business, even housing. The Party indoctrinated the people through compulsory classes, and whipped up sentiment against capitalists, especially Americans. That was not difficult because of the monopoly U.S. companies had over the sugar and banana plantations that were basic to the island's economy, although there had been a lot of good will toward U.S.A. In fact, American journalists had helped to popularize Castro's campaign.

After Spanish Catholic priests and Jehovah's Witnesses openly opposed the new regime, many religious leaders--some evangelical pastors included--were rounded up as enemies of the revolution and herded into forced labor camps under the most primitive living conditions. (Strong public opinion outside Cuba brought their release within a couple of years.) Dissidents were jailed or shot. Some 700,000 Cubans, about one-tenth of the population, fled the country.

That was 30 years ago. What would I find now? I was unprepared for the surprises of the next couple of weeks.

My traveling companion to Cuba was the Canada Director of Worldteam (formerly West Indies Mission), Albert Ehmann. This was Al's first visit to Cuba also. We landed at the nation's tourist resort town, Varadero. The government had converted the seaside mansions of wealthy American business tycoons into tourist hotels. (U.S.A. had severed all relations and discouraged Americans from visiting Cuba. The penalty was $50,000 fine or one year in jail if the visit was unauthorized.) However, Canada maintained diplomatic ties, and each year 45,000 Canadians joined tourists of other nationalities to fly into Varadero to escape northern winters and bask on sparkling beaches. Low tour fees included fares, meals, and accommodation, and Cuba happily picked up the tourists' foreign exchange, insisting on U.S. dollars. Most tourists returned north with plenty of exposure to the sun but practically none to the people of Cuba, for they didn't get beyond the tourism boundaries. We had other goals for our visit.

After we landed, immigration did stamp a visitor's visa in our passports. Then we stood in line for customs inspection. I watched officials search through the suitcases of a tour group ahead of us. They peered in cosmetic bags, unwrapped packages, and leafed through books and papers, going through everything meticulously. Al and I had nothing to hide, but we hoped that our Scripture portions and other items wouldn't be confiscated. One missionary visitor to Cuba had told us his literature had been confiscated because, as the customs officer politely pointed out, some leaflets asked prayer for Communist countries.

Albert and I were next. We picked up our bags to put them on the inspection counter, but an official told us to keep moving. A security guard pointed us to a door. I thought we were being singled out for special checking, but it turned out to be the exit. Apparently the tour group was taking too long to process, and the officers decided to hurry things up.

Somewhat in disbelief, we found ourselves outside, bags in hand, being embraced by two smiling Cuban pastors. They had come to escort us to the convention site, two hours' journey away, in the middle of the island. "We welcome you!" Pastor Jose said as we climbed into his small Russian Lada. "Only we are sorry our request for Rev. Fuller to speak at our convention has been rejected. We are appealing the decision."

I, too, appealed the decision in silent prayer as we drove past fields of tall green sugar cane and neat adobe houses. I was still better off than another mission executive I met later. He told me he'd not been allowed to leave his hotel and tourist area during a week's visit. But a few other evangelical visitors had been able to visit widely.

Once we'd left the tourist area, we began seeing large billboards supporting the revolution. One showed a soldier aiming his Russian-made AK 47 submachine gun, under the declaration: THE ENEMY WILL NOT FIND US UNORGANIZED, UNARMED, OR UNPREPARED.

OPPORTUNITIES, NOT PROBLEMS

It was high noon as we came to the Karl Marx Park.

"There's a restaurant in here," Jose said. "Let's have lunch." We got further acquainted over a plate of chicken, rice, and beans. The waitress put a glass of water at my place, but Jose cautioned me against drinking it. Instead, he ordered bottled mineral water. While we were dining, I noticed a mouse running along the top of the partition beside us.

"Many visitors ask us about the problems we have with Marxism," Jose stated before we could ask any questions, as if he expected every foreigner to bring up the subject. "But we don't talk about those things. There are always people who look at the negative only, but the Holy Spirit wants us to reflect on His truth and on positive things."

"Some visitors are not wise in the critical things they write," added the other pastor, Esteban. "That doesn't help us as Christians. Every country has bad things that can be said about it, but there are also lots of good things."

Zealous but unwise visitors had caused problems. One party of nine pastors arrived as tourists, but they preached in churches without permission. Also, by publicly distributing used clothes, they embarrassed sensitive government officials. The leader of the group was held in prison for three days, and the pastors were sent home on the next plane. "It's O.K. for foreigners, who simply are sent home," our Cuban friends said; "but for the rest of us who have to live here, it's not pleasant taking the consequences."

We assured the two pastors we had come to learn more about the people and the Lord's work, and in no way did we want to cause harmful repercussions. (Most names in this chapter are not the actual names of the people interviewed.) Reassured, Esteban shared with us that after the revolution he and several other Cubans had tried to reach Florida, 80 miles away, in an open boat. They had sailed to within six miles of one of the Florida Keys when a Cuban patrol vessel picked them up. Result: a term in a corrective camp.

"I guess the Lord wanted to show me that my place was here in Cuba, witnessing for Him," Esteban said as we finished our meal with a favorite Cuban dessert of salty cheese covered with guava sauce. I thought that Esteban's and Jose's faces both reflected endurance and a touch of sadness.

"Did you feel you had been prepared to live under Marxism?" I asked, remembering missionaries who told me they regretted not having prepared pastors theologically for ministry in a Marxist society.

"In no way!" Esteban replied. "We were all afraid, not knowing what was going to happen. We thought it was going to be like China or Russia, with pastors being tortured, imprisoned, and killed."

Jose added that his own uncle had traveled throughout the island warning Christians about the results of Communism as seen in Russia and China, especially as they affected the church. Jose respected his uncle and understood his concern, but he felt it would have been better to teach believers how they could live and witness under Communism.

"Most missionaries left suddenly," Esteban continued. "We don't blame them for that, because we know the American Embassy closed and advised all Americans to leave. Suddenly we were like orphans. The majority of mainline denomination pastors left the country, but our evangelical pastors stayed.

"We felt extremely isolated. We didn't have any cases to compare ourselves with. Was our situation typical of other countries under Communism? We had no Christian books available, no tracts to give out (even if distribution had been permitted), no public evangelism was allowed, and our local Christian broadcasts were stopped. We didn't have permission to repair our churches or build new ones. Many believers thought the changes taking place in Cuba meant the death of the church."

"What did you do?" I asked.

"I went to my knees in prayer and Bible study," Esteban answered. "The books of Acts and Revelation showed me that trials were natural for the church, and that it prospered in adverse conditions. I struggled in prayer until finally God gave me peace and showed me I could be a real Cuban and a real believer without fear."

"How about your family?" I asked as we continued our drive.

"We kept very close," Esteban answered. "One of my brothers taught in the university to help financially while I continued pastoring. He had to struggle with the ideologies around him, and at one time he was dismissed because of my witness. But we went to the authorities and showed them that this was a kind of discrimination. They reinstated him."

"How did you raise your children in this context?" I asked.

"Our children had to go through the entire school system, and also nursery and day care, since my wife was working. Of course they were taught atheistic concepts. But in our home we constantly discussed the Word of God with them, and we found that little children can sort things out much better than we think. All our children are following the Lord."

Esteban said that when he was allowed to visit Miami recently, he was shocked to find some Christian Cubans facing the problem of their children rebelling and being involved in immorality, drugs, and violence.

"So following the Lord doesn't depend on the kind of government you live under," Esteban continued. "However, I've had to struggle with my own guilt feelings. Good things were happening in my country as a result of the revolutionary government: employment, medical services, free education, better housing, and so on. Yet these things were being done in the name of atheist ideology. This was a problem for all of us evangelicals to sort out. We had to dig deeply into God's Word for ourselves, to understand what were the positive principles of the revolution that we could accept, and what were our own scriptural principles we couldn't compromise."

A VISION FULFILLED

"Here's where the conference is being held," Jose announced as we arrived at the site. The simple auditorium was packed with a cross section of young and old, black and white. The conference leader, Carlos, opened the meeting without fanfare. I noticed in all services that introductions were minimal, with no eulogy of speakers or musicians. Simplicity marked the services. Worshipers dressed casually but neatly. Business sessions were marked with openness, every *centavo* of money carefully and publicly accounted for.

At the close of the day, I heard an appeal I'd never before heard at a conference: Carlos asked those present not to come back the next day! Albert whispered that that was to give room for others, because attendance was limited to 350 people, allegedly for safety reasons.

"Actually, there were about four hundred present tonight," Carlos told us afterward. "We'll be asked about that, but we couldn't stop the extra 50 coming in!"

The next morning the Bible study was led by a Cuban pioneer missionary, Bartholomew Gregory (B.G.) Lavastida. One hundred years old, he challenged his listeners to dedicate their lives to Christian service. At the end of his message, several responded to make a commitment and others came forward to seek salvation.

Pastor Lavastida also shared his vision of seeing a thousand Cubans come to the Lord before the end of the year. "I believe God is keeping me alive so I can talk personally with Fidel Castro about my Saviour!" he stated publicly.

"I knew there were informants in the service this morning," the centenarian told us in his home afterwards. "They have to have something to report back to their superiors, so I thought I'd give them that message to relay to President Castro!"

Lavastida's father had been a military officer in the army of the Cuban liberator, Jose Marti, who led the struggle for independence from Spain. After the father was murdered by political enemies, a friend tried to persuade young B.G. to enter politics to help fulfill his father's vision. Instead, he entered the Presbyterian ministry, preaching the gospel throughout the island. The future of the nation depended on its youth, he felt, remembering Jose Marti's vision of a pine forest: Although it burned to the ground, new young pines sprouted from the scorched soil and flourished. Lavastida saw a spiritual application and started a Bible school called *Los Piños Nuevos* (The New Pines). An evangelist at heart, he invited a young missionary, Elmer Thompson, to work with him as a Bible teacher to disciple young converts. That was the beginning of the West Indies Mission, which today goes under the name of Worldteam

And now this century-old leader, his face shining with

youthful energy, was telling us about his vision for spreading the gospel throughout the island under a Marxist regime.

PERMISSION GRANTED

"I've just had a phone call from Havana," Carlos announced, coming up to me with a big grin. "We've got permission for you to preach twice!"

My mind quickly went over the notes I had prepared for teaching from the Book of Philippians in four sessions, as originally requested. How was I going to condense that into two sessions?

"Tonight you will preach as long as you wish," Carlos continued, as if he'd read my mind. "Then tomorrow you will take the entire morning. That will give us the 'twice'!"

Even though the sessions were long, the pastors and church members eagerly took notes of my exposition: "The Citizen of Heaven Living on Earth."

"We have few Bible study helps," one told me afterward. "I've always wanted to preach on Philippians. Now I'm going to use your outline in my church."

Carlos was one of the pastors who had been placed in a concentration camp in the sixties. He and other pastors were thrown in with social misfits, homosexuals, and criminals. Each morning he was awakened at four and sent out to cut sugar cane or hoe the land. The prisoners were allowed only one change of clothing a month, and had to put their clothes back on wet after washing them in the river at night. They spent evenings attending indoctrination classes. Food was sparse, sometimes only one small meal for a whole day. Interrogation and intimidation were common. At night the believers met secretly in the cane fields to pray and encourage each other.

When the camp commander found that Carlos could type, he assigned him to his office. Carlos showed him his Bible right away and told him that he was an evangelical pastor. In spite of this, the commandant was so pleased with Carlos' work that he made him responsible for the bookkeeping of several camps, giving Carlos many opportunities for witness and counseling.

Once the commandant sent to him a Catholic priest who was suffering from depression.

The change in the commandant's attitude toward Carlos was typical of the change in the government's attitude to evangelicals in general. When Cuba gave opportunity to all remaining religious leaders to leave in the 1980s, many evangelical pastors stayed on, to the surprise of the government. Evangelicals won their way by proving they were hardworking, law-abiding citizens who could be trusted.

In one town a hospital superintendent, hearing that a Christian was being assigned to his hospital, exclaimed derisively, "Don't tell me we're going to have another Christian in town!" The governor of the province happened to overhear this remark and rebuked the superintendent. "You can be thankful we're having another Christian in town," he said. "Christian medical staff are more faithful and do better work than others." President Castro once told a gathering of students they should "work like the Christian students."

"Now that people see we make good citizens, we're able to protest against discrimination on the basis of the Constitution," Carlos explained. "If believers are discriminated against, or if we can't get permission to repair a church, we go to the local authorities and lodge a protest. President Castro has publicly said the revolution will have failed if there is discrimination against one black person, or one woman, or one Christian. So we use that to make a point when necessary."

There are only whites and blacks on the island, I was told. The conquistadors wiped out the Cubanacan Indians, after whom the island was named. Estate owners imported black slaves to harvest the sugar cane and cotton crops.

All Cubans must carry an identification paper, which includes information on whether a person is religious or not. Although the Constitution says there should be no discrimination on the basis of religion, local zealots try to intimidate people. I met Felicia, a Christian student, who was told she could not study for a profession unless she gave up her religion.

"But that's the most precious thing to me!" she told them.

When Felicia's mother, Maria, found that her daughter was

being pressured at school to give up her faith, she boldly told the principal and teachers that if they wanted to say anything about her daughter's religion, they should say it to her and not to Felicia.

"I know the Lord will answer my prayers and protect my children," Maria told me.

CUBANS AT HOME

After the conference, the pastors all wanted Albert and me to visit their churches, and Carlos had to settle the argument as to where we would go and how long we would stay. We had only another week, and it was filled with daily travel, from one end of the tropical island to the other. This gave us a fascinating overview of a simple-living, hospitable people, proudly self-sufficient. We drove past plantations of sugar cane and fields of tobacco. Brilliant bougainvillaea, flame of the forest, poinsettia, and hibiscus added their brilliant hues, while banana, mango, guava, and coconut trees provided year-round fruit. Some farmhouses were roofed with palm fronds, but most had tile roofs. Occasionally we passed sugar factories that had cut back production because of poor harvest. Outside one town, a large billboard announced: "New Communists arise where problems die."

The government was seeking to control prices. Fuel and many commodities were sold at two prices: the government-controlled price (available with ration cards), and the free market price, which was about double. The problem was that commodities selling at the government price were often limited, so that people sometimes had to buy at the free market price. There was no private ownership of stores, and little of residences. The government rented out rooms in houses at controlled rates--about 10 percent of the wages of each employed person in a family. The majority of people were neatly dressed. Some spent a whole month's wages on a dress or a pair of trousers or a pair of shoes.

I marveled at the number of old cars. Since the government had not allowed any new cars from U.S.A. or Western Europe to be imported since 1959, Cuban mechanics used their ingenuity to keep old vehicles running. We saw a 1939 Buick operating well as a taxi. One car we rode in had no generator, so it was not used at night. There were cars from the forties and fifties that would have fetched high prices in North America as antiques. People don't sell them, even though they could get $20,000 for a car from the fifties.

Transportation becomes a problem for pastors who have to itinerate. One pastor we met is responsible for three churches 16 miles apart. It takes him three hours to get to one of them by bus, because of bus changes. He can't afford to buy a bicycle, and he's not allowed to keep a horse in the city.

At the time of my visit, the average pastor received between $150 and $250 per month, depending upon the size of his congregation. A teacher received around $200, and a medical doctor $320 per month. Banks give two percent interest on deposits up to $2000. Over that, interest is reduced to one percent up to $5000, after which only 1/2 percent interest is given. However, prices of rationed goods and basic food are kept low so that no one need go hungry, even though the diet may be simple.

On Cuban coins is the slogan: "Country or death--we will win." Public speeches often finish with this slogan. Instead of peace doves on signs in the towns, we were confronted with signboards showing soldiers with machine guns, and revolutionary slogans reminding people to stay alert against imperialism. A postage stamp commemorated the revolution with a soldier looking through a gunsight.

In town I found that the bookstore was well stocked with 36 volumes of Lenin's writings. Nearly everything was published in Russia. A neighborhood store displayed a simple shirt made in China, selling for the equivalent of US $30. A number of television programs are produced in Russia, but U.S. films and baseball games are big TV favorites.

As we drove farther into the countryside, we passed cowboys riding horses. A farmer prodded two huge bullocks pulling a wooden sled. Men and women waved at us from the top of a load of tobacco leaves being hauled into town by a tractor.

We found an evangelical church in each town we visited.

Most were in disrepair, because for 20 years it had been virtually impossible to get a permit to make repairs. Now permits were beginning to be available. The houses of believers were small and simple, sometimes covered with rough wood slabs, but most had flowers planted outside.

We were almost embarrassed by the hospitality of the Christians, who had so little. Inevitably they welcomed us with demitasse cups of black Cuban coffee. Breakfast at one pastor's house consisted of cocoa, fried bananas, dry bread, and two scrambled eggs shared among six. The pastor's wife, Anna, asked if we'd like some Russian peaches, and set before us a bowl filled with what looked like peach halves in syrup. They seemed very soft, but certainly had a peach flavor. Then the pastor and his wife laughed and explained that Anna had made the "peaches" out of flour. Her moulds were orange skins turned inside out. When the paste jellied, she scooped out the middle, where the peach stone would have been, and added peach-flavored sugarcane syrup. She got the flavor essence from her son, who rinsed out empty flavor bottles at the local sugar mill.

The pastor's house had green doors and pink and blue interior walls. He explained that it wasn't possible to get paint at the time, so they used whatever leftover colors they could find. On the outside of the front door was a small metal plaque: *Solo Cristo Salva* ("Only Christ Saves"). I noticed that motto on the doors of believers all over the island.

"EACH DAY IS A SURPRISE"

At the end of one service in a country chapel, a young man presented Albert and me with a Scripture poster. I was amazed that the believers should give us these when Scripture posters could not be purchased in the country. When I examined mine more closely, however, I discovered it had been made from a secular poster, the previous wording having been cut off. It was a sunset scene, across which the words were inscribed: "You established the sun, and it knows where to set" (Psalm 74:16; 104:19). It was such a simple statement, but meaningful to believers living in an atheistic country--the sun witnesses to the handiwork of the Creator, who orders all things.

We were intrigued to find that the Christmas tree, which had pagan origins in Europe, has become a symbol of identification for Cuban evangelicals. Some New Pines churches leave a yule tree up all year as a witness to their belief in the Saviour's birth.

I was impressed by the number of young people we saw in the churches. Perhaps our biggest surprise came when we dropped in on a "social gathering" at the home of a lecturer at a university. The room was full of faculty and students singing Scripture choruses! They told me that since publication of the book *Fidel and Religion,* many Christians are less afraid to talk about their faith. Someone gave me a copy of the book, which was written by a Brazilian priest, based on interviews with the Cuban president. In it, Fidel espouses liberation theology, but also makes favorable comments concerning evangelicals. He states that there should be no discrimination against Christians.

One of the students we met was Raul. He became a Christian after hearing the gospel at an evangelical church. At the university one lunch hour, he found himself seated at a table filled with black students from Africa. Before starting to eat, Raul bowed his head to give thanks. When he looked up, he found the black students staring at him. "Why did you bow your head?" they asked.

"I was thanking God for my food," Raul replied calmly.

"Are you a Christian?" the Africans demanded. Raul declared that he was.

"So are we!" they exclaimed. After lunch they took Raul to their rooms and showed him their Bibles. It was the beginning of a long friendship. I met several of those Africans at the "social gathering." One of them, Samson, told me he had spent a year studying at an SIM Bible school in Africa. Others told me that Samson was the most active Christian witness. Cuba provides scholarships for about 100,000 foreign students, many from Africa. For some of them, it is an opportunity to share their faith in Christ rather than to lose their faith to atheism.

"Each day in Cuba is a surprise box!" Carlos commented. "We don't know what the future may hold. Things that seem impossible today may be possible tomorrow."

There was a time when church members could meet only on certain days, but now they can meet any day of the week, as long as they do so in their registered buildings. Whereas the mainline denominational churches have dwindled in membership, the evangelical churches are growing. Carlos told us that there are Christians scattered throughout the villages; many do not have churches or pastors or Bible teachers.

HISTORIC HAVANA

At last we were headed for Havana, the capital, nearly two million in population. We sped along an eight-lane divided highway for the last 100 miles. Occasionally the highway is closed while Air Force Migs practice landing on it. Movable concrete barriers are scattered along the median for use in case of an attempted aerial invasion.

Havana's colonial Spanish architecture sparkled in the tropical sunshine. A group of boys and girls, their red scarves identifying them as members of the Communist Youth Association, stood on an old fortification overlooking the harbor as their leader pointed out historic sites. Havana was Spain's main shipbuilding center in the 18th century and was renowned for its wealth and culture. Cuba's original flags and historic war paintings were on display at the museum.

I dropped in on a completely different world: the Cuban Dollar Store. I was curious to see this anomaly which the government maintains in order to earn foreign exchange. Only foreigners are supposed to shop there, but since other foreigners were taking Cuban friends in with them, we took in two of our friends. They said their children had never seen most of the goods displayed. We were able to purchase loudspeaker equipment for one of the churches.

After having seen empty shelves in run-down stores throughout the island, I suddenly felt I was in a fantasy world.

It was a kind of Cuban Hong Kong, fulfilling the same foreign currency role as Hong Kong does for China. Russians, as well as people of other nationalities, were snapping up consumer goods ranging from cosmetics to electronic gadgets. In spite of the anti-American slogans I had seen elsewhere, the magic key which opened this glittering world to anyone was the U.S. dollar.

The two-storey building was full of shoppers. I noticed a black man and concluded that he, like me, was a foreigner, since he was shopping in the Dollar Store. He told me a little nervously that he came from Tanzania, and that he was studying engineering.

"Do you have a Bible?" I asked him.

"No," he replied, keeping his voice low. "You know, here in Cuba it's very difficult to be found reading a Bible."

"But don't you know there are many Christians in Cuba?" I asked. He was surprised to hear that, and more so when I introduced my two Cuban friends as believers. As we parted, I encouraged him to read the Bible and trust Christ as his Saviour.

"I'm glad I met you!" he exclaimed, then disappeared quickly into the crowd.

"I'M A BELIEVER--IN MARXISM"

I'd asked for an interview at the Department of Religious Affairs. At the Central Communist Party Headquarters in the *Plaza de la Revolucion* we were welcomed by Comrade Julio Ortiz, responsible for foreign relations. After exchanging pleasantries about our two countries, I asked what Cuba's attitude was toward Christianity.

"Before the revolution there was crime, there were drugs and beggars, there was poverty, unemployment," the bullet-headed official told us. "Mafia money built some of the tourist hotels for prostitution and gambling. Foreigners came to Cuba because of the 100,000 prostitutes on the island. Now prostitution has been banned, and Cuba is seeking to build a nation with right ethics and industriousness. The revolution has overcome many of the problems. Would you not say that Cuba is more Christian now than before the revolution?"

I replied that true Christians oppose the evils he mentioned, and we commended the government for trying to overcome them. However, I added, the Christian faith revolutionizes an individual's inner life through salvation and gives him or her the power of the Holy Spirit to resist sin.

(At the time, Castro was boasting that Cuba was drug free. Later the nation was stunned when several senior security officials, including one of Fidel's original revolutionaries, were executed for their part in an international drug ring. The director of customs was jailed for corruption.)

"I'm a believer--a believer in Marxism!" Comrade Ortiz parried. "Comrade Fidel states in the book, *Fidel and Religion*, that he does not believe religion is the opiate of the people."

"Does that book express the government's position or just the president's position?" I asked.

Before Ortiz could answer, a young man whom I took to be the Communist Party advisor held up two fingers.

"The book expresses both positions," Ortiz replied quickly.

I said I'd seen religions, including Christianity, in practice on six continents. In many cases, religious systems put people to sleep, because religion without the Spirit of God is self-deceiving. God's Holy Spirit, not a religious system, gives us spiritual life, I explained.

I said that evangelicals are unhappy about the way evil is sometimes done in the name of Christianity. They feel that true Christians should be the best citizens. I quoted the apostle Paul's description of people who have an outward form of godliness, but whose lives deny the power.

"Have you experienced the power of the living Christ in your life?" I asked.

"I don't have time to go into philosophical matters!" Comrade Ortiz replied tartly. "You have your convictions and I have mine."

I told Comrade Ortiz I had a copy of *Fidel and Religion* in Spanish only, and I couldn't read it. In vain I had looked everywhere for an English edition.

"I'll find one for you," he told us as we were leaving. "I'm a man of my word. I'll send it around to where you are staying."

That evening a messenger brought us a copy of the book in English. He also presented us with an enlarged photograph of President Castro.

PLUS AND MINUS

By the end of my visit, I had met pastors and members from a wide cross section of church denominations. I asked them what they saw as the beneficial results of the revolution. They listed accountability, frugality, simple life style, curbing of vices, free education and health services, and improved rural living conditions. Isolation from foreign resources had made them more reliant on the Lord.

I then asked what problems they felt resulted from the revolution.

"We don't need to talk about problems!" they usually replied.

"But every system in every country has advantages and disadvantages," I explained. "My own country has problems. If I tell people at home that Cuba has no problems, they won't believe me when I tell them the good things."

Reluctantly they listed farm collectivization, family problems ending in divorce, bureaucracy, shortages of consumer goods, and suspicion caused by the system of informants. Believers particularly, feel the pressures of atheistic ideology and isolation from evangelicals worldwide.

"How do you help your people cope with these problems?" I asked several evangelical pastors.

"Since we have to live with these factors, we don't look on them negatively as problems," they explained. "We see them as opportunities for the gospel. There are helpful lessons we can learn from problems."

Among the lessons they listed were self-control, purity, integrity, personal Bible study, witness, and a more scriptural lifestyle. Distinctions between believers and nonbelievers had become more obvious.

The pastors explained that there are two extremes of reaction among Cuban churches. One is to be against everything the government does because it is Communist. The other is to accept everything as being good because it is from the government. Some pastors have successfully appealed regulations. One was that application to conduct a funeral must be made 15 days before the funeral was to take place. Some pastors pointed out that it was impossible to know when a person was going to die, in order to apply 15 days ahead. Besides, they didn't have refrigerated mortuaries. The regulation was dropped.

"There was much attempt to control us at first, but not so much now," one pastor told me. "We evangelicals teach our members to be Christians first of all and then good Cubans, and to obey the laws but also to evaluate what they are told. We used to pray for a change of government. Now we pray that the Lord will enable us to live for Him under whatever government He allows us to have. God is sovereign and has the solution to every problem."

"BEING A CHRISTIAN IS A PRIVILEGE!"

Before we left Cuba, Albert and I met with two of our Cuban friends in Lenin Park for a time of fellowship and prayer. "I don't imagine the authorities ever thought Lenin Park would be the site of a prayer meeting!" I remarked.

"This isn't the first time we've had prayer here," they replied. "We often come for Bible study and prayer with other believers."

Then our friends saw us off at the airport with a warm Cuban embrace. We boarded our flight wondering how to evaluate what we had seen. Obviously, Cuba is very much an island, in a category of its own in Latin America. Historically it has always been strongly materialistic, making it more open to atheism. Indian traditional religion was wiped out with the last of the aborigines.

Cuba's historical role in Spain's strategy for the Americas provided a backdrop to Fidel Castro's ambition to export his revolution. Unquestionably, Cuba had fomented political unrest elsewhere, but Latin America hadn't embraced Cuba's revolutionary leadership as expected. From reading *Fidel and Religion,* I gathered Castro has come to realize that religion is inbred in most of Latin America. Is he embracing liberation theology as a new strategy to spread revolution? He is quoted as saying: "Liberation theology is doing more to promote revolutionary change in Latin America than all the millions of books on Marxism have been able to achieve."

Whatever that means, I left Cuba feeling more concern for the self-indulgent Christianity of my own nation than for the vibrant New Testament church I had just been with. The church of Jesus Christ is not simply subsisting in Cuba; it is a virile, witnessing, growing body. As a student in Havana told me the day before, "In Cuba it is not considered a privilege to be a Christian. But to us believers, it *is* a privilege!"

I also left Cuba with disturbing questions about other Latin American countries. Would pastors and believers there be any more prepared than Cuban Christians were, should their governments turn Communist? What would happen to un-taught, superficial believers? Moreover, what lessons should we learn from the Cuban experience? Whether in democratic or totalitarian societies, were believers identifying with the needs of suffering people? Were they living New Testament lives, being "salt and light"?

In Cuba I'd seen the impact of Communist ideology on a whole nation. Fidel Castro had a crusading zeal to export his revolution to the rest of the world. Was there a Latin American evangelical counterpart to that zeal?

In my travels in South America I heard evangelicals talking about COMIBAM, an acronym for the name of a missions conference with a vision for the whole Spanish-Portuguese world, and beyond. Appropriately, the site for this conference was to be the continent's largest country: Brazil. Perhaps there I would get a continental perspective on the missionary vision of evangelicals.

I will also make you a light of the nations, so that my salvation may reach to the end of the earth.

ISAIAH 49:6 (NASB)

20

LIGHT

TO THE

NATIONS

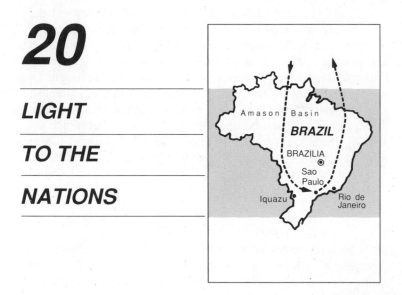

THE GIANT

Brazil at last! I had flown around it and over it, for Brazil borders all South America's nations except Chile and Ecuador. I had landed in its interior in transit to other countries. I had stepped across its border to view Iguazu Falls. I had heard it described as both "a quiet giant" and "the South American imperialist." I had read all the superlatives:

•Largest country in South America: nearly half of the continent's total area, larger than either contiguous U.S.A. or Western Europe; fifth largest in the world.

• Spanning three time zones.

• Possessing half of South America's entire population.

• Boasting the world's mightiest river and falls.

• The world's largest coffee and sugar producer, and second largest iron ore producer.

• Owing the largest national debt in the "two-thirds world."

"Brazil" is a Tupi-Guarani word meaning "glowing coal," the name of a local hardwood. The full name of the country is actually the United States of Brazil. South America's only Portuguese-speaking nation, it now stretched out below me as our aircraft headed for the city of Sao Paulo in the southeast. The purpose of my visit to this giant in the sun was to attend South America's first continentwide missions conference involving the Spanish and Portuguese world. I thought it significant that this historic conference was being held in a nation which is itself overcoming tremendous problems and beginning to reach out to the rest of the world after centuries of isolation.

MIGHTY AMAZON

I looked down at the mottled green carpet of jungle threaded with tributaries of the Amazon. That mightiest of rivers drains a basin nearly the size of Australia, and although slightly shorter than the Nile, has a volume 60 times the Nile's. The Amazon is so powerful that ships can draw fresh water from its flow one hundred miles off the Atlantic coast. Seagoing ships can navigate 2300 miles upriver with cargo for Iquitos in Peru, only 500 air miles from the Pacific. (Amazon is a name from Greek mythology meaning "without breasts." It was given the river after a Catholic missionary thought he saw such women fighting the conquistadors. There has never been confirmation of such warriors. Did the missionary see Indian men with long hair?)

I spotted an irregular patch below us, like parquet tiles laid on a green floor. They were fields of an agricultural project. I wondered how it got there without any roads, but there was a river, the jungle highway. At one time Brazil used that highway to ship out tons of rubber. It lost its world monopoly after

English entrepreneurs smuggled out rubber seedlings, cultivated them in London's famous Kew Gardens, then planted them in Malaya in East Asia.

Apart from an occasional plantation, I saw little other sign of life, for the leafy forest roof hid the few Indians who still inhabit the basin. Throughout the country their numbers continue to dwindle. At the beginning of the century there were half a million in 230 tribes. Now estimates vary from 100,000 to 200,000, in 140 tribes.

Even though these represent only one-tenth of one percent of the country's population, they have become the focus of powerful interests. Industrial and agricultural developers have their eyes on the land. Government agencies adroitly label some budget items as "Indian projects," to get better funding. Discovery of oil makes the government sensitive to any influence that might arouse the aborigines. Missionaries have been suspect at times. Actually, missions have helped preserve some of the Amazon's dying cultures. I learned that Wycliffe Bible Translators (Summer Institute of Linguistics) had just presented the New Testament to the Guarani in their own tongue. Until recently many Indians had been ashamed of speaking Guarani because Portuguese was considered the superior language. When Wycliffe began work among the Guarani, the Indians wouldn't admit they had a language of their own. Wycliffe's work has made them proud of their tongue, and now there are thriving Guarani churches in Brazil.

A real threat to the remaining Indians as well as to the whole nation is the rampant deforestation caused by farmers seeking to grow food to feed their families. Once the jungle is cut down, the poor soil becomes unproductive, leading to further "slash and burn" clearing. One major proposal to develop mining and industry would flood an area the size of Great Britain by constructing 150 dams. During the eighties, the government subsidized clearing of a forested area larger than France. "The forest is our pharmacy, our hardware store, and our supermarket," says Paiakan, headman of the 9000 Kaiapo Indians. "The rivers are our refrigerators. We Indians will die out if the forest is cut down and the rivers are polluted."

Scientists worry about the effects of forest destruction on world ecology and climate, for the Amazon basin has one-third of the globe's remaining rain forest, covers 10 percent of the world's land surface, and contains half the world's botanical species.

Some Brazilians argue that North Americans and Europeans cut down *their* forests for farmland, and now they shouldn't hinder Brazil from meeting its land needs. The government is caught between ecological and societal concerns. Nationwide, 50 million Brazilians are chronically undernourished. Millions in the northeast suffer from alternating drought and flood. Other millions border on starvation in the shantytowns of Brazil's major cities. Of the 145 million population, 72 percent live in cities.

Dying minorities in the jungle, or dying masses in the slums--both add up to a national tragedy for Brazil.

BRAZIL'S "LOCOMOTIVE"

Our flight descended toward the largest of those cities: Sao Paulo. The flight attendant pronounced the name almost like "San Pawlo," because Portuguese vowels are nasal. "Sao" sounds like a nasal Spanish "san": Both mean "saint." I was headed for "St. Paul, Brazil."

I wasn't prepared for the extent of the city sprawling below us. Three times the size of Paris, it is the most populous city in the Southern Hemisphere: 10 million in the city proper, and 16 million in the entire metropolitan area (22 million projected for the end of the century). On the outskirts, miles of rusty shacks lead to squalid factories, followed by gray high-rise apartments surrounding clusters of office towers in the city core.

When I arrived at my hotel, rudimentary but affordable, I looked out on a patchwork of tile roofs. Rows of apartment and office buildings ranked one behind the other, up an incline to an Eiffel-like tower, lit at night by floodlights that turned the scudding clouds into a halo over the congested city. A large neon sign showed the temperature to be 20 C (about 68 F) at 11 p.m. Most of the electricity for those lights came from the hydroelectric dam I had seen in Paraguay. The city of Sao Paulo alone uses seven times as much power as the entire country of Paraguay.

"The locomotive which pulls the rest of Brazil," some call Sao Paulo. It produces 40 percent of the nation's industrial products. Many of the residents *(Paulistanos)* leave for work at 6 a.m. and return home by 10 p.m., spending three or four hours of that time on crowded buses and underground trains.

The rest of the nation is easier going. A Brazilian described the *marajas* syndrome to me. Taken from the word for an Indian prince, or *maharajah*, who lives off the labors of others, the term refers to people appointed to government office because of family connections, or to repay a favor. They, in turn, hand out positions to unqualified relatives. Some *marajas* never show up in their offices except to collect their salary.

Unfortunately, hardworking Sao Paulo has one of the highest murder rates for any city worldwide, and a higher-than-average incidence of AIDS. Fifty percent of the population is under 26 years of age, and 2.4 million children live on the streets, a number equaling the entire population of many a city in North America. Of Latin America's 60 million street children, half live in Brazil. Seven million Brazilian children are totally abandoned. The rest of the street children may have parents, or have shacks to sleep in, but they gain their livelihood off the streets.

Police cruised the streets in tiny Volkswagen "bugs," still being produced in Brazil. They looked top-heavy with large flashing lights on top. I sensed the crime atmosphere when I went to cash travelers checks. Armed guards stood at the alert in front of banks. At a money changer's office, the woman who approved my transaction had three security monitors that showed who was entering the lobby or walking along the hall. A security man escorted me to another room to collect my money. A guard inside looked us over through a one-way mirrored window before letting us in. I was advised not to change much money at a time because the currency *(cruzado)* was changing daily against the dollar. Wages in Brazil are quoted at a monthly instead of annual rate, because of the fluctuating currency. Brazil holds the record for Third

World national debt. International bankers hold their breath lest the nation default in payments. That could start a disastrous financial reaction around the world.

In a large pedestrian mall, men and women made a meager living holding up advertising signs for local stores. In spite of high unemployment, some of the signs advertised jobs, but they all required skills. Shoeshine boys confronted me everywhere, for in Latin America shiny shoes are considered essential for self-respect. On the pavement lay a man without arms or legs, a dish for coins beside him.

MELTING POT

The people were of all colors, for Brazil is a true melting pot of races--more than any other nation I've been in. Portuguese discovered the area around 1500. Early settlers were wealthy landowners from southern Portugal who disdained work but freely cohabited with indigenous Indians and imported African slaves. At one time there were twice as many blacks as whites in the country. A new, mixed race emerged, so that today Brazilians proudly declare, "Every good Brazilian family has at least one African in its history."

In 1808 Brazil became the seat of the Portuguese Empire for a while, when the monarchy fled from Napoleon's army. After 1850, millions of other Europeans arrived, mostly from Italy, Spain, and Germany. Now Asia has added to the nation's racial diversity, with a million Japanese forming the largest Asian group.

African culture comes through in a multitude of ways: dances such as the samba (borrowed from an Angolan fertility rite), food such as bean cakes deep-fried in palm oil, and religious rituals (voodoo). Probably half the population practices some form of spirit worship or occultism. Along the beaches of Rio de Janeiro, devotees leave food offerings to the goddess of the sea, exactly as West African spirit worshipers do. "Voodoo" comes from the West African Fon word, *vodu*, for "spirit." I was intrigued to find that the Brazilian name for the god of thunder and lightning, *xango* is the same as the ancient name *shango* used by the Yoruba people among whom Lorna and I had lived in Africa. Slaves brought over the words and form of worship.

Tourists probably know more about Rio, on the Atlantic coast 200 air miles to the east of Sao Paulo, than any other Brazilian city. A necklace of dazzling beaches and picturesque rocks strung between mountains and ocean, it lives up to the promises of travel brochures. It is also the site of an annual four-day spectacle known as Carnaval.

The event originated in pre-Lenten festivities of the Roman Catholic Church and is celebrated throughout Latin America with parades, fireworks, and family feasts.

Rio outdoes the rest of the continent in city decorations and colorful, costumed events. But for many, *Carnaval* (literally, "farewell to flesh") has become the last opportunity to indulge base passions before the pre-Easter period of self-denial. Rio is known for its orgies during *Carnaval,* as men and women abandon themselves to drunkenness and sex. The day after the festival, newspapers list revelers who expired of exhaustion or died in brawls. But survivors don't worry about their excesses. The next day any priest can grant absolution--for a fee.

SHORT-LIVED LIBERTY

What a different history Rio and Brazil could have had if the early Protestant settlement of 1555 had survived! Over in France at that time, my own ancestors, Protestant Huguenots, were being imprisoned and even burned alive as heretics. Seeking freedom to worship, a group of men sailed with the colonial official Vice Admiral Nicholas Villegaignon to the South American coast and settled on an island off what is now Rio de Janeiro. That was 65 years before the pilgrim fathers landed in North America. The settlers held the first continuing public Protestant services in South America. In 1557 they conducted the first Protestant weddings, a revolutionary thing to do considering that Catholic governments did not recognize Protestant marriage ceremonies.

The Huguenots rejoiced in the liberty of this haven as they prayed and sang their hymns. Their joy and liberty were short-lived, however. Villegaignon turned out to be a treacherous villain. He had specifically recruited Huguenots, but his real motive was not to provide liberty. He needed them to build his new colony, for the Protestants had a reputation for reliable, hard work.

Although he had been a friend of John Calvin as a boy and later professed conversion, Villegaignon now reverted to Catholicism and declared Calvin a heretic. Forbidding the Protestant settlers to propagate their faith, he became known as "the Cain of the Americas." Finally, he allowed the Huguenots to sail back to France, carrying sealed orders to French magistrates to burn them as heretics. Three who stayed in Rio and worked among the Indians were strangled and thrown into the sea for their heresy.

Thus tragically ended South America's pioneer Protestant mission. The corrupt and cruel Catholicism of the day, straight out of the Inquisition, settled over the land like a suffocating blanket. It was nearly three hundred years later that pioneer Henry Martyn, on his way to India as a missionary, visited Brazil's coast and wrote about the spiritual needs he witnessed.

"What happy missionary shall be sent to bear the name of Christ to these western regions?" Martyn cried. "When shall this beautiful country be delivered from idolatry and spurious Christianity? Crosses there are in abundance, but when shall the doctrine of the Cross be held up?"

That was in 1805. In 1893, when evangelists from the Keswick conference in England called in at ports along the coast (see chapter 14), they quoted Martyn's challenge in their report, *The Neglected Continent.*

George and Mary Allan and a host of others read that report and responded. And here in Brazil, in the city of Sao Paulo, I was going to see how the gospel had spread throughout the continent.

MISSION FIELD BECOMES MISSION FORCE

"COMIBAM marks the transition of Latin America from a mission field to a mission force!" declared energetic Argentinian Luis Bush. A great cheer went up from three thousand men and women who had gathered from all over Latin America, and from Spain and Portugal. I knew right then that I was in the midst of a truly Latin event, one that pulsated with promise.

COMIBAM stood for *Congreso Misionero Ibero-Americano* (Iberoamerican Missions Conference--Iberian being a generic term for Spanish and Portuguese, with roots in the Iberian peninsula of Europe).

Delegates met at Sao Paulo's Anhembi Exhibition Hall, advertised as the largest conference complex in the world. They cheered as young people paraded across the platform with the flags of the delegates' nations. After years of planning, the first Iberian missions conference was a reality.

Luis Bush, chairman of the coordinating committee, and his wife, Doris, had told me their vision for COMIBAM when we dined together earlier.

"We don't want a great structure," said Bush. "We want COMIBAM to be a facilitator, to help Iberoamericans who feel God's call to be missionaries. They need to know how to go about it. Their churches need to know how to send them out. They're full of questions: Where are the needs? How should they prepare? How can their churches support them?

"One of the big questions concerns family. We Latin Americans are very close-knit, so parents have a lot of concerns about their children and grandchildren going away to some other land. At COMIBAM we want to help find the answers to those and other questions."

Luis Bush brought wide experience to his role. Born in Argentina, he grew up in Brazil and worked in Chicago, U.S.A. He found Christ as Saviour while attending the church of Russell Shedd, son of Bolivian Indian Mission pioneer Leslie Shedd.

After graduating from Dallas Theological Seminary, Luis pastored a church in San Salvador, where he organized a Central American missions conference. Some people said it couldn't be done in San Salvador, but one thousand young people and two hundred pastors took part. Luis Bush is now president of Partners International (formerly Christian Nationals Evangelism Commission).

The COMIBAM concept grew out of a meeting in Mexico

sponsored by CONELA, the Latin American Evangelical Fellowship. Venezuela was planning a missions conference, and other countries were interested. Why not call a missions conference for all Spanish and Portuguese language countries "Iberoamerica"? From the start, Latin Americans took leadership, and agencies like CONELA, World Evangelical Fellowship, Lausanne Committee for World Evangelism, and Partners International helped sponsor the conference. SIM, other missions, and local churches helped pay travel costs for their own church and mission delegates.

"I confess I was the Doubting Thomas on the committee!" Al Hatch (chapter 1) told me. "Remember, I talked with you in Pasadena about the dwindling numbers attending conferences these days? But look at the people here--three thousand! And most have come at their own expense, some traveling overland for days to get here. I believe this shows there is a real movement of the Spirit of God concerning world missions."

SIMers Myron Loss and Terrill Nelson told me about the three tiring days they and Bolivian friends had spent traveling by bus and train. They had to camp at the Brazilian border one night while Immigration demanded visas for the Bolivians, who had been told they wouldn't need visas. They had lots of time for fellowship en route!

There were men and women from all over: Nicaraguans mingling with Hondurans, Cubans with Chileans, Quechuas in woolen shawls, and Argentines in business suits. Pastors made up the largest group (25 percent), with youth next (nearly 22 percent). As host, Brazil had the largest number present, but little Uruguay was very evident with a busload of men and women, some sipping tea from their indispensable *mate* cups.

The sponsors invited a number of mission agencies and churches from other continents to help share the vision for world evangelization. In fact, it was evident from the first that the conference was not saying that the missionary torch had passed from the hands of "northern" missions, but that Latin America wanted to hold the torch too.

"We are all a product of mission," declared Dr. Manuel Ferreira of the Assemblies of God, Brazil, in an emotional salute. "Evangelical churches cannot forget those who have given birth to them. Intercessors, guardians of the faith--they have opened their hearts and pocketbooks, giving what God has given them. We owe much to those churches, missions, and missionaries. It's our responsibility to intercede for them."

"We cannot take any glory to ourselves," said Wade Coggins, Executive Director of the Evangelical Foreign Missions Association (North America), replying on behalf of all missionaries. "But we realize that in recognizing the ministry of foreign missionaries, you have honored those who have given their lives for the gospel in South America, both in early days and more recently, such as Chet Bitterman of Wycliffe." (Bitterman was murdered by guerrillas in Colombia, where Coggins had served with C&MA.)

Latin American speakers challenged today's generation to take the gospel to others. "We've laughed at mistakes missionaries among us have made," Luis Palau told them. "Now it's our turn to make our own cross-cultural mistakes and be laughed at." An African mission leader, Panya Baba (invited to represent the Third World's largest indigenous denominational mission, the Evangelical Missionary Society, founded in Nigeria by SIM in 1946), told delegates about opportunities in Africa. "We've found unreached people we didn't even know existed. Although we now have over seven hundred Nigerian missionaries, we can't meet the demand. We need help from Latin America and other lands."

"The Argentine football player Maradona came to us in Italy to win a perishable crown," declared a young Italian evangelist. "But if you come with the gospel, you'll win an eternal crown!" The audience clapped and cheered.

Brazil's Edison Queiroz spoke on "The Church and Missions." He told how a visitor had remarked about their new church building. "This is our leftover building," Queroz told the visitor. "Our members didn't think they could keep up their missionary giving and also build a larger church. But we made a commitment to meet our mission responsibilities first. So this church was built from the leftover money!"

Queiroz asked how many delegates were prepared to

commit their lives to God for missions. Nearly everyone stood. Then he asked how many had already done so. The rest of the audience stood to their feet.

But what did commitment to missions really mean? Delegates had the opportunity to find out at 80 workshops held daily, covering topics from Islam to TV evangelism and to the care of missionary children, the latter being one of the most crowded workshops. Some of the workshops were led by leaders I'd met during my travels, like Arnoldo Canclini of Argentina and Guillermo Milovan of Uruguay. There were display booths advertising a multitude of ministries and missionary tools. Television and radio topped the list, for Brazil alone has 85 evangelical TV and radio stations. There are over three hundred Spanish-language denominational publications in Latin America.

CATCHING UP IN MISSIONS

"We're behind some other parts of the world in missions," Bush told us in a press session, "but we're getting the vision."

"What do you see as problems?" a journalist asked.

"The preparation of missionaries is one," Bush replied. "Churches and schools need to face that. Then there's the need for mission structures through which Latin Americans can serve. And, of course, the problem of finance concerns us all. These are poor countries, and even if they can raise support, they may not be able to transmit it out of the country. The encouraging thing is that our churches are now looking for solutions, not just asking questions. And that's where experienced missions can help."

Jonathon dos Santos, president of the Brazilian Association of Cross-Cultural Missions, told me about Latin America's many indigenous missions. The slight but dynamic Brazilian directs one of them, the Antioch Mission, which trains, sends, and supports missionaries in Angola, Bolivia, England, Hong Kong, India, Israel, Paraguay, and Portugal. The Peruvian mission *Asociacion Misionora Evangelica a las Nacionas (AMEN)* has missionaries in London and Paris. Project Magreb sends Argentines to North Africa. COMIBAM lists 180 indigenous Latin American organizations that call themselves missions.

"There are different definitions of missions," Al Hatch explained. "Maybe only half of the 180 listed are cross-cultural and missionary-sending. What we're seeing take place is very encouraging, but we need to realize that the vast majority of evangelical churches in Latin America have yet to be touched with the challenge of world missions."

Adding to the Latin atmosphere of COMIBAM were musical groups that made the auditorium vibrate with amplified guitars. A Quechua group played bamboo flute melodies. The way delegates threw themselves into the singing reminded me of the "gusto" I had witnessed at the football stadium in Buenos Aires: waving, clapping, swaying to the rhythm. In Sao Paulo, it seemed a very natural Latin expression.

The catchy theme chorus, sung by three thousand enthusiastic men and women a dozen times each day, still rings through my head: "Iberoamerica shall proclaim; it will take the light to the nations!"

At the close of the day, participants huddled together in small prayer groups. Arms around each other's shoulders, tears coursing down their cheeks, they poured out their hearts for the spiritual needs they had heard about during the day. Haitian pastors asked prayer for outreach in "the Voodoo Capital of the World," *Plain-du-Nord.*

There devotees worship *Ogoun,* the god of war, whose name and worship were brought to Haiti by West African slaves. Haitian officials recently rededicated their Republic to Satan.

"Praise God!" delegates shouted when told that the evangelical population of both Costa Rica and Guatemala is around 25 percent. But they also prayed earnestly as they heard of the harassment and imprisonment evangelical pastors face in some other nations.

Participants from SIM-related churches took the opportunity to get together one lunch hour. About sixty, mostly from South America but with several from Africa, met to share prayer requests and to rejoice in the common bonds they had through the work of SIM.

"The thing which unites us is the blood of Jesus Christ," said Nathaniel Olutimayin, then chairman of the Evangel Fellowship of SIM-related churches. "But we are also united through the work of the missionaries who brought us the gospel."

"OBEDIENCE IS THE KEY"

I wanted to talk with a Brazilian pastor and a Brazilian missionary to get their insights. "Here's the man you should talk with," said Allen Thompson of Worldteam, introducing me to a tall young man. "Ebenezer Bittencourt is both a pastor and missionary. Besides, he wants to talk with you about your book, *Mission-Church Dynamics.*"

"How did you hear about the book?" I asked Ebenezer when he and I found a quiet place to talk.

"When I went to U.S.A. to study," he replied. "Columbia Biblical Seminary uses it as a textbook. It expanded my horizon. I like your chapters on church-centered and mission-centered approaches. As a Brazilian pastor I was too much of a church-centered man. We nationals look just inside our churches. We are very self-centered. But many missionaries are too mission-centered. They overlook the local church. I've used your book to help both missionaries and pastors. You point out that Christ himself must be the center, not a mission agency or church denomination."

I'd heard that the church was growing at five times the population rate, and that 16 percent of the population is evangelical. But Ebenezer told me it wasn't all easygoing.

"There's rapid growth in some parts," he said. "But my own church is in a resistant area of the city, and it's had a sad history. I went there last year, but it still has only 80 members."

This young pastor, son of German and Indian descent, told me some of the pastoral problems he faces. Voodoo worship ranks high as a barrier to evangelism. In the church are other problems. Women don't want their husbands to get involved, because the women don't understand what the men are doing.

Believers are untaught but don't want to learn Portuguese, which is necessary so they can read the Bible and Christian books. Others say that since Jesus is coming back anytime they don't want to waste their time studying.

"Most Brazilian Christians are untaught and superficial, leaving them open to cults or syncretism," Ebenezer told me. "One evangelical church with 10,000 members sells holy water and healing handkerchiefs to raise funds. Seventy percent of Christians are charismatic. We can learn a lot from their aggressive witness, but many tend to be legalistic, placing believers under a kind of bondage to their leaders instead of teaching the Scriptures and letting the Holy Spirit guide them. This hinders the spread of the gospel among the educated class, who think evangelicals are very simplistic and naive."

I asked Ebenezer how he answered the allegation of Communists and liberation theologians that evangelicals are interested only in making church members, and not really in helping people.

"There's a history to that," he explained. "Charismatics in particular felt that believers shouldn't do anything but preach. They didn't have any community programs. Because of their interpretation of Romans 13 about being subject to higher powers, they didn't protest if they saw the poor being mistreated. So evangelicals looked good in the eyes of the government, whereas modern Catholics looked bad because of their political activism. But now evangelicals are beginning to realize that as citizens they should play their part in changing the country--of course by vote, not by violence.

"We have a lot of poor people in our church, and we don't have enough money to look after them. But we must do what we can. Our churches are poor; inflation is running 40 percent and people's wages aren't keeping up. That's why I think it's good to have big churches in a city, so members can work together to finance projects. Urban evangelism is expensive.

"We have to teach the people to give sacrificially. One pastor I know hadn't had a salary increase for seven years, even though the government had raised the minimum national wage five times. He had to take a part-time job and not give full time to the church. Then the elders wondered why it didn't grow!"

Ebenezer's church has sent one of their members as a missionary to Portugal, handling his care through an established mission there. Ebenezer is also a part-time missionary with Worldteam, supervising their local missionaries. He feels this helps to model missions for his members.

I asked Ebenezer how he felt about COMIBAM. "It's very encouraging," he replied. "A lot of people are being exposed to missions for the first time. They see they can do it themselves. But I hope their response won't be based just on the emotional appeal of the need of the world. We need to stress obedience to God's command. And we need to hear about the responsibilities of the local church in fulfilling the Great Commission."

This was an evangelical patriot I was talking with. He told me about his deep concern for his nation, for justice and integrity rather than carnage and corruption. Most of all, he was a pastor with a vision for his community and for the world. He saw the key to be *obedience to God's command.*

I heard Luis Bush declare the same to the COMIBAM delegates: "Missions does not depend on political or economic power, but on obedience and faith in the Word of God. As Latin Americans, we are saying, 'Lord, we are willing to be your servants, your instruments to take the torch and to be a light to the nations.'"

It was a gigantic challenge. Not to tie down the sun, as the ancient Indian priests sought to do, but to beam the sunlight of the gospel, the redemptive light of the Eternal Son, into the still dark corners of Latin America and the world.

In Brazil I saw and heard a lot that set me thinking.

Then the righteous will shine forth like the sun in the kingdom.

Matthew 13:43

21

TYING

DOWN

THE ISSUES

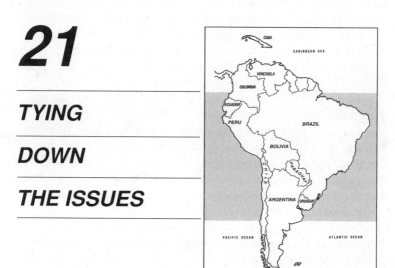

Once more I lifted toward the sun, leaving the South American continent behind. Now at last I had time to sit back and evaluate my odyssey. Would Isaias, the Peruvian elder, think I had told "what it's really like"?

To visit all those countries was a privilege. To interview the whole spectrum of society--from peasant to professor, from shepherd to senator--was an education. To see the great needs of Latin America, to sense the spiritual forces at war and to see the gospel at work--I found all that very challenging. But what did it all mean?

THE CONTINENT

I had discovered a continent grander than I imagined. It has the world's longest mountain chain, mightiest river, deepest gorge, highest falls, and largest rain forest. It also is much larger in proportion to the rest of the world than shown on standard maps. Because of the problem of drawing a global world on flat paper, traditional maps make South America seem smaller than it is. For instance, most maps give the impression that Brazil is smaller than Greenland. Actually, Brazil is six times larger. (Greenland is about the size of Mexico.)

From Latin America came agricultural products we take for granted today: potatoes, cocoa, rubber, vanilla--even chicle for chewing gum. Remedies such as quinine came from its forests, but also products that are health hazards: tobacco and cocaine. Travelers jokingly refer to diarrhea as "Montezuma's revenge." But the real revenge of Montezuma II, the last Mexican emperor, could be the harmful effects of tobacco and cocaine on our society.

Whereas Europe drastically changed the course of the Americas in the last five centuries, Latin America has in turn profoundly affected the rest of the world for both good and ill.

PEOPLE AND SOCIETY

East and West truly meet in Latin America. The original inhabitants came from Asia millenniums ago; Europeans and Africans began arriving half a millennium ago. Today's Latin Americans are actually new races dating from the sequence of events triggered by the Columbus expedition of 1492. The result is a melting pot of proportions found in no other continent. Yet, each country has its distinctive national character. Each has been shaped by its proportion of ethnic mix, its geography, and its history. There is no truly typical Latin American nation; there are just common factors.

Latin American society is in flux. Stereotypes are collapsing. Social movement is upward, across, and down. Change and uncertainty produce trauma as well as opportunity. An easygoing lifestyle may in fact hide deep resentment and anger. In spite of identification with cultural roots and current ideologies, intellectuals still search for that elusive yet extremely important element called "identity." Corruption is endemic, but that is true in many parts of the world. In terms of societal problems, Latin America is "one of the most difficult areas of the contemporary world," as Peruvian theologian Samuel Escobar told me.

POLITICS

In general, the political scene has been shaped historically by a strong sense of independence, nostalgic ties with Europe, and an emotional underlay of aboriginal roots. Governments often reflect a tension between fascination with the economic success of the United States of America and resentment of its perceived power. Compounding the tension are external international rivalries and the internal tragic violence of right wing death squads and left wing terrorists.

Although Catholic influence and Communist infiltration have been obvious factors in Latin American politics, not many people realize how dramatically the introduction of a Protestant element altered the dynamics of society. By their very presence, Protestants forced a closed church-state system to open, leading to a more pluralistic society. Protestant egalitarian and democratic concepts have contributed to change, but left wing ideology and right wing ecclesiology have both turned change into political advantage. Unfortunately, evangelicals, not always certain of their identity in society, have too often reacted negatively to change when they could have been at the heart of some of it, not with placards but with godly practice. However, some are providing "salt and light" in their political arena.

COMMUNISM

Communism's dialectic of class struggle conveniently builds on the injustices of Latin America's history. Communists can point to blatant illustrations of class abuse, evident in the stark contrast between the wealthy few and destitute many. It is easy for us who are not from Latin America to label social agitation as Communist influence, but it may simply reflect great human need that Christians themselves should address. Communism is quick to "capitalize" on real issues. To many downtrodden people who have seen the worst side of capitalism, Communism, unfortunately, seems to contrast very favorably. However, in some left wing countries disillusionment is setting in as revolutionary governments fail to produce better results than their capitalist predecessors. Their economy will further deteriorate as Russia reduces financial aid.

It remains to be seen how much the amazing changes in Russia and Europe will affect Latin America ideologically. Some socialist regimes like to think they practice a purer ideology than European Communists. After all, doesn't Latin America boast a Communist party older than Russia's? Maoists such as the Shining Path don't consider Marxists as true revolutionaries, anyway. And the father figure of the Shining Path movement, Jose Carlos Mariategui, declared, "We must bring Indo-American socialism to life with our own reality."

Evangelicals need to realize that God can keep them and prosper their witness under Communist regimes, as the Cuban experience demonstrates. While some liberal theologians' solution to the Communist question is compromise, the evangelical solution is fidelity to the Word of God and faithfulness as citizens. The answer to atheistic Communism is genuine Christian living based on the scriptural principles of justice, integrity, and love.

DRUG TRADE

Latin America's economic morass has given impetus to the drug trade, threatening to destroy the very fiber of society, from coca-growing peasant to drug-bribed official. For many poverty-stricken farmers, drug growing seems the only means of survival. Depressed economies are especially vulnerable; one estimate is that a million South Americans are employed directly or indirectly by drug traffickers. A judge who earns $230 a month may be offered $50,000 to dismiss a drug case; refusal to accept could mean death. And for the drug lords, the conquistador's lust for gold lives on in today's greed for quick profits from drugs. In one recent year the total value of all legal exports from one South American country was $5.25 billion, but drug lords in that land raked in an estimated $4 billion, untaxed.

Sadly, the moral degeneracy of so-called Christian lands outside Latin America helps stimulate the market that makes the drug trade profitable. It is also a two-way commercial trade; many of the chemicals needed to produce cocaine come from North America (also from China and Brazil), and on the black market they can have a higher profit margin than cocaine itself. In some lands political terrorists help farmers get the best price for their drug crop, and they protect traffickers--for a fee. International Mafia connections turn the drug scene into a global nightmare.

THE ECONOMY

Poverty is the most pervasive image presented by Latin American society. Blame is placed on factors ranging from multinational foreign companies to the rich elite and corrupt governments. I also heard Latin Americans blame the easy-going personality of (a) Latins, or (b) Indians, or (c) blacks. The drug trade may keep some farmers alive, but it doesn't contribute to funds needed to run their country. In some nations, top officials stay in their offices only long enough to skim off finances for their foreign bank accounts. World prices and international trade compound the problems. Meanwhile, as inflation and national debt spiral upward, the world's banks hold their breath lest a default in repayment should trigger economic problems around the world.

The religio-political mindset of both church and government in the past gives perspective to Latin America's economy today. While Catholic bishops denounce economic imperialism as the cause of their nations' problems, they do not recognize the root of those problems in their own system. They are therefore unable to explain why North America has surpassed South America economically, when Latin America had all the initial advantages: earlier settlement, more initial cash wealth, more natural resources, larger cities, more population, and stronger government.

I was intrigued by the thought that the divergent paths that

North and South America took were in some respects determined at the time of the Reformation. North America was initially settled by northern Europeans who were radically affected by the Reformation. South America was initially settled by southern Europeans who violently rejected the Reformation. Of course there were other factors which determined the destinies of North and South America. For instance, the North American settlers came to make a home and stay; South America's conquistadors came to exploit and leave.

It is not within the scope of this travelogue to provide an in-depth analysis of socioeconomic problems. However, at the risk of oversimplifying, let me list the historical factors which have made an impact on Latin America's development, for these factors have helped shape the context which the gospel must penetrate:

•*National inferiority complex.*

This was brought about by the domination of successive waves of conquerors, whether Indians or Europeans.

•*The patron, or boss, system.*

This predated the colonizers, but was intensified by them and encouraged dependency on others.

•*The suffocating influence of a medieval church-government relationship in the past.*

The terror of the Inquisition, apart from its religious effect, helped stifle initiative and change in society. Also, Latin America did not generally benefit from the Protestant work ethic which motivated many of the North American colonists.

•*The concept of limited good.*

The Spanish and Portuguese colonists came out of a static medieval economy based on the ancient philosophy of limited good: One community could improve its status only at the expense of the status of another community. In northern Europe that concept was eventually overcome by the Calvinistic byproducts of growth and entrepreneurship. But today the concept of limited good continues to keep many Latin Americans from seizing opportunity. It induces envy and resentment of success, and it raises expectations of handouts from those who have improved their lot. It also lends itself to the Communist concept of class struggle, and of sharing common poverty rather than stimulating common growth.

Although I am not from U.S.A., I was interested to note the influence of the concept of limited good on attitudes toward the United States. The concept would imply that the highly successful U.S. economy has been achieved at the expense of Latin America. This produces resentment, but at the same time the patron mindset looks to U.S.A. to bail out the countries. (Somehow blame has not yet been placed upon Japan, even though some of my American friends jokingly tell me that Japan now owns most of U.S.A.!)

• • • • • •

To suggest that Latin America's economic problems are not basically the fault of North America is to fly in the face of popular thinking, abetted by pronouncements of the Council of Catholic Bishops and governments of both the ideological left and right. A contrary view might also seem to overlook the arrogance and selfishness of other nations, including my own. Those sins I have to confess. But after examining the figures and the conclusions being bandied about, I suspect that Latin America's economic ills are caused by more than some foreign bogey. Are they not at least partly the result of the same religio-politico-economic system that crippled some European countries? It is a system built on privilege and bureaucracy rather than true entrepreneurship and free enterprise.

In suggesting this, I cannot ignore the devastating effect of interest rates and world prices on current conditions. Nor can we overlook the desperate state of Latin America's poor. They need the economic assistance of the rest of the world. But the good news is that Latin America also has within it the resources and ability to improve economically. And the best good news is that emancipation from spiritual slavery can have good effects upon the quality of life of individuals and nations.

EVANGELICALS AND THE POOR

Although today's Catholics and liberal Protestants sometimes act as though they had discovered the poor, we should not forget that it was the plight of spiritually and physically oppressed Indians that spurred evangelical pioneers into action. To use a currently popular phrase, they had a definite "bias for the poor." I am thankful to see today's evangelicals continuing to meet physical as well as spiritual needs. Many have a deep concern for their poverty-stricken communities.

However, there are allegations that evangelicals disregard the plight of the poor. I believe there are several reasons for this perception:

1. Marxists and liberal theologians misunderstand the evangelical emphasis on the need for personal salvation of the individual, and on the priority of eternal life over temporal benefit. Atheists and universalists don't have those priorities, since they don't admit the eternal lostness of the sinner or accept the need for spiritual regeneration. They therefore tend to discount that which evangelicals do to help the poor; it does not fit their framework and is overshadowed by spiritual priorities.

2. Evangelical approach to helping the poor is developmental. They seek to improve conditions within the system, until the system changes because of changed people within it. That view is anathema to those who believe that development only bolsters fascist regimes and that structures and systems can be changed only by revolution.

It is interesting to note that both evangelicals and political revolutionaries say, in essence, that society can only be changed by changing people. However, for atheists or liberals, "the new man" is a political revolutionary who overthrows the structure and ushers in a new, just society. It is essentially a class struggle, the revolutionary being allied with the lowest class to overthrow the upper classes. For the evangelical, "the new man" is produced through the "new birth," and he then works to bring about justice within his society. It should be a classless struggle, the church being identified with God's justice against sin in every level of society.

3. Some evangelical churches have had a simplistic attitude to their society, leading to an unscriptural dichotomy. Although rightly giving priority to preaching the gospel, they have neglected to be salt and light in their neighborhoods. Like the

Thessalonian believers who decided they didn't have to work because Jesus might come back at any moment, these Christians think they don't need to change their society because it will one day be destroyed. Their neglect of the societal implications of the gospel has left a theological vacuum that liberation theology has filled with its own distortion of the truth. Evangelicals need to speak out on these issues, not just to rebut arguments but to demonstrate scriptural concern and solutions.

4. Although pioneer missionaries purposely ministered to the poor and succeeded in bringing about social change as a result of spiritual change, in recent years missionaries have not always identified well with the poor. They know that Jesus did, and that He condemned the oppressive rich. But the lifestyle of the average missionary, although moderate in the context of his or her own land, appears affluent in contrast to conditions of the poor. That lifestyle may be appropriate in outreach to educated urbanites, but should not characterize the missionary in a context of poverty. As Samuel Escobar told me, "In the last decade Latin America has become poorer and more indebted, and national pastors have had to become more frugal. However, the evangelical missionary enterprise, with few exceptions, has not taken one step in the direction of a simpler lifestyle."

This is a vexing and complicated question that needs to be addressed. However they live, expatriate missionaries will be looked upon as affluent. But evangelicals should seek ways of identifying with people in their need, and not flaunt their relative affluence.

5. Because theologically liberal churches have espoused the cause of the poor and have linked it with a social gospel, some evangelicals have shied away from the topic of Third World need, lest their constituencies identify them with liberalism. As a result, their supporters have not understood the scriptural place of ministering to people in physical need as a valid facet of the gospel. That creates an unscriptural dichotomy. Our hearts must beat with the message of eternal life, while our hands are busy ministering to the needs of people in Jesus' name.

6. Right wing governments have usually allowed religious liberty. In fact, some governments may have encouraged Protestant missions in order to reduce the political power of the Catholic church. Evangelicals are so concerned about the atheism of left wing politics that they sometimes openly favor right wing governments. Radicals see this as favoring oppressors of the poor.

7. Evangelicals may simply not know what to do in the face of injustice and poverty. They don't want to join political demonstrations or identify with Communist causes. The poverty is so enormous and their resources are so limited that they may simply give up. But evangelicals should encourage creative programs.

8. One result of the new birth is a kind of upward mobility, simply because the convert has broken destructive life patterns and established new goals, even as the Protestant enclaves of northern Europe became known for their industrious entrepreneurship. While this change of attitude has positive benefits, it can also have the unfortunate result of making comfortable people forget others trapped in the poverty cycle.

Although some evangelicals may forget their roots as they improve their lot, many are increasingly involved in assisting the poor through practical self-help programs, along with their witness to the saving grace of Christ. The majority of evangelicals are poor, and can easily identify with the cause of the poor. They also can understand the context of liberation theology, but for the most part they do not espouse its politico-economic solutions.

• • • • • •

Evangelical missions and churches can ignore the reality of poverty, with all its implications, only at their peril. They need to understand what the Scriptures really say on this topic, and what the people themselves are saying. They need to bring Scripture to bear on the real problems of society instead of leaving the field open to those who handle the problems in the opposite way, interpreting Scripture through societal problems. Evangelicals need to prepare believers, on the one hand, to face the problems of their society and, on the other hand, to answer the specious arguments of radical ideology disguised under the name of religion. (See Liberation Theology, below.)

CATHOLICS

Catholicism in Latin America is different from the Roman Catholic Church elsewhere. Latin Americans don't appreciate the term "Roman"; they feel closer to Madrid or Lisbon than Rome, and prefer to be called simply Catholics. John Mackay, in his classic book, *The Other Spanish Christ,* points out that Iberian (Spanish and Portuguese) Catholicism was greatly influenced by Moorish concepts from North Africa, making it different from Catholicism in the rest of Europe. Sociologist Octavio Bunge called the Spanish religion "anti-Christian Catholicism." It was ritualistic, not requiring intellectual understanding or ethical practice. As Mackay so ably states, the only Christ that the Indians of Iberoamerica saw was either an infant or a corpse--in both cases a helpless object of pity. The *life* of Christ, the Holy Saviour living among mankind without sin, was entirely missing. Consequently, imported Catholicism was a religion without relevance to ethics or morality.

Although Latin America has been considered chiefly Catholic, its underlying religion is spirit worship related to ancient Asian shamanism and African traditional religion, including voodoo in some communities. Covering that is a veneer of Catholic Christianity. The sequence leading to complete syncretism between Christianity and paganism is easy to follow:

1. According to ancient belief, the supreme God abandoned man. Some tribal traditions say this was because of divine caprice. Others say it was because the people rejected Him.

2. The earth mother was left to provide the good things humans needed. Therefore, offerings and sacrifices to her are necessary. The Indian peoples identify her with the Virgin Mary, who, according to Catholic doctrine, never died.

3. The Devil and his demons constantly seek to harm humans; therefore they must be warded off by fetishes. The help of saints is needed to do this.

4. Jesus became a symbol of death, not life, and was easily identifiable with the god of the dead, who, in some ancient beliefs, was the son of the sun and moon--the Inca. Catholic parades displaying the dead Jesus fitted in with the custom of carrying the mummies of Incas through the streets on special occasions.

5. Quechuas, traditionally preoccupied with death, naturally related to the morbid expressions of suffering and death found in medieval Catholicism. These were identified with acts of penance to obtain forgiveness for sins.

6. In the same kind of tradition as the sacred role of the Inca emperor (the sun god's representative on earth), the Pope is the grand patron, the guardian of the faithful, and dispenser of salvation to those who obey the Catholic church. Obedience to this authority is more important than living according to the ethics of one's faith.

7. The rites and institutions of pagan religion were easily identified with Catholic ones. For instance, under the Incas there were convents for priestesses, a priesthood, a confessional, penance, and sacred water purification.

8. When Catholicism crossed the Atlantic, it brought the concept of limited good mixed with merit theology. This has resulted in a religion with materialistic goals, which can easily relate to either traditional Indian religion or Marxism. Indian animists were accustomed to propitiating their gods and spirits in hope of getting things.

• • • • • •

People in countries where Catholics are not dominant have difficulty understanding Latin American Catholicism. An honest description may seem harshly critical because in North America and Europe the Catholic church has become more tolerant. Even in Latin America some lay Catholics have become more open to the gospel. After Vatican II, some priests who once urged crowds to stone evangelicals actually helped distribute Bibles. There are evangelical elements among Catholics, especially among those called charismatic.

However, there has been a backlash on the part of Catholic elements in Latin America due to the rapid growth of evangelicals, who are seen as a threat to the Catholic church. The Pope's several visits to Latin America reflect this concern. On his tour of Mexico in 1990, he publicly warned Catholics to shun "Protestant sects" (a term increasingly used by Latin American Catholics to describe Protestants, in place of the term, "separated brethren"). In one of the countries I visited, a radical Catholic group which calls itself The Second Inquisition threatened one mission board with violence unless they withdrew all foreign missionaries. A government department requested all non-Catholic organizations to register the names and addresses of their leaders. Evangelicals see this as an attempt to intimidate non-Catholics.

Worldwide, Catholics have launched Lumen 2000, a global evangelism plan which is tied in with the 500th anniversary of Columbus's discovery of the Americas--a celebration resented by many educated Latin Americans. The plan "affirms the Pope's conservative revisionism," according to Eugene Stockwell of the World Council of Churches. When the sponsors of an evangelical consultation on AD 2000 evangelism, held in Singapore in 1989, invited Catholics to report on Lumen 2000, Latin American evangelical delegates strongly objected. They submitted a Statement of Concern, which included the following points:

> *In our Iberoamerican continent, the religious-political force of the Roman Catholic Church . . . is in fact the most fierce opponent to all evangelistic efforts on our [Protestant evangelical] part. . . . Iberoamerican Roman Catholicism is to the present day incompatible with our evangelistic vision: Mary more than ever [holding] the first place in the faith, tradition [superceding] the Bible, salvation by works over the . . . finished work of the Lord Jesus Christ on Calvary, the supreme authority of the Pope, religious syncretism. . . . We recognize the work of the Holy Spirit in the life of non-Protestant/nonevangelical people and churches. However, we cannot cooperate with the structures they represent.*

LIBERATION THEOLOGY

Liberation theology is a very understandable reaction in an

area of the world which is saturated with dogmatic religion and totalitarian politics, coupled with desperate poverty. In northern Europe and North America, Protestantism provided an avenue for gradual democratic change--although it also gave rise to permissiveness and liberal theology. However, in the totalitarian context of Latin America, it was inevitable that yearnings for social revolution resulted in a dogmatic theology of liberation, espousing violence.

Although liberation theology developed along separate streams of Protestant and Catholic thinking, the common aim is establishment of a socialist system peopled with "new" men and women in a classless society. Central American evangelical theologian Emilio A. Nuñez C. points out that liberationists use poverty as "the taking-off point for Latin American theology, and Marxist analysis is seen as the best instrument for understanding the situation of poverty." Liberation theologians believe that the present system cannot be improved, but that the entire structure of society must be changed--with violence if necessary. In the process, they have redefined such familiar terms as "gospel," "salvation," "church," and "theology," using sociological rather than scriptural definitions. Liberal theologian Hugo Assmann makes the seemingly contradictory statements that the theology has been developed "in the light of the Word of God," but that Scripture has been rejected as an unreliable "source of criteria."

Some liberation theologians reason like this:

• God has a bias toward the poor and is found in the oppressed. Therefore, identification with poverty and suffering becomes the means for knowing God.

• The institutional church embodies the privileged. It therefore does not witness to the world; rather, the poor of the world, who embody God, must "evangelize" the church to struggle against oppression.

• Jesus became an example of the struggle because He identified with destitute people against powerful religious leaders. He was put to death by the powerful.

• Jesus' death is exemplary, not vicarious. He showed us that we should oppose oppression. By following His example and struggling against oppression, we find salvation and become children of God.

Somewhere in the theological subconscious of Latin America there may lurk the memory of medieval holy wars, in which Muslims and Christians fought for what they saw as a divine cause. Is liberation theology advocating a contemporary holy war? At the time of the Iberian conquest of the Americas, political domination was advanced in the name of religion. Now political revolution is being urged in the name of religion.

We must admit, however, that liberation theology points out real problems. Evangelicals are also concerned about these. Ironically, liberation theology has arisen because of two theological vacuums, one Catholic and one evangelical. *Iberian Catholicism* left a vacuum of morals in society. The Christian life was not applied to justice and ethics.

Evangelicals are perceived as leaving a vacuum of praxis-- while they have labored among the poor, they have not always demonstrated how the Scriptures apply to the poor. The average Latin American therefore thinks evangelicals are otherworldly, preaching an irrelevant gospel. *Liberation theology* tries to fill the vacuum. It is not just a new theology but a new way of *doing* theology, which affects the Latin American church's way of perceiving itself and of deducing its theology: from society rather than from Scripture. Evangelicals urgently need to communicate the relevance of the Scriptures to the needs of daily life and to express scriptural theology in terms understandable to Latin America.

EVANGELICALS

Latin America has one of the world's fastest growth rates for evangelicals. In what was once considered the world's only Catholic continent, about 10 percent of the population is now Protestant, and the majority of them are classified as evangelicals. Although sometimes still lumped together with cults, evangelicals now have fairly wide recognition.

I couldn't help feeling that this is God's "fullness of time" for Latin America. The response to the gospel is unquestionably the work of the Holy Spirit. And I believe He is using several factors to bring this about:

1. The broken dominance of the Catholic Church.
2. Disillusionment with politics.
3. Anxiety over violence and disintegration of society. When distressed people have the opportunity to understand the gospel, increasingly they look to it for spiritual solace rather than to the promises of liberation theology. However, many suffer from terrorism and are coerced into joining godless movements.
4. Economic problems. The uneducated were always poor, but the educated now feel the economic pinch as well. Their materialistic self-assurance has been shattered.
5. Ending of isolation. Latin American countries increasingly feel the impact of external ideas, which open them to change.
6. Land reform. The freeing of farmers from the control of feudal landlords is opening them up to making their own choices in life.
7. Vernacular Bible translations. People are not only reading the Spanish and Portuguese Bibles more, but many now can read in their own vernaculars.
8. Communication by radio. Millions have become aware of the gospel by radio and television.
9. A grassroots lay movement. Increasingly believers are mobilizing to evangelize their people.
10. Evangelical training programs. Believers are being instructed in the Scriptures, and leadership is being developed.

• • • • • •

An estimated 75 percent of Latin American evangelicals call themselves either charismatic or Pentecostal. The Latin American personality, with its warmth of expression, is very responsive to charismatic ministry. Meetings are marked by joy and vitality, in contrast with the depressing morbidity of traditional Catholicism. The reason some evangelical leaders question the large numbers of conversions reported by certain evangelists is that their ministry seems based on emotion, without an accompanying understanding of what salvation means. Emilio Nuñez warns against "a cheap gospel" being preached by some evangelists. Emphasis on the phenomenal also finds ready response, especially in the context of a superstitious Catholicism with its underlay of shaman spirit worship. Moreover, culture may demand response to anything that a persuasive person, such as an evangelist, asks people to do. Televangelists are powerful speakers, and probably the leadership quality most admired by Latin Americans is oratory. All this raises questions about the meaning of numerical growth.

"Years ago I spoke with Ecuadorian evangelical theologian Rene Padilla about these stories of growth," comments William (Bill) D. Taylor, Executive Secretary of the World Evangelical Fellowship's Missions Commission. "He replied, 'We must ask our church growth friends two questions: What is church? What is growth?'"

Inflated statistics are sometimes circulated by enthusiasts outside Latin America. For instance, a widely circulated report gave the membership of one Argentine church as 20,000. The pastor could not understand where the figure came from. He said the actual membership was 2500.

A number of evangelical leaders I met questioned whether reports of popular response to the gospel represent true conversion, and how much of it really adds to the church. At the same time, Samuel Escobar pointed out that much of Latin America's evangelical growth doesn't fit the mold of traditional ecclesiology. "People are desperate and they turn to the gospel for solace," he told me. "They don't think about whether they are orthodox or not. They don't come to the Lord through the traditional channels of dogmatism, or systematic theology. Rather, they seek the Lord out of personal anxiety and poverty. As society around them crumbles, they find stability and identity in the community of believers. This grass roots movement is the spiritual hope of the future."

This folk Christianity is a move in the right direction, away from sterile churchianity and Christo-paganism. The movement presents a challenge to Bible-based evangelicals to teach the Scriptures. In fact, that is the number one need throughout the churches. Unfortunately, much church leadership lacks training. An established pattern of lay leadership through elders has much to commend it, but it can result in vested interests perpetuating weak leadership--a kind of "limited good" cycle. At the other end of the spectrum, the pastoral model frequently seen in Latin America follows the caudillo, or boss, concept: authoritarian, dictatorial. Traditionally, both pagan and Catholic priests reflected prestige and dominant authority instead of servant leadership. Evangelicals have to overcome the effects of three religious traditions:

•Among aborigines, an animistic shamanism that mediated between the people and the gods.

•A priesthood that controlled everything through a hierarchy.

•Financial giving that was not of grace or stewardship, but was legislated and was considered meritorious.

With this kind of background, believers urgently need scriptural leadership development.

All told, evangelicals are the hope of Latin American society. One major contribution is their strong family emphasis. A Colombian survey asked what a person moving into the city would buy once he had met his subsistence needs. The average laborer would buy a transistor radio, but the study showed that an evangelical would likely buy a table, because of his family values.

The rising interest in evangelism and missions is encouraging. I found it easy to be carried away with the excitement of what is happening in some circles, especially in a conference such as COMIBAM. Yet I realized we must not become either triumphalistic or complacent. For one thing, church growth is uneven; some communities and sectors remain untouched by the gospel. And cults are increasingly active. Mormons, for instance, report that they are sending thousands of missionaries to Argentina.

Where there is rapid church growth, much of it is tall but not deep. The harvest is threatened by winds of Catholic backlash, plagues of cults, viruses of African spiritism, and fires of Marxism.

THE FUTURE

What will characterize Latin America in the coming decade? Poverty, the drug trade, and violence will likely increase in the coming years. In countries which already find difficulty feeding their people, it seems that the standard of living will continue to fall due to pressures exerted by the horrendous interest on national debt and the population's 2.3 percent annual growth rate. Politicians and economists see no easy solutions to the chaotic societal problems.

While some Catholic elements increasingly become populist in philosophy, there could be a backlash from the Catholic church, trying to maintain authoritarian power--a tension between revolution and reaction. As Catholicism continues to lose its authoritarian grip and people become increasingly disillusioned with both religion and politics, the Latin American trend toward materialism and atheism will increase. Some will turn to Communism in its different forms. Marxism is attractive as a reaction to the "opiate" of religion; it is true that God may use it as judgment on ritual religion. But Marxism or Maoism or Trotskyism can never provide the healthful climate needed for the emancipation of Latin American society. In the end, Communism self-destructs. While it denounces the abuses of capitalism, it is bankrupt itself. Likewise, capitalism, unless it is governed by moral and spiritual values, results in oppressive greed. Latin America has seen the worst illustrations of that.

To fill the spiritual vacuum, people will look either to spiritism or the cults, unless they are presented with the gospel made relevant to their lives.

Latin America's unsettled conditions give ideal opportunity for witness. There may be danger and hardship, but traditional barriers to the gospel are breaking down. A changing society is more open than a static society. The urgent need is for the gospel to be demonstrated in society as the real answer to human need. Latin Americans need to see families that stay together in love, men and women who withstand corruption, communities that care for the poor, and believers who, in a world of despair, radiate a vibrant faith.

Evangelicals must put forward the scriptural alternative to sterile churchianity, empty materialism, and poisonous Marxism. Where Iberoamerican Catholicism is a religion without morality, God's people must demonstrate newness of life in Christ. If Latin America's spiritual problem is the result of a destructive, stifling religious system--Christianity without a living Christ--the solution must be in permeating society with a living faith. It must be an internalized faith, providing the ethics, the moral force, and the spiritual liberty that lead to societal freedom. Neither Communism nor churchianity nor the hybrid of liberation theology can produce the kind of internal, personal revolution that is needed to change society.

Both Iberoamerican Catholicism and Communism hold out the same basic promise of material gain. Catholics teach that by penance and by prayers to the Virgin, the faithful can get what they ask for. Communists boast that man can get whatever he wants without God. Several popular televangelists preach a prosperity theology that amounts to materialism. But Christ's true disciples are living their faith by taking up the cross of Jesus daily.

In terms of what Latin American believers may be called to endure, will the coming century be the first or the last? Whatever the times and seasons, the Church of Jesus Christ is to be salt and light in the midst of poverty, injustice, and anarchy. The experience of first century believers in Rome and twentieth century believers in Cuba gives hope for whatever may befall Latin America. That hope is found, not in the ancient custom of "tying down the sun" or in its modern counterparts, but in the power of the Spirit of Christ at work in and through believers.

WHAT DOES THIS MEAN TO MISSIONS?

In this context, missions in Latin America face their greatest opportunity--not an opportunity to establish foreign churches and extend their influence; not to pose as paternalistic benefactors of less fortunate people, but as true fellow servants with Latin Americans in the outreach of the gospel. Today's missionaries from outside Latin America have opportunity for partnership which the pioneers didn't have. Those courageous pioneers dared to preach salvation by faith, even at the risk of imprisonment or death. They worked with Latin Americans, but the latter's number was nothing like the army of believers available today. South and Central America have produced outstanding spiritual leaders who are ministering effectively in their own lands. And some are taking the gospel to the heart of places like Chicago, Hong Kong, London, and Sydney.

Missions need to see themselves as true partners with these leaders--not to be indulgent or patronizing but to seek advice, to plan strategy, to cooperate in joint projects. Latin American churches also want to be involved, to minister and not just be ministered to. They want a Latin American agenda, not one drafted in North America or Europe. Missions need to find ways of working with the churches without competing with them, of strengthening them without making them reliant on outside help.

As Wade Coggins challenged both expatriate and Latin American delegates at COMIBAM: "Let's go forward together!"

Such a partnership raises basic questions:

•*What kind of missionaries are needed?*

Men and women who will demonstrate the servanthood of Christ, not just foreign expertise. To be most effective, they should live a simple lifestyle. That doesn't mean living in a grass hut when trying to reach city highrise dwellers, but in every context it means identifying with the conditions the people face--practicing a lifestyle appropriate for a disciple.

•*What kind of help is needed?*

Physical needs are obvious, but the most frequent answer I received was "leadership and missionary training." Believers are witnessing; people are turning to Christ. But they are untaught. They don't have pastors and teachers trained in the Scriptures. The most common criticism I heard of missions was that they should have encouraged the development of national leadership sooner than they did.

•*Are there unevangelized peoples? Can missions help to win them to Christ?*

Evangelical leaders answer "Yes" to both questions. They want missions to help train national missionaries. They also need specialists such as linguists to translate Scriptures, radio programmers to develop broadcasts, and agriculturists to help farmers find alternatives to the drug trade. They're asking for missionaries to help them reach into new areas, and to evangelize subcultures which have been resistant to the gospel.

•*Where are the unreached people?*

Although there are still small linguistic groups which can be reached only by missionaries deciphering their language-- and that work must continue--large unreached populations live in urban centers and speak Spanish, Portuguese, or one of the major Indian languages. Even though the Scriptures are readily available in these languages, cultural or religious walls have isolated millions from the gospel.

"By the end of the century, most of the 'hidden peoples' of the world will live in cities," SIM General Director Ian Hay has stated. In 1900 only five percent of Latin Americans lived in cities; now about 70 percent of the population is urbanized, and there are 35 "world class" Latin American cities of over a million inhabitants each.

Targeting the cities does not mean the job is completed elsewhere, nor does it mean that missions have lost their vision to spread the gospel in every tongue. But the current emphasis on urban evangelism is really a corrective for previous neglect. Escobar points out that for the most part Protestant denominations deferred to the Catholics. Their missionaries preached to the aborigines, not to people of Spanish descent in the urban centers of Catholic power. Evangelical missionaries did successfully challenge Catholic domination of large Indian populations such as the Quechuas; but city dwellers, held in the grip of traditional, ritualistic religion, have only recently begun to open up to the gospel. Today they constitute Latin America's missionary frontier.

The stereotype of unreached people in Latin America is that of primitive rain forest dwellers. That may partly be due to the fact that missions generally steered clear of the major cities. It may also result from the unfortunate tendency of people to associate missions with the wild and the exotic. The fact is that today the great masses of unreached Latin Americans are men and women of European-Indian descent who live in the towns and cities. Ministering in these urban jungles may not seem as romantic a task as in leafy jungles, but it will be as demanding. In these days it could be more dangerous, and it will certainly be more costly. It will take patience and innovative methods. It will demand love and commitment. Many unevangelized people dwell in Latin America's highrise apartments and shuttered villas. For the most part, they are still shut out from effective witness that would lead to their salvation and the establishment of churches. Only obedience to the Saviour's command will take His disciples to them. It is not an easy step for most evangelical churches. With their perception of having a lower class status, they are hesitant to witness to the educated class, and they lack natural contacts.

"If we can win professionals, intellectuals, and business people to Christ, we can make an impact on the upper social levels and on society in general," says Ruben Ramirez of InterVarsity Christian Fellowship in Colombia. When he saw the aggressive tactics of Marxists, he committed himself to witness among Colombian students--an assignment not without danger.

Then there are expatriate communities like the Japanese, Chinese, Russians, and Jews.Uprooted from their own lands, they provide an ideal opportunity for Christian witness, but for the most part have been left untouched by the gospel.

The church of Jesus Christ faces an unusual challenge in Latin America. Instead of opposition from patently non-Christian religions like Islam or Buddhism, which dominate some areas of the world, the gospel in Latin America faces its greatest opposition from a syncretistic Christianity: Christo-paganism. Because it is called Christian, its errors are more subtle, and its departures from the truth become blurred. The gospel must therefore be the sharp sword of truth wielded in love, as it was in pre-Constantine Europe when it had to stand out starkly in contrast to paganism as well as Judaism. The early church did this through the witness of Spirit-filled disciples whose lives pointed the way to the risen Lord, not to institutionalized religion.

That is the task today: not programs, not institutions, not political demonstrations, but the Spirit of God released in the lives of disciples witnessing in a confused and hostile environment. Churches and missions must seek ways to help believers internalize Biblical truth and demonstrate it within their culture. Then the gospel will make an impact on the entire fabric of society and on its ills: poverty, violence, drugs, corruption, immorality, oppression.

WHAT HAD I REALLY SEEN?

Scenes flashed across the screen of my mind, like slides in a projector:

•Burning zeal and commitment in the eyes of a young Communist couple.

•Tears streaming down the face of a woman as she tenderly touched a figure of the dead Jesus.

•The artist explaining the mural of her "fragmented" people.

•Worshipers of material gods--men and women scurrying along city streets to amass wealth that would only become devalued paper.

•Crowds having their bags of rocks blessed by both Catholic priest and pagan shaman.

I wept inwardly as I thought of these lovable people on a fabulous continent, and the opportunity the gospel had lost five hundred years earlier. Under the sign of the cross, missionaries crossed the sea and imposed on a hapless people a religion that denied true Christian grace. Was the Spanish invasion God's scourge on an earlier religion that had corrupted creation rather than glorified the Creator? If so, those who called themselves by the name of Christ did not temper judgment with God's mercy. Many demonstrated lust for power and wealth instead of love and servanthood, rape instead of redemption. It was a gross distortion of the gospel.

I wept again as I thought of what my own people are doing today: my fellow northerners creating a market that helps support a tragic scourge in Latin America--the drug trade. My mental slide projector clicked again and I looked into the face of the child who had watched his drugged brother kill his baby brother.

I could never settle into complacency after an odyssey like this. I must become part of God's answer to Latin America's need. I can't undo what happened five hundred years ago. But I can go, or help others go, to demonstrate the power of the risen Christ. I can't stop the drug trade, but I can challenge God's people to use their own income to produce life in the place of death and to help alleviate suffering, through backing the work of the gospel. I can join hands with emerging evangelical forces in Latin America to press on with the task.

There were two more slides in my memory's projector: the evangelical leader punching his fist into his hand and exclaiming, "Come over and help us--now!" And the Peruvian elder asking me to tell others what things are really like.

FIVE CENTURIES AFTER COLUMBUS

It is five centuries since Columbus happened on the Americas, starting a chain reaction which has affected the entire world. Columbus evidently was a devout Christian who considered that his name, Christopher ("Christ bearer"), was an ordination from God to be an evangelist. This conviction and his extensive Bible studies about prophecy and the end times spurred him on to find the unevangelized peoples of the earth. In his diary he wrote: "The fact that the gospel must still be preached to so many lands in such a short time--this is what convinces me."

And so Columbus set out, in his own words, "in the name of the Lord Jesus to spread His name and gospel everywhere." As he approached the New World, he did not know that a prophecy was circulating among several of the aboriginal ethnic groups that "the Great White Father, King of Gods, Ruler and Teacher of Men" would return imminently to destroy those who rebelled against Him, and to set up a new civilization.

What a momentous juncture in history: an explorer with an evangelist's heart coming face to face with a people who possessed a prophecy about a dramatic spiritual change! Here was potential for one of history's greatest breakthroughs of the gospel.

But something went terribly wrong. The conquistadors who followed Columbus had a different agenda from the explorer. As to the pagan prophecy, the Spaniards fulfilled its warning of destruction, tragically enough; they also initiated a new civilization. But they failed to bring the liberating power of the gospel to the peoples of the western hemisphere. Instead, they presented a distorted Christ, not the Saviour of the Bible. Spiritually, it was a lost moment in history. While we cannot regain that exact moment, God is giving evangelicals today an opportunity beyond anything Columbus could have conceived.

"Five hundred years ago we Spaniards sent to South and Central America a lie," radio evangelist Luis Rodriguez of Spain told Bruce Woodman of South America Crusades. "Now we would like Latin Americans to send back to us the truth."

STRUGGLING TO TIE DOWN THE SUN

"When the whole world was still in darkness, the sun miraculously gave birth to a son," a Latin American guide had told me. Through the centuries of war and peace, his people had struggled to control the sun and placate the fearsome spirits.

But their world was still in darkness.

Then came a false light: the sun of another religion, a sun that scorched to death instead of giving life.

Fitfully at first, the true light appeared. Then the radiance of the only begotten Son of the eternal Father broke across the continent. Darkness was still in the hearts of men and women--of the majority of them--but the light was there to be seen, to be felt, to be drawn to. It was Christ in the lives of Latin Americans.

The Andean Indians believed that the sun god had commissioned the Inca to enlighten the people. The sun came back daily to check that his commission was being obeyed. I had to ask myself if we in our generation--we who have received the true light--are obedient to the Son of Righteousness, our Saviour, to fulfill His commission. Are we faithfully witnessing, in the expectation of His return?

The sun god's messengers traversed thousands of miles in relays, bearing sacred messages from the son of the sun. Should we be any less diligent than the Inca's messengers in taking the sacred message of our salvation into the farthest reaches, the highest hills, the deepest valleys, the simplest huts, and the tallest buildings?

For in Latin America, men and women are still struggling to gain control of a terrifying world and a hopeless eternity.

Struggling to tie down the sun.

APPENDIX

TIE DOWN THE SUN

STATISTICS: SOUTH AMERICA AND CUBA
(Source: SIM International Research and Education Department; 1990 population estimates)

ARGENTINA
Capital: Buenos Aires
Area: 2,775,700 sq. km/1,072,162 sq. miles
Population: 32.3 million
Urban population: 85%
Infant mortality: 3.2% (before age 1)
Literacy: 93-94%
Religions:
> Catholic 88.8%
> Protestant 5.6%
> Jewish 2.0%
> Non-religious 1.8%
> Marginal Christians 1.6%
> Muslim 0.2%

BOLIVIA
Capitals: La Paz (administrative)
> Sucre (legal)
Area: 1,098,160 sq. km/424,162 sq. miles
Population: 7.3 million
Urban population: 49%
Infant mortality: 11% (before age 1)
Literacy: 63-75%
Religions:
> Catholic 92.0%
> Protestant 4.0%
> Baha'i 2.6%

BRAZIL
Capital: Brasilia
Area: 8,544,866 sq. km/3,286,487 sq. miles
Population: 150.4 million

Urban population: 74%
Infant mortality: 6.3% (before age 1)
Literacy: 76%
Religions:
>Catholic 73.1%
>Spiritism pervasive
>Protestant 17.4%
>Other Catholic 2.0%
>Non-religious/Atheist 1.4%
>Buddhist 0.3%
>Muslim 0.1%

CHILE
Capital: Santiago
Area: 756,945 sq. km/292,383 sq. miles
Population: 13.2 million
Urban population: 84%
Infant mortality: 1.9% (before age 1)
Literacy: 90-95%
Religions:
>Catholic 63.4-89%
>Protestant 11-23%
>Non-religious 6.7%
>Marginal Christians 2.3%
>Traditional 0.8%

COLOMBIA
Capital: Bogota
Area: 1,143,316 sq. km/439,737 sq. miles
Population: 31.8 million
Urban population: 68%
Infant mortality: 4.6% (before age 1)
Literacy: 86%
Religions:
>Catholic 93.0%
>Protestant 3.1%
>Non-religious/Atheist 1.2%
>Tribal religions 1.1%

Baha'i 0.1%
Muslim 0.2%

CUBA
Capital: Havana
Area: 114,966 sq. km/44,218 sq. miles
Population: 10.6 million
Urban Population: 72%
Infant mortality: 1.2% (before age 1)
Literacy: 95%
Religions:
>Non-religious/Atheist 57.0%
>Catholic 38.0%
>Spiritist 3.0%
>Protestant 2.4%

ECUADOR
Capital: Quito
Area: 283,561 sq. km/109,483 sq. miles
Population: 10.7 million
Urban population: 54%
Infant mortality: 6.3% (before age 1)
Literacy: 74-88%
Religions:
>Catholic 91-95%
>Protestant 3.4%
>Marginal Christians 0.8%
>Non-religious/Atheist 0.7%
>Traditional 0.6%

FRENCH GUIANA
Capital: Cayenne
Area: 91,000 sq. km/35,100 sq. miles
Population: 0.9 million
Urban population: 73.4%
Infant mortality: NA
Literacy: 82%
Religions:

Religions:
> Catholic 67.2%
> Non-affiliated 13.0%
> Protestant 6.5%
> Non-religious/Atheist 5.0%
> African Traditional 3.5%
> Chinese religions 1.3%
> Muslim 1.0%
> Baha'i 0.7%

GUYANA

Capital: Georgetown
Area: 215,800 sq. km/83,000 sq. miles
Population: 0.8 million
Urban population: 33%
Infant mortality: 3% (before age 1)
Literacy: 90%
Religions:
> Hindu 35.6%
> Protestant 28.0%
> Non-affiliated 10.0%
> Catholic 9.4%
> Muslim 9.0%
> African Traditional 3.0%
> Non-religious/Atheist 2.0%

PARAGUAY

Capital: Asuncion
Area: 405,752 sq. km/157,048 sq. miles
Population: 4.3 million
Urban population: 43%
Infant mortality: 4.2% (before age 1)
Literacy: 82-85%
Religions:
> Catholic 96.0%
> Protestant 2.3%
> Traditional 0.7%
> Atheist 0.6%

PERU
Capital: Lima
Area: 1,284,640 sq. km/496,222 sq. miles
Population: 21.9 million
Urban population: 69%
Infant mortality: 7.6% (before age 1)
Literacy: 80%
Religions:
> Catholic 95%
> Protestant 3-4%
> Other 1-2%
> Traditional 1%

SURINAME
Capital: Paramaribo
Area: 163,896 sq. km/63,037 sq. miles
Population: 0.4 million
Urban population: 66%
Infant mortality: 4% (before age 1)
Literacy: 80%
Religions:
> Hindu 27.4%
> Catholic 21.6%
> Protestant 19.9%
> Muslim 19.6%
> Spiritist 5.5%
> Non-religious/Atheist 4.0%
> Baha'i 1.0%

URUGUAY
Capital: Montevideo
Area: 176,215 sq. km/68,037 sq. miles
Population: 3 million
Urban Population: 87%
Infant mortality: 2.2% (before age 1)
Literacy: 94%
Religions:
> Catholic 60.5%

Non-religious/Atheist 35.0%
Protestant 3.1%
Jewish 1.7%

VENEZUELA
Capital: Caracas
Area: 915,574 sq. km/352,144 sq. miles
Population: 19.6 million
Urban population: 83%
Infant mortality: 3.3% (before age 1)
Literacy: 88.4%
Religions:
Catholic 90.0%
Protestant 2.6%
Non-affiliated 2.3%
African Traditional 2.2%
Non-religious/Atheist 1.5%
Muslim 0.4%

ALLAN, George. *Reminiscences.* Cochabamba, Bolivia: Bolivian Indian Mission, n.d.

ANDERSON, Gerald H. ; STRANSKY, Thomas F. *Mission Trends No. 3--Third World Theologies.* Grand Rapids, MI: Wm. B. Eerdmans Publishing Co. and Paulist Press, 1976.

ARIAS, Esther; ARIAS, Mortimer. *The Cry of My People.* New York, NY: Friendship Press, 1980.

Atlas de COMIBAM. Sao Paulo, Brazil: COMIBAM, 1987.

BAKKE, Ray. *The Urban Christian.* Downers Grove, IL: InterVarsity Press, 1987.

BAZLEY, Barbara. *Hidden Gold.* Basingstoke, UK: Marshall Pickering, 1985.

BAZLEY, Barbara. *Hearts Aflame.* Basingstoke, UK: Marshall Pickering, 1988.

BELL, Inez J. *The Kantuta Blooms in Bolivia.* Toronto, ON: Canadian Baptist Overseas Mission Board, 1971.

BELLI, Humberto. *Breaking Faith.* Garden City, NJ: Crossway Books, 1985.

BETTO, Frei. *Fidel and Religion--Conversations with Frei Betto.* Sydney, Australia: Pathfinders Press/Pacific and Asia, 1986.

BINGHAM, Hiram. *Lost City of the Incas, the Story of Machu Picchu and its Builders.* London, UK: Phoenix House Ltd., 1951.

BROOKS, John (Ed). *The 1986 South American Handbook.* Bath, UK: Trade and Travel Publications Ltd., 1985.

BRUNDAGE, Burr Cartwright. *Empire of the Inca.* Norman, OK: University of Oklahoma Press, 1963.

BURNS, E. Bradford. *Latin America: A Concise Interpretive History.* Englewood Cliffs, NJ: Prentice-Hall, 1982.

CASSON, Lionel; CLAIRBORNE, Robert; FAGAN, Brian; KARP, Walter. *Mysteries of the Past.* New York, NY: American Heritage Publishing Co. Inc., 1977.

CHILTON, David. *Productive Christians in an Age of Guilt Manipulators--A Biblical Response to Ronald J. Sider.* Tyler, TX: Institute for Christian Economics, 1981.

COOK, Frank S. *Seeds in the Wind.* Opa Locka, FL: The World Radio Missionary Fellowship, Inc., 1961.

COSTAS, Orlando E. *The Integrity of Mission, The Inner Life and Outreach of the Church.* San Francisco, CA: Harper & Row, Publishers, 1979.

COSTAS, Orlando E. *The Church and Its Mission: A Shattering Critique from the Third World.* Wheaton, IL: Tyndale House Publishers, 1974.

DABBS, Norman H. *Dawn Over the Bolivian Hills.* Toronto, ON: Canadian Baptist Foreign Mission Board, 1946.

DE SOTO, HERNANDO. *The Other Path.* New York, NY: Harper & Row, Publishers, 1989.

DEIROS, Pablo Alberto. *Historia del Cristianismo.* El Paso, TX: Casa Bautista de Publicaciones, 1980.

DUSSEL, Enrique D. *A History of the Church in Latin America: Colonialism to Liberation* (1492-1979). Grand Rapids, MI: Wm. B. Eerdmans Publishing Co., 1981.

DWYER, AUGUSTA. *Into the Amazon: Chico Mendes and the Struggle for the Rain Forest.* Key Porter Books, 1990.

ESCOBAR, Samuel. *La Fe Evangelica y Las Teologias de la Liberacion.* El Paso, TX: Casa Bautista de Publicaciones, 1987.

ESCOBAR, Samuel; DRIVER, John. *Christian Mission and Social Justice.* Scottsdale, PA: Herald Press, 1978.

FRIZEN, Edwin L. ; COGGINS, Wade T. (Eds). *Christ and Caesar in Christian Missions.* Pasadena, CA: William Carey Library, 1979.

FROST, Peter. *Exploring Cuzco, A Traveller's Guide to Peru's Most Famous Region.* Cambridge, MA: Bradt Enterprises, 1984.

FULLER, W. Harold. *Mission-Church Dynamics.* Pasadena, CA: William Carey Library, 1980.

GARCIA, Jose Ferreira. *De Los Llanos Amazonicos a la Cumbre de Los Andes.* Lima, Peru: Editora Universal S.A., 1989.

GUINNESS, Lucy E. ; MILLARD, E.C. *South America, The Neglected Continent.* England: E. Marlborough & Co., 1894.

GUNDRY, Stanley N. ; JOHNSON, Alan F. *Tensions in Contemporary Theology.* Chicago, IL: Moody Press, 1976.

GUNTHER, John. *Inside South America.* New York, NY: Harper & Row, Publishers, 1966.

GUTIERREZ, Gustavo. *A Theology of Liberation.* Mary-Knoll, NY: Orbis Books, 1973.

HARTZLER, Dan. *"New Age Goes Latin"* Latin American Evangelist, Vol. 68, No. 2.

HAWTHORNE, Sally Reese. *Cloud Country Sojourn.* London, UK: Marshall, Morgan & Scott, Ltd., n.d.

HAY, Ian M. *Foundations, Scriptural Principles Undergirding SIM.* Toronto, ON: SIM International, 1988.

HILLYER, H.S. *Discovery.* Toronto, ON: Evangelical Publishers, 1947.

HUDSPITH, Margarita Allan. *Ripening Fruit. A History of the Bolivian Indian Mission.* Harrington Park, NJ: Bolivian Indian Mission, 1958.

HUNDLEY, Raymond C. *Radical Liberation Theology. An Evangelical Response.* Wilmore, KY: Bristol Books, 1987.

ISAIAS, Juan. *The Other Side of the Coin.* Grand Rapids, MI: Wm. B. Eerdmans Publishing Co., 1966.

JOHNSTONE, Patrick. *Operation World.* Bromley, Kent: Send the Light, and Pasadena: William Carey Library, 1986.

KESSLER, J.B. *A Study of the Older Protestant Missions and Churches in Peru and Chile.* Holland: Oosterbann and Le Cointre N.V., 1967.

KIRK J. Andrew. *Theology Encounters Revolution.* Downers Grove, IL: InterVarsity Press, 1980.

KIRK, J. Andrew. *Liberation Theology.* London, UK: Marshall, Morgan & Scott, 1979.

LANNING, Edward W. *Peru Before the Incas.* Inglewood Cliffs, NJ: Prentice-Hall Inc., 1967.

Lausanne Occasional Paper No. 17, Christian Witness to Traditional Religionists of Latin America and Caribbean. Pattaya: Lausanne Committee for World Evangelization, 1980.

Lausanne Occasional Paper No. 21, Declaration on Evangelism and Social Responsibility--An Evangelical Commitment. Grand Rapids, MI: Lausanne Committee for World Evangelization and World Evangelical Fellowship, 1982.

LOSS, Myron. *Culture Shock, Dealing with Stress in Cross-Cultural Living.* Winona Lake, IN: Light and Life Press, 1983.

Lost Empires, Living Tribes. Washington: The National Geographic Society, 1982.

MACKAY, John A. *The Other Spanish Christ.* New York, NY: The MacMillan Company, 1932.

MAKOWER, Katherine. *Don't Cry For Me.* London, UK: Hodder and Stoughton, 1989.

MASON, J. Alden. *The Ancient Civilizations of Peru.* London, UK: Pelican Books, 1957.

MAUST, John. *Peace and Hope in the Corner of the Dead--A Story of Tragedy and Hope from Ayacucho, Peru.* Miami, FL: Latin America Mission, 1987.

MAYERS, Marvin K. *A Look at Latin American Lifestyles.* Dallas, TX: Summer Institute of Linguistics, Inc., 1976.

McFARREN, Peter; PRADA, Teresa; PRADA, Ana Rebeca. *Insider's Guide to Bolivia.* La Paz, Bolivia: Fundacion Cultural Quipas, 1988.

McINTYRE, Loren. *The Incredible Incas and Their Timeless Land.* Washington: The National Geographic Society, 1975.

McLAURIN, J.B. *The Journey of Many Prayers.* Toronto, ON: Canadian Baptist Foreign Mission Board, circa 1950.

MERRICK, Earl C. *Bolivia, A Source Book for Mission Study.* Toronto, ON.: The Canadian Baptist Foreign Mission Board, n.d.

METRAUX, Alfred. *The History of the Incas.* New York, NY: Random House, Inc., Pantheon Books, 1969.

MIRANDA, Jose. *Marx and the Bible.* Maryknoll,NY: Orbis Books, 1974.

NASH, Ronald H. (Ed) *Liberation Theology.* Milford, MI: Mott Media, Inc., 1984.

NEELY, Lois. *Come Up to this Mountain, The Miracle of Clarence W. Jones and HCJB.* Opa Locka, FL: World Radio Missionary Fellowship, Inc., 1980.

NELSON, Wilton M. *Protestantism in Central America.* Grand Rapids, MI: Wm. B. Eerdmans Publishing Co., 1984.

NIDA, Eugene A. *Understanding Latin Americans.* Pasadena, CA: William Carey Library, 1974.

NORDYKE, Quinton. *Animistic Aymaras and Church Growth.* Pasadena, CA: William Carey Library, 1972.

NUÑEZ C., Emilio A. *Liberation Theology.* Chicago, IL: Moody Press, 1985.

NUÑEZ C., Emilio A.;TAYLOR, William D.*Crisis in Latin America: An Evangelical Perspective.* Chicago, IL: Moody Press, 1989.

ORR, J. Edwin. *Evangelical Awakenings in Latin America.* Minneapolis, MN: Bethany Fellowship, Inc. 1978.

PADILLA, Rene C. *Mission Between the Times.* Grand Rapids, MI: Wm. B. Eerdmans Publishing Co. ,1985.

Pass the Word -- 50 Years of Wycliffe Bible Translators. Huntington Beach, CA: Wycliffe Bible Translators, Inc., 1984.

PEARSON, B.H. *The Monk Who Lived Again--A Tale of South America.* Winona Lake, IN: Light and Life Press, 1946.

PAYNE, Will; WILSON, Charles T.W. *MissionaryPioneering in Bolivia, with some account of work in Argentina.* London, UK: Echoes of Service, (1904)

READ, W.R. ; INESON, Frank A. *Brazil 1980, The Protestant Handbook.* Monrovia, CA: World Vision, 1973.

READ, W.R. ; MONTERROSO, V.M., JOHNSON, H.A. *Latin American Church Growth.* Grand Rapids, MI: Wm. B. Eerdmans Publishing Company, 1969.

Reader's Digest Book of Facts. London, UK: The Reader's Digest Association Limited, 1985.

RICHARDSON, Don. *Eternity in Their Hearts.* Ventura, CA: Regal Books, 1981.

ROBERTS, W. Dayton. *Strachan of Costa Rica.* 1971.

RYCROFT, W. Stanley. *Religion and Faith in Latin America.* Philadelphia, PA: The Westminster Press, 1958.

SAVAGE, Mary. *Introducing Bolivia.* Andes Evangelical Mission, n.d.

SCOPES, Wilfred. (Ed) *The Christian Ministry in Latin America.* Geneva: Commission on World Mission and Evangelism, World Council of Churches, 1962.

SHEREDA, Edith. *Feeling After God.* London, UK: E. Marlborough & Co., 1894.

SHEREDA, Edith. *The Indian War Cry.* Loizeaux, 1942.

SHEREDA, Edith. *Among the Bolivian Indians.* New York, NY: The Bible Truth Press, n.d.

SIDER, Ronald J. *Rich Christians in an Age of Hunger.* Downers Grove, IL: InterVarsity Press, 1977.

Sixty Years in Bolivia. Six Decades of Canadian Baptist Missionary Progress in South America. Toronto, ON: Canadian Baptist Foreign Mission Board, circa 1959.

SMITH, W. Douglas, Jr. *Toward Continuous Mission.* Strategizing for the Evangelization of Bolivia. Pasadena, CA: William Carey Library, 1978.

SNYDER, Darlene. *Bolivia, the Beggar Sitting on a Gold Throne.* Typewritten report, 1971.

STEYNE, Philip M. *Gods of Power.* Houston, TX: Touch Publications, 1989.

STILLWELL, H.E. *Pioneering in Bolivia.* Toronto, ON: American Baptist Publication Society, n.d.

The Cambridge Encyclopedia of Latin America and the Caribbean. New York, NY: Press Syndicate of the University of Cambridge, 1985.

The Two Souls of Peru. Washington: National Geographic Society, Vol. 161, No. 3, 1982.

THOMPSON, Hazel Fay. *Smoke from Bolivian Fires.* Toronto, ON: The Canadian Baptist Foreign Mission Board.

TURNBULL, Johnson. *From Mule to Jet in Bolivia.* Toronto, ON: Baptist Women's Missionary Society of Ontario and Quebec, 1971.

WAGNER, C. Peter; McCULLOUGH, Joseph S. *The Condor of the Andes.* Queensland, Australia: Evangelistic Literature Enterprise, 1987.

WAGNER, C. Peter. *The Protestant Movement in Bolivia.* Pasadena, CA: William Carey Library, 1970.

WAGNER, C. Peter. *Defeat of the Bird God.* Grand Rapids, MI: Zondervan Publishing House, 1967.

WILLEMS, Emilio. *Latin American Culture: An Anthropological Synthesis.* New York, NY: Harper & Row Publishers, 1975.

WINTEMUTE, H.E. *The Religion of Bolivia.* Toronto, ON: The American Baptist Publication Society, n.d.

YAMAMORI, Ted. *Toward the Symbiotic Ministry, God's Mandate for the Church Today.* Scottsdale, AZ: Food for the Hungry, Inc. (Reprint from "Missiology, An International Review" Volume V, No. 3, July, 1977).

YAMAMORI, Tetsunao. *God's New Envoys.* Portland OR: Multnomah Press, 1987.

ZAPATA, Virgilio A. *El Evangelista.* Guatemala: Editorial Latina, 1988.

ABOUT SIM

SIM is an amalgamation of three missions which had their roots in the 1890s:

Andes Evangelical Mission (South America)
International Christian Fellowship (Asia)
Sudan Interior Mission (Africa)

Interdenominational in membership and affiliation, SIM draws missionaries from nations around the world. They pursue the two-fold objective of evangelizing unreached peoples and discipling them into missionary-minded local churches.

Under the motto, "By Prayer," SIM missionaries use a wide range of skills in a variety of ministries to accomplish this task. Its acronym stands for Society for International Ministries.

SIM offices will gladly provide current lists of personnel needed and of strategic projects in Africa, Asia, and South America.

SIM PURPOSE STATEMENT:

The Purpose of SIM
is to glorify God
by evangelizing the unreached and
ministering to human need,
discipling believers into churches
equipped to fulfill Christ's
Commission.

SIM NOW:
To keep informed of SIM ministries in South America, Asia, and Africa, write for a free subscription to this 16-page magazine.
CATALOG: SIM offices will gladly send you a catalog of published materials and audiovisuals. Sample titles:

BOOKS
Fire on the Mountains
by Raymond Davis. The miraculous birth of the church in southern Ethiopia.

The Winds of God
by Raymond Davis. How Ethiopian evangelists reached throughout southern Ethiopia.

Tread Upon the Lion
by Sophie de la Haye. The story of West Africa pioneer Tommy Titcombe.

Condor of the Andes
by Peter Wagner and Joe McCullough. The story of South America's first missionary pilot.

AUDIOVISUALS
The Race
A challenging documentary of results of the spiritual race begun by three missions in the 1890s, culminating in today's SIM.

Power by Prayer
A Biblical look at intercessory prayer. 26 mins. VHS video, 16mm film.

No Unreachables
"Unreachable people" who are now part of the church. 26 mins. VHS video, 16mm film.

Talking Guidance, Talking Mission
Personal guidance experiences. 29 mins. VHS video.

Showing That We Care
Meeting human need through development ministries. 29 mins. VHS video, 16mm film.

Who Sends Them?
The local church and missions. 23 minutes. VHS video.

FOR CHILDREN
Rick-a-Chee
series, by Edna Menzies. Six large- page illustrated stories about a small African boy.

Never Hide a Hyena in a Sack
by Ines Penny. Biblical lessons in life from African folklore.

SIM OFFICES:

Australia:
PO Box 371, Miranda, NSW, 2228
Canada:
10 Huntingdale Blvd., Scarborough, Ontario, M1W 2S5
East Asia:
116 Lavender Street, #04-09 Pek Chuan Bldg. ,
Singapore 1233
Europe:
Case Postale 42, 1000 Lausanne 20 Sevelin, Switzerland
Great Britain:
Joint Mission Centre, Ullswater Crescent, Coulsdon,
Surrey CR5 2HR, England
New Zealand:
P.O. Box 38588, Howick

Southern Africa:
   Private Post Bag X1, Clareinch, Cape Town 7740,
   Republic of S.Africa
USA:
   P.O. Box 7900, Charlotte, NC 28241-8819

ABOUT THE AUTHOR

W. HAROLD FULLER, D. Lit.

Born of missionary parents in British Columbia, Canada, W. Harold Fuller had his first contact with the Caribbean and Latin America while in the Canadian Navy. He studied journalism under the American Newspaper Institute and Bible and Missions at Prairie Bible Institute before going to Africa with SIM in 1951.

Dr. Fuller has used his writing skills in Christian journalism as well as in mission administration. Traveling widely in the interests of missions, he has lectured on six continents. In 1989 Biola University, California, awarded him an honorary doctorate of literature for his "contribution to worldwide ministry through leadership and missiological publications."

Author Fuller became involved in South America when Andes Evangelical Mission joined SIM in 1982. His administrative travels as Deputy General Director for SIM, and his extensive research in Latin America have brought together a wealth of information, written in a gripping narrative style.

Notes: